Culture in
Second Language
Teaching and Learning

THE CAMBRIDGE APPLIED LINGUISTICS SERIES

Series editors: Michael H. Long and Jack C. Richards

This series presents the findings of recent work in applied linguistics which are of direct relevance to language teaching and learning and of particular interest to applied linguists, researchers, language teachers, and teacher trainers.

In this series:

Culture in Second Language Teaching and Learning

Eli Hinkel

Seattle University

CAMBRIDGE
UNIVERSITY PRESS

CAMBRIDGE UNIVERSITY PRESS
Cambridge, New York, Melbourne, Madrid, Cape Town, Singapore, São Paulo

Cambridge University Press
40 West 20th Street, New York, NY 10011–4211, USA

www.cambridge.org
Information on this title: www.cambridge.org/9780521644907

First published 1999
6th printing 2006

Printed in the United States of America

A catalog record for this publication is available from the British Library

Library of Congress Cataloging in Publication Data

Culture in second language teaching and learning / Eli Hinkel (ed.).
p. cm. – (Cambridge applied linguistics series)
Includes bibliographical references and index.
1. Language and languages – Study and teaching. 2. Second language
acquisition. 3. Language and culture – Study and teaching.
I. Hinkel, Eli. II. Series.
P53.C77 1999
418′.007 dc21   98-53640
                                                           CIP

ISBN-13 978-0-521-64276-7 hardback
ISBN-10 0-521-64276-0 hardback
ISBN-13 978-0-521-64490-7 paperback
ISBN-10 0-521-64490-9 paperback

Contents

Contributors

Lawrence F. Bouton, University of Illinois, Urbana-Champaign
Martin Cortazzi, University of Leicester, Leicester
Joan Kelly Hall, University of Georgia, Athens
Linda Harklau, University of Georgia, Athens
Eli Hinkel, Seattle University, Seattle
Lixian Jin, De Montfort University, Leicester
Elliot L. Judd, University of Illinois, Chicago
Yamuna Kachru, University of Illinois, Urbana-Champaign
James P. Lantolf, Cornell University, Ithaca
Kenneth R. Rose, City University of Hong Kong
Ron Scollon, Georgetown University, Washington, D.C.
Suzanne Scollon, City University of Hong Kong

Series editors' preface

The relationship between language and culture has been a focus of attention from a variety of disciplinary perspectives for many years. Linguists, anthropologists, sociologists, psychologists, and others have sought to understand whether and how cultural factors influence aspects of human behavior such as perception, cognition, language, and communication. Within language teaching, cultural factors have occasionally attracted the interest of both theoreticians and practitioners. Robert Lado was one of the first to suggest that cultural systems in the native culture could be compared with those in the target culture and serve as a source of transfer or interference in much the way other types of contrasting linguistic systems do. Others have examined a range of different aspects of second language use that are subject to culturally based influences, including classroom interaction, roles of teachers and students, and teaching styles. Textbooks in language teaching methodology and classroom texts, however, typically offer a very rudimentary perspective on cultural factors in teaching and learning, if they are dealt with at all, and culture is often identified by an occasional reference to the folklore and customs in the learner's native culture.

This book seeks to reexamine the relationship between culture, language teaching, and learning by showing how cultural factors influence many different aspects of second language learning and use. Among the issues discussed are students' classroom behaviors and teachers' expectations and how they may reflect different norms for culturally appropriate behavior; differences between L1 and L2 modes of conceptual and lexical organization; the interpretation of conversational implicature in conversation by speakers of different cultural groups; the influence of cultural factors on writing and learning to write in a second language; differences between L1 and L2 rhetorical paradigms in written discourse in L1 and L2; and differences in speech act interpretation across cultures. The chapters present original research on these issues and examine implications for teaching and learning.

The book serves not only to focus awareness on the role of cultural factors in language learning and teaching but also to develop an appropriate pedagogy to address the kinds of issues identified. This involves finding ways for the ESL curriculum to engage students and teachers in an exploration of how language and culture interact. Culturally focused consciousness-raising activities in the teaching of writing and speaking are offered as one approach. Teacher educators will find that many of the chapters also invite a reexamination of teacher education curricula to provide teachers with a deeper understanding of some of the culturally based concepts, beliefs, and discourse practice learners bring to the language classroom.

Culture in Second Language Teaching and Learning makes a useful contribution to our understanding of culture within the context of second language learning and clarifies a range of important issues that are often little understood by teachers and teacher educators. The book is therefore a welcome addition to the Cambridge Applied Linguistics Series. It adds a further dimension to our understanding of the nature of communicative competence and shows how functional L2 competence involves recognizing and learning how to use culturally specific norms for written and spoken discourse.

Michael H. Long
Jack C. Richards

Acknowledgments

This book took almost four years to become a book. During this time, many people gave me their assistance and wisdom. I am especially indebted to Susan Carkin, without whose foresight, friendship, support, and inspiration this volume would have probably never happened. Robert Kaplan, a mentor and a friend, helped in innumerable ways. His generous guidance was instrumental at crucial junctures. I am thankful to Jack Richards for his patience and insight when the book needed resuscitation. My heartfelt appreciation goes to Rodney Hill, a documentation manager at Microsoft Corporation. His knowledge of linguistics has grown dramatically during the past few years, when he read the many versions of outlines, drafts, and chapters.

Eli Hinkel

Introduction
Culture in research and second language pedagogy

Eli Hinkel

Culture and language

It may not be an exaggeration to say that there are nearly as many definitions of culture as there are fields of inquiry into human societies, groups, systems, behaviors, and activities. Over the years, the many explicit and implicit definitions of culture in second language pedagogy have led to what R. Scollon (1995, p. 382) calls "miniaturization of the concept of culture so that researchers study and write about the culture of the school or even the culture of the classroom." Similarly, Flowerdew and Miller (1995) refer to ethnic culture, local culture, academic culture, and disciplinary culture when they discuss the specifics of academic demands on nonnative speakers of English (NNSs) faced with a second language (L2) medium of instruction. In part, the small-scope definitions of culture are a result of teachers' and researchers' increased realization that a detailed analysis of the relationships between various norms of discourse is necessary to improve the quality of teaching and learning.

Even within the explorations and the teaching of language, the term *culture* has diverse and disparate definitions that deal with forms of speech acts, rhetorical structure of text, social organizations, and knowledge constructs. Culture is sometimes identified with notions of personal space, appropriate gestures, time, and so forth. Although these concepts are certainly manifestations of cultural norms, the impact of culture as discussed in this volume is both broader and deeper, defining the way a person sees his or her place in a society.

In her study of culture and the individual, Rosaldo (1984) points out that culture is "far more than a mere catalogue of rituals and beliefs." She argues that cultural models derive from the world in which people live and the reality that they construct. She further observes that those who live outside a culture, that is, researchers, ethnographers, and anthropologists, cannot provide its complete interpretation because an individual's sense of self and assumptions about the world and society "ultimately depend upon one's embeddedness within a particular sociocultural milieu" (p. 140). She emphasizes that culture shapes and binds one's social and cognitive concepts, and that these concepts are not likely

1

to be understood and appreciated by outsiders. In Rosaldo's terms, the cultural world, with its social order and constraints, serves as a background against which a people's subjectivities are formed and expressed.

Applied linguists and language teachers have become increasingly aware that a second or foreign language can rarely be learned or taught without addressing the culture of the community in which it is used. Thomas (1983, 1984) observes that nonnative speakers are often perceived to display inappropriate language behaviors and often are not even aware that they do. She cautions that violations of cultural norms of appropriateness in interactions between native and nonnative speakers often lead to sociopragmatic failure, breakdowns in communication, and the stereotyping of nonnative speakers. Thomas (1983, p. 91) points out that teachers must draw on research to "develop ways of heightening and refining students' metapragmatic awareness, so that they are able to express themselves as they choose."

This volume focuses on culture as it applies to language research and the applications of its findings in language pedagogy. In addition, it focuses on second language learning and the ways in which people's worldviews affect their learning, understanding, production, and interaction in a second language and a second culture. The contributors to this collection of articles approach the notion of culture as it applies to social norms, worldviews, beliefs, assumptions, and value systems that affect many, if not all, aspects of second or foreign language use, teaching, and learning. The collection brings together research in anthropology and social cognition, as well as second language learning, acquisition, and teaching. The authors take the position that multidisciplinary studies on culture carried out in various domains of applied linguistics, sociolinguistics, interaction and pragmatics, and rhetoric and writing can inform second and foreign language learning and teaching. Conversely, the environments in which languages are learned and taught often serve as research grounds where the impact of culture can be investigated.

Studies of culture and sociolinguistics

This introduction touches briefly on just a few of the studies that have contributed to an understanding of the relationships between culture and language. The list of references included in the book gives a better idea of the scope of work that has been undertaken in the last few decades.

In the early 1900s, linguists who researched the structure of Amerindian languages (Boas, 1911) noted that relationships among thought, abstract notions, and language as a means of expressing thoughts and notions were complex. Edward Sapir in the 1920s concluded that a language and the culture of its speakers cannot be analyzed in isolation. Language can be seen as a way to describe and represent human experience and understanding of the world (Sapir, [1921] 1961), and members of a language community share systems of beliefs and assumptions which underlie their constructions of the world. These constructions, views of objective phenomena, beliefs, and histories are communicated through language, thus establishing a connection between language and the culture of a community. Sapir's explanation extends beyond lexis to language as a referential framework of expression: "in all language behavior there are intertwined, in enormously complex patterns, isolable patterns of two distinct orders. These may be roughly defined as patterns of reference and patterns of expression" (p. 11).

In the tradition of Boasian linguistics, independently of Sapir, Whorf (1956) concluded that language systems, discourse, and lexis reflect ways of looking at the world and its various realities. To Whorf, lexicon reflected the thought processes that separated Amerindian worldviews and beliefs from those of Europeans in terms of their definitions of time, space, and natural phenomena. Although languages often have distinct grammatical features, it may be misleading to define differences among languages solely in terms of lexical descriptions and grammar rules. The Sapir–Whorf hypothesis of linguistic relativity pertains to conceptually abstract notions of lexical and grammatical, as well as referential and expressive, systems.

The study of culture further developed in the rather distinct domains of anthropology and sociolinguistics. In general, anthropologists are concerned with culture as the way of life of a people, the social constructs that evolve within a group, the ways of thinking, feeling, believing, and behaving that are imparted to members of a group in the socialization processes. In his book *The Interpretation of Cultures,* which has since become a classic, Geertz (1973) states that language and its uses within a group are of interest to social anthropologists inasmuch as they are a significant part of human behavior that represents symbolic action in regard to the social structure and interactions within the group. He further notes that behavior articulates culture and determines how language is used to express meaning. In general terms, through the analyses of language uses, anthropologists seek to gain access to cultural frameworks and thus acquire an understanding of the conceptual world within which the members of the group live.

Culture theory, developed on the basis of social anthropology, delves into conceptual properties of culture and cultural meaning systems, as well as symbolic representations of self and manifestations of beliefs and emotions (Shweder, 1984). Because concepts, thoughts, and identities are often expressed through language, culture theory is also concerned with language acquisition and socialization into a group. In light of culture theory, language is often viewed as a complex system that reflects what meanings are attached to behaviors and how they are expressed (Gardner, 1984). On the other hand, some cultural anthropologists believe that language use may have little to do with the true causes of human behavior and often serves to mask them (Stigler, Shweder, & Herdt, 1990).

In the 1960s and the 1970s, investigations of the connections between language and culture produced such impressive and seminal works as Hymes's (1964) *Language in Culture and Society,* Gumperz (1972) on interactional sociolinguistics, Kaplan (1966) on rhetorical patterns accepted in different cultures and styles of writing, and E. Hall (1976) on behavioral and cognitive constructs. The studies carried out at the time did not, however, always establish the relevance of their conclusions to second or foreign language pedagogy. In part for this reason, many teacher- and student-training methodologies, then and now, have not included findings that deal with the effects of the first culture on second and foreign language learning. In 1981, John Lyons noted that "[t]here are certain aspects of the interdependence of language and culture that are not as widely appreciated as they ought to be" (p. 325).

Hymes (1970, 1971, 1972a) and Gumperz and Hymes (1972) held the view that uses of language and its analyses are inseparable from the society, specific sociological situations, the interlocutors' social backgrounds and identities, and social meanings that are "encoded linguistically" (p. 18). Hymes (1972b) notes that in linguistics, a descriptive theory of speech and interaction has to consider the "speech community," to be "all forms of language, including writing. . . ," and "speech events." According to Hymes, speech events are governed by social and linguistic norms for the use of speech, as well as communicative content, form, setting, and goals. He further comments that speech events and acts "are not all universal" and may be contingent on the social structure, values, and the sociocultural order of the community. In his benchmark articles, Hymes (1967, 1972b) first introduced the notion of "communicative competence" that has subsequently had a great deal of influence on second language research and teaching methodologies. He pointed out that communicative competence included both "speaking" and behavioral competence and "interpretation" of speech and behaviors according to the norms of the speech community (Hymes, 1972b, pp. 53 and 64 respectively).

In the 1980s, research into manifestations of culture in second and foreign language teaching and learning focused on the effects of body language, eye contact, and other overt behavioral and communicative paradigms. Comparisons of culturally defined behaviors addressed such general topics as posture, movement and eye contact (Morain, 1986), limitations of lexicon in referring to tangible concepts (e.g., colors and quantities), relationships that do not exist outside Anglo-American societies (e.g., terms of kinship and the structure of the extended family), and punctuality (Condon, 1986).

At the time, many classroom teachers and language teaching method-ologists described appropriate techniques for addressing cultural behav-iors while teaching second language linguistic skills. Damen's (1987) work approached the influence of culture on interaction and communication, moved beyond overt and recognizable cultural behaviors, and urged class-room teachers to become ethnographers of their students' cultures to provide insights into learner knowledge and expectations. Her view of cul-ture focused predominantly on the anthropological understanding of culture and briefly touched on cultural values, beliefs, and assumptions that invariably find their way into instructional settings. According to Damen's definition, beliefs and values represent distinct paradigms, and she defined beliefs as intellectual acceptance of the "truth or actuality of something" (p. 191), including experiential and religious beliefs among other culturally derived patterns of thinking. She states that values "bring affective force to beliefs" and center on ideas of "good, proper, and pos-itive, or the opposite" (p. 191).

Damen's definition of cultural values and beliefs may seem to imply that teachers and learners are aware of these beliefs and values and can examine them intellectually. However, one of the prominent qualities of cultural values, assumptions, and norms acquired in the socialization process is that they are presupposed and not readily available for intel-lectual scrutiny. As Stewart (1972, p. 16) explains,

[t]he typical person has a strong sense of what the world is really like, so that it is with surprise that he discovers that 'reality' is built up out of certain as-sumptions commonly shared among members of the same culture. Cultural assumptions may be defined as abstract, organized, and general concepts which pervade a person's outlook and behavior.

To members of a particular culture, these assumptions appear self-evident and axiomatic. They are not, however, necessarily shared by members of other cultures whose values are also based on unquestioned and unques-tionable fundamental notions and constructs. In this sense, conceptual-izations of reality and social frameworks in different cultural communi-ties may occasionally be at odds to varying degrees.

Current perspectives

Kramsch (1991) notes that in many language classrooms culture is fre-quently reduced to "foods, fairs, folklore, and statistical facts" (p. 218). Like Thomas (1983, 1984), Kramsch emphasizes that the impact of culture on language learning and use is far more complex than "the four Fs" (ibid.) and that research and language teaching need to link "the teaching of language to that of culture" (p. 236). It is probably simplistic to imply that culture can be examined, taught, and learned through exercises for reading newspaper headlines and help-wanted advertisements or that customs, cuisines, and courtesies delineate the extent of the impact of culture on one's linguistic and interactive behaviors, although they can serve as springboards to more in-depth discussions.

A substantial body of research has emerged that points to a likelihood that many aspects of second and foreign language learning are affected by the interpretive principles and paradigms in learners' natal culture (Moerman, 1988; de Bot, Ginsberg, & Kramsch, 1991); that is, a second language learner's understanding of conceptualizations and constructs in second culture is fundamentally affected by his or her culturally defined worldviews, beliefs, assumptions, and presuppositions.

Culture and language are inseparable and constitute "a single universe or domain of experience" (Kramsch, 1991, p. 217). In her book *Context and Culture in Language Teaching,* Kramsch (1993a) states that cultural awareness and the learning of a second culture can only aid the attaining of second language proficiency. Kramsch indicates that the teaching of culture implicitly or explicitly permeates the teaching of social interaction, and the spoken and the written language. In her view, second and foreign language learners necessarily become learners of the second culture because a language cannot be learned without an understanding of the cultural context in which it is used. She cautions, however, that even the nonnative speakers who have had many years of experience with second culture may have to find their "own place" (p. 257) at the intersection of their natal and target cultures.

In the current understanding of the place of culture in second and foreign language pedagogy and learning, the work of Michael Byram has played a prominent role. In the late 1980s, Byram (1989) observed that culture represents "hidden" (p. 1) curriculum in second and foreign language teaching. He indicates that language teaching can rarely take place without implicitly teaching the culture of its speakers because language invariably refers to their knowledge and perceptions of the world, the concepts of culture, and cultural learning. Byram points out that communicative competence involves "appropriate language use which, in part at least, is culture specific" (Byram, 1989, p. 61).

Buttjes and Byram (1991) approached the teaching of language and culture as integrated and advocated intercultural mediation to serve as a source of "'causal knowledge' about culture" (Buttjes, 1991, p. 9). Byram (1991, p. 22) specified that the analysis of sociological, structural, and cultural aspects of language enhances "the language awareness component" of learning and contributes directly to the learner awareness of language and proficiency as a whole.

As Byram and Morgan (1994) observe, the teaching of culture often represents an aspect of language teaching that is unfamiliar to language teachers whose professional training largely focuses on structural facets of language. Although applied linguists and practitioners may have become aware that cultural variation is closely tied to language use, training in pedagogy rarely addresses the many influences of culture on language learning and teaching. Advanced language proficiency and linguistic skills do not necessarily point to a developed cultural proficiency (Barro et al., 1993). The conceptualization of culture as inextricable from ethnolinguistic identity (Gudykunst, 1989) and "notions of personhood" (Collier & Thomas, 1988, p. 104), however, leaves open the question of whether adult learners can be fully socialized in a second culture.

Explicit instruction of adults and attempts to speak "like a native" (Saville-Troike, 1989, p. 26) cannot take the place of the socialization process (Scollon & Scollon, 1995). The conceptualization of sociocultural frameworks and the structure of L1 beliefs, knowledge, presuppositions, and behaviors remain predominantly first culture-bound even for advanced and proficient nonnative speakers (Barro et al., 1993; Byram, 1989; Kramsch, 1993a). Byram and Morgan (1994, p. 43) state that "[l]earners cannot simply shake off their own culture and step into another . . . their culture is a part of themselves and created them as social beings. . . . Learners are 'committed' to their culture and to deny any part of it is to deny something within their own being."

Byram and Morgan (1994) state that "[i]t is axiomatic in our view that cultural learning has to take place as an integral part of language learning, and vice versa" (p. 5). They further call for the development of a theory that necessarily brings the learning of culture into the research that deals with second and foreign language teaching and learning. Byram and Morgan conclude that "the mere acquisition of linguistic competence is insufficient" and that teachers need to integrate current research findings into their transmission of knowledge to learners. Hymes (1996) similarly calls for introducing ethnography and research on influences of culture on language into education and states that both disciplines can draw on and change one another. He notes that although "schools have long been aware of cultural differences," culture has often been considered "invisible" (p. 75) in everyday interaction, as have the norms of speaking, the community values, and the sociocultural expectations of an individual's roles. According to Hymes, language plays a crucial role in the social life of the community, and a lack of cultural understanding among members of several communities often leads to social inequality that has yet to be recognized.

PART I:
CULTURE, INTERACTION, AND LEARNING

The purposes of communication and learning are often derived from cultural frameworks that have been in place for centuries and are often assumed to be so basic that they are rarely questioned. The chapters in Part I explore the influence of culture and culturally determined constructs on the assumptions associated with interaction, teaching, and learning, and the ways in which the learning of a second culture can be carried out. Together, these chapters present concepts considered crucial in applied linguistics: assumptions and presuppositions that members of divergent cultures take for granted, and lexical meanings that are not shared by members of various language communities but can be learned through immersion in a second culture. The work included in Part I draws on methodologies for applied linguistics analysis established in the domains of ethnography, originally outlined by Hymes and Gumperz and Hymes in the early 1970s, lexical organization, originated by Whorf in the 1950s, and the principles of pragmatic analysis and implicature specified in the seminal work of H. P. Grice, carried out in the 1970s.

In Part I, the broad picture of presupposed cultural constructs in second language learning draws on the Sapir–Whorf hypothesis pertaining to culturally determined values and beliefs. The studies that followed the foundational work on the effect of culture on language indicate that worldviews and subsystems of sociocultural meanings constitute major aspects of culture. Sapir observed that language behaviors are an intrinsic part of the socialization process, and language use needs to be understood as cultural and social phenomena with systematic regularities. In this sense, the learning of a second language necessarily entails readjusting these linguistic and cultural systems to some degree. Such readjustment requires understanding of the worldviews held in the second language community; the degree and difficulty of the readjustment depends on the extent of the differences between the learner's first and second language. As Hymes and Geertz proposed in the 1970s, communication between members of different cultural communities necessarily involves the interactants' systems of social and cultural identity and the subsystems of sociocultural norms. Whorf's hypothesis of lexical reflections of reality and their acquisition by nonnative speakers proposed that the readjustment of the cultural systems of worldviews and beliefs may not be always attainable for adults. The three chapters in Part II analyze the divergent worldviews that exist between learners' first and second language cultural systems and determine the extent to which their readjustment is possible.

The chapters in Part I reflect the influence of culture on aspects of interaction and learning that often appear mundane. Yet, the sociocultural behaviors of individuals follow the norms of the community and represent a convergence of philosophical, historical, and normative facets of culture. In interactions among members of different cultures, divergent concepts of appropriate behaviors and meaning interpretations can affect participants' conduct in social contexts. Nonnative speakers of a language are faced with the need to attend to normative paradigms and interactional practices, in addition to the linguistic parameters of imparting meaning and understanding. The findings in these studies indicate that although nonnative speakers can acquire certain culturally determined concepts and aspects of behavior, others may not be easily taught or learned.

In Chapter 1, Suzanne Scollon focuses on students' classroom behaviors and teachers' expectations of the classroom learning. Interaction between members of different cultures necessarily involves their systems of social meanings and normative behaviors, as noted by Hymes in the 1960s and 1970s. Suzanne Scollon employs an ethnographic approach to classroom interactions between students and teachers to exemplify the cultural constructs that underlie the views on the goals of education in Chinese and Western classrooms and that shape the behavior of students and teachers. She traces the cultural assumptions tacitly affecting the learning processes to the philosophical precepts stemming from the teachings of Socrates and Confucius. She asserts that these precepts have come to permeate students' and teachers' behaviors and expectations in such routine classroom tasks as presenting material to students and signaling beginnings and ends of lessons, as well as the complex notions associated with acceptable communicative exchanges between students and their educators. Scollon argues that the Socratic method of education underlies many daily activities in the Western classroom and emphasizes the art of rhetoric as a search for knowledge and education. In her view, this approach differs considerably from the Confucian educational philosophy, in which rhetorical reasoning is secondary and the primary goal is to gain wisdom and act in accordance with the moral code that the teacher communicates to the student. Furthermore, Scollon emphasizes that the assumptions of group identity and harmony maintenance, ubiquitous in the cultures that embrace Confucian philosophy, may appear to be a paramount goal for Chinese students operating in L1 or L2 that is not necessarily shared in the Anglo-American Socratic teaching and learning tradition.

In Chapter 2, James P. Lantolf discusses the cognitive aspects of learning a second culture and demonstrates that conceptual thinking is closely tied to the acquisition of lexical abstractions and generalizations. Lantolf points out that the organization of concepts and the development of conceptual thinking often form the basis for the way that objects and processes can be perceived in different cultures. The lexical development of second language users has proved to be a fertile ground for investigating the acquisition or lack of acquisition of concepts and meanings common in the second language culture but absent from the first. Lantolf's overview of several large-scale experiments demonstrates that these concepts can be acquired with mixed success. He notes that immersion in the second culture seems to play an important role in the learners' ability to construct conceptual organizations and lexical paradigms similar to those of native speakers, whereas the classroom learning of a second (or foreign) language does not necessarily produce proximate outcomes. When adults are immersed in a second culture, they acquire the new cultural constructs and models of meaning that rely on the conceptual organization and the lexical domains prevalent in the language of the second culture. However, current research has not yet been able to identify the role that cognition plays in second culture learning and acquisition. Lantolf cautions that it is not known what happens when people appropriate the conceptual and lexical modes of organization accepted in the second culture. It is also not clear whether a connection exists between linguistic proficiency and the cognitive ability to acquire modes of the second culture and its conceptual constructs.

Similar to Lantolf, in Chapter 3, Lawrence F. Bouton investigates the learning of meanings and conversational implications in L2 interactions. They point out that culturally defined contexts of interactions and the roles of the participants underlie the learners' ability to interpret conversational implicature and that members of different cultures appear to have diverse expectations of their interactional roles. Based on the notion of interactional competence developed by Hymes and the conversational principles stipulated by H. P. Grice in 1975, Bouton endeavors to find out whether the value of implied meanings is similar in conversations in various cultures. The author presents a longitudinal study to determine whether nonnative speakers are able to derive the same implied meanings in English expressions that native speakers do. He further investigates the length of time needed for nonnative speakers to develop the knowledge and skills that approximate those of native speakers. His findings indicate that conversational implicature presents various degrees of difficulty to nonnative speakers and that instruction can improve and speed up their ability to discern the implied meanings. He also found that nonnative speakers who received no instruction required almost three years to reach the level of competence attained by the nonnative learners who had been explicitly taught to deal with conversational implicature in the second culture. Similar to Lantolf, Bouton concludes that nonnative speakers can attain knowledge of the lexical and implied meanings in a second language and a second culture, but their progress appears to be somewhat constrained.

1 Not to *waste words* or *students*

Confucian and Socratic discourse in the tertiary classroom

Suzanne Scollon

The Master said, "To fail to speak to a man who is capable of benefiting is to let a man go to waste. To speak to a man who is incapable of benefiting is to let one's words go to waste. A wise man lets neither men nor words go to waste." *Analects* XV.8. (Lau, 1983, p. 151)

At a tertiary institution in Hong Kong, a foreign teacher is lecturing to a class of students, who listen attentively, occasionally commenting to each other in Cantonese on what the teacher has said. The teacher, disturbed by the talking, stops and waits for the students to stop. The students, sensing the teacher's discomfort, become silent, and the teacher resumes lecturing. Gradually, the students learn that the teacher expects them to be silent when she is lecturing. At the end of the lecture, the teacher asks whether there are questions. One student asks a question, and, as the teacher responds, the other students start talking among themselves. Soon it becomes noisy enough that the teacher either has to move toward the student in order to continue the discourse or ask the other students to be quiet. In either case, it is not long before students begin to ask whether they are permitted to leave. The teacher must then decide whether the class is over and if so, either give nonverbal permission and continue talking, or cut off her conversation at least momentarily to announce that the class is dismissed. If not, she may hurriedly give instructions regarding the assignment for the next class. She cannot help feeling that the students are being rude or showing lack of interest in the class. She may feel that she is wasting her breath if one student has raised an important question and the others are not listening to her response.

In another classroom, a Cantonese teacher is lecturing in English. Students are commenting to each other on what he says. As they get more

Paper presented at preconference institute on Culture in Teaching and Learning, TESOL, March 8, 1994, Baltimore, Maryland. The work reported here is part of an ongoing ethnographic study of Intercultural Problems of Identity in Discourse conducted by Ron Scollon and myself with the support of City Polytechnic of Hong Kong, Hong Kong Baptist College, and Lifelong Learning, Ohio University. I would like to acknowledge these institutions while assuming responsibility for my observations and conclusions. These observations were discussed in a group that met over a period of months in the spring semester of 1993. I would like to thank Timothy Boswood, David Li Chor Shing, and Ron Scollon for those discussions of classroom participation formats.

interested in the lecture, their talk becomes louder. The lecturer continues to speak, unconsciously becoming louder and louder in order to be heard over the students. Finally, he calls for their attention, and they quiet down. As the lecture continues, they again begin speaking to each other, now in subdued tones. He lectures until the end of the period, concluding by saying if they have any questions they can ask him later.

Almost every Western teacher new to Hong Kong experiences classes that resemble the one first described. In contrast, most Chinese teachers are unaware of students talking to each other in the classroom unless it becomes loud enough to interfere with their lessons. As a Chinese-American English teacher engaged in ethnographic research, I became interested in this difference in perception and began to pursue it in discussions with my collaborator Ron Scollon and other colleagues. We were puzzled both by this communicative pattern and by the fact that it was imperceptible to Chinese teachers.

Socratic and Confucian discourse

In teaching contrastive rhetoric during a period when democratic reforms were being hotly debated in Hong Kong, I began with the definitions of Aristotle and explained that he inherited from his teacher Plato, who wrote down the dialogues of his teacher Socrates, the ideal of using rhetorical skills to create discourse that facilitates in the establishment of truth. I was struck by Plato's location of the beginning of rhetoric in the origins of democracy in Syracuse in the fifth century BCE (Perelman, 1992, p. 759). Exiles who had been dispossessed of their lands by a despotic government had to go to court on their return in order to reclaim their property. As there were no written records, a democratic legal system was founded, with claims settled orally. This became the prototype for legal and democratic discourse still widely used today. The speaker pleads his case using argumentative discourse to an audience whose members participate in and judge a controversy. As skill in argumentation did not come naturally, teachers began to specialize in the teaching of rhetoric. Known as Sophists, they became influential with the growth of Athenian democracy. This new need, education for public affairs, gave rise to a new genre, the public lecture. The development of the art of rhetoric meant that eloquence became expected in lecturing, whether the subject was medicine, astronomy, or politics.

There developed a split between dialectic, the art of logical argument, on the one hand, and rhetoric, the art of persuasive speaking, on the other. Socrates was critical of rhetoric, which, in his view, was not concerned with truth but with utilitarian ends. His view of education was that its goal should be not efficiency and power but a search for knowledge and understanding. He is credited with the greatest literary achievement of the fourth century BCE, the Socratic method of teaching.

Dialogue is at the heart of the Socratic method, which is alive today not only as a subject for law students and philosophers but in much of the Western day-to-day experience of discourse inside and outside the classroom. Much of Western education is preparation for such events as oral dissertation defenses and other examinations, and ultimately job interviews. Citizens are assumed to need to be able to respond to questioning in court, soliciting the services of legal, medical, financial, or social welfare workers, or when crossing borders. In all of these settings, one needs to read between the lines to figure out what is being asked. Often this is done with question-and-answer sequences.

China, having no tradition of democracy, has only recently developed oratory, according to Oliver (1971), who demonstrates that there were persuasive speakers in ancient China, but they were individuals such as ministers speaking to their ruler one-on-one, unlike Greek politicians. The teaching of Confucius was tailored to the needs of individuals preparing for positions in administration. As Oliver points out, the ancient Chinese made no division between dialectic and rhetoric. As far as voicing one's opinion is concerned, Confucius has this to say:

When the Way prevails in the Empire, the rites and music and punitive expeditions are initiated by the Emperor. . . . When the Way prevails in the Empire, the Commoners do not express critical views. *Analects* XVI.2. (Lau, 1983, p. 163)

When everything is as it should be, the emperor is in charge, but the educated minister is free to speak his mind. When chaos prevails, one speaks out at his peril.

When the Way prevails in the state, speak and act with perilous high-mindedness; when the Way does not prevail, act with perilous high-mindedness but speak with self-effacing diffidence. *Analects* XIV.3. (Ibid., p. 133)

In keeping with his lack of interest in speaking out, Confucius had no faith in litigation:

In hearing litigation, I am no different from any other man. But if you insist on a difference, it is, perhaps, that I try to get the parties not to resort to litigation in the first place. *Analects* XII.13. (Ibid., p. 113)

Although it could be argued that the modern classroom and its modes of communication have been superimposed on students and teachers who hold assumptions handed down from the time of Confucius in the sixth and Socrates in the fifth centuries BCE, I will make no attempt to trace the historical development of the Socratic method or the Confucian method. Rather, I use these terms as labels for what I see as distinct ways of teaching in dyads or small groups based on cultural assumptions about teaching and learning. I will compare and contrast the two traditions in terms of the goals, philosophical assumptions, use of language in communication, and roles of teacher and students. Then I will describe their contact beginning in the nineteenth century and conclude by making suggestions about discourse in teaching and learning today.

The goal of education

Socrates and Confucius shared the educational ideal of upholding virtue. Socrates, although belonging to the Greek tradition of education, was critical of Athenian democracy, and made a virtue of thinking for oneself rather than following tradition:

I have heard a tradition of the ancients, whether true or not they only know; although if we had found the truth ourselves, do you think that we should care much about the opinions of men? *Phaedrus* [274]. (Jowett, 1990, p. 138)

He was concerned with ethical character and conduct and the practical use of reason for the sake of justice.

Until a man knows the truth of the several particulars of which he is writing or speaking, and is able to define them as they are, and having defined them again to divide them until they can be no longer divided, and until in like manner he is able to discern the nature of the soul, and discover the different modes of discourse which are adapted to different natures, and to arrange and dispose them in such a way that the simple form of speech may be addressed to the simpler nature, and the complex and composite to the more complex nature – until he has accomplished all this, he will be unable to handle arguments according to rules of art, as far as their nature allows them to be subjected to art, either for the purpose of teaching or persuading; – such is the view which is implied in the whole preceding argument. *Phaedrus* [277]. (Ibid., p. 140)

For Confucius, though he shared Socrates' interest in ethical conduct, training in virtue meant passing on the best of the Chinese tradition, which took precedence over thinking for oneself.

The Master said, "The *Odes* are three hundred in number. They can be summed up in one phrase, 'Swerving not from the right path.'" *Analects* II.2. (Lau, 1983, p. 11)

The Master said, "I transmit but do not innovate. I am truthful in what I say and devoted to antiquity." *Analects* VII.2. (Ibid., p. 57)

When under siege in K'uang, the Master said, "With King Wen dead, is not culture invested here in me? If Heaven intends culture to be destroyed, those who come after me will not be able to have any part of it. If Heaven does not intend this culture to be destroyed, then what can the men of K'uang do to me?" *Analects* IX.5. (Ibid., p. 77)

Although he presented himself as merely a transmitter, it is widely recognized that Confucius transformed the ancient tradition in a creative way (Chen, 1990). Concerned about the widespread belief that Confucianism teaches blind, rigid obedience to authority, Chen writes, "Few great persons in world history have been more misunderstood and misinterpreted to the West than the person of Confucius" (p. 460). Hall and Ames (1987, p. 48) also show that creativity is a recurring theme in the interplay between "learning" [*xue*] and "reflecting" [*si*], citing *Analects* XIII.36: "In doing what is authoritatively human [*jen*], do not yield even to your teacher."

The emphasis on reasoning was not a high priority of Confucius. As Hall and Ames state, "thinking for Confucius . . . is fundamentally *performative* in that it is an activity whose immediate consequence is the achievement of a practical result" (1987, p. 44).

The Master instructs under four heads: culture, moral conduct, doing one's best and being trustworthy in what one says. *Analects* VII.25. (Lau, 1983, p. 63)

He did acknowledge the necessity of thinking, however:

The Master said, "If one learns from others but does not think, one will be bewildered. If, on the other hand, one thinks but does not learn from others, one will be in peril." *Analects* II.15. (Ibid., 1983, p. 15)

The purpose of learning and wisdom is to be able to do what is right:

The Master said, "The man of wisdom is never in two minds; the man of benevolence never worries; the man of courage is never afraid." *Analects* IX.29. (Ibid., 1983, p. 85)

The main difference between Socrates and Confucius is that the former was interested in truth and universal definitions, his method centering on following out the consequences of a hypothesis, whereas the latter was more concerned about action. One learns in order to gain wisdom so that one may act appropriately. Instead of emphasizing truth, Confucius emphasized the consequences of using the right names in the doctrine of rectification or *zheng ming*:

When names are not correct, what is said will not sound reasonable; when what is said does not sound reasonable, affairs will not culminate in success; when affairs do not culminate in success, rites and music will not flourish; when rites and music do not flourish, punishments will not fit the crimes; when punishments do not fit the crimes, the common people will not know where to put hand and foot. Thus when the gentleman names something, the name is sure to be usable in speech, and when he says something this is sure to be practicable. The thing about the gentleman is that he is anything but casual where speech is concerned." *Analects* XIII.3. (Ibid., p. 121)

According to Hansen (1985), Western theories have assumed that truth arises from the faculty of reason, a doctrine that is not found in traditional

Chinese: observing rites
Western: reason ⇒ free action

Chinese moral theories. He asserts that although Mencius believed that all men could distinguish right from wrong, this faculty was held to be innate and had nothing to do with reason. Confucius conceived of man as a being who was realized and perfected through participation in the rites. In Western doctrine, reason is accompanied by belief and desire. Reason operates on beliefs by means of inferences and explanations, and on desires in the judgment of outcomes in deliberating practical matters. Thus, it forms the basis of voluntary, free action.

In associating names with desires rather than focusing on beliefs, Chinese philosophers focus on making distinctions, using social convention to condition appropriate attitudes and desires. Hansen views the rectification of names as a powerful means of shaping behavior. Western beliefs, by contrast, are structured as propositions or sentences that are creatively manipulated by the autonomous individual and thus less subject to social control. The individual's repertoire of words is finite, learned as part of socialization into a speech community by which he unconsciously absorbs attitudes associated with each word. Sentences, though, are not learned but formed in the process of reasoning that is part and parcel of explaining one's beliefs. This process of reasoning is nurtured by means of the Socratic method, in which parent or teacher asks leading questions in order to pursue truth by following a line of argument.

In his concern with consequences rather than truth, Confucius used rhetorical rather than leading questions. Rather than engaging in lengthy dialogues, he emphasized the importance of care in speaking:

The Master said, "The gentleman desires to be halting in speech but quick in action." *Analects* IV.24. (Lau, 1983, p. 35)

The Master said, "In antiquity men were loath to speak. This was because they counted it shameful if their person failed to keep up with their words." *Analects* IV.22. (Ibid.)

"To make friends with the straight, the trustworthy in word and the well-informed is to benefit. To make friends with the ingratiating in action, the pleasant in appearance and the eloquent is to lose." *Analects* XVI.4. (Ibid., p. 163)

The roles of the teacher

Socrates thought of himself as a midwife.[1] In the *Theaetetus*, he says, "These are the pangs of labor, my dear Theaetetus; you have something within you which you are bringing to the birth" [148] (Jowett, 1990,

---

1 Shelley Wong called my attention to *Theaetetus* in her paper "Dialogic Approaches to Teacher Education in the Teaching of English Writing to Speakers of Other Languages," in David C. S. Li, Dino Mahoney, and Jack C. Richards (Eds.), *Exploring Second Language Teacher Development* (City Polytechnic of Hong Kong, 1994).

p. 515). Just as in the Greek tradition a midwife was required to be past childbearing age, Socrates claimed to be beyond giving birth to brilliant ideas. His role in relationship to the youth is to lead him to the truth by means of questioning. "Then now is the time, my dear Theaetetus, for me to examine, and for you to exhibit" (ibid., p. 513). In this he expresses the pattern of linking dominance with spectatorship and subordination with display or exhibition; that is, the student, being subordinate in relation to his dominant teacher, is expected to exhibit erudition in order to earn his praise. Bateson (1972) associates this pattern of what he calls "end linkage" with the American national character.

In order to get at the truth, Socrates proceeds by asking a line of questions, "not in order to confute you, but as I was saying that the argument may proceed consecutively" (Jowett, 1990, p. 256). In the *Gorgias,* he leads the rhetoricians on, refuting and being refuted, in order to establish truth, reassuring them that he does it for this purpose only and not out of animosity. Of course, he does more refuting than being refuted, and more often than not his interlocutor agrees with him. In the *Phaedrus,* for example, he sets up a straw man to refute.

Confucius nowhere in the *Analects* pursues a line of questioning. Most typically his students ask a question, which he answers. At times he responds with a question, which he proceeds to answer:

Tzu-chang asked about going forward without obstruction. The Master said, "If in word you are conscientious and trustworthy and in deed singleminded and reverent, then even in the lands of the barbarians you will go forward without obstruction. But if you fail to be conscientious and trustworthy in word or to be singleminded and reverent in deed, then can you be sure of going forward without obstruction even in your own neighbourhood? When you stand you should have this ideal there in front of you, and when you are in your carriage you should see it leaning against the handle-bar. Only then are you sure to go forward without obstruction."
Tzu-chang wrote this down on his sash. *Analects* XV.6. (Lau, 1983, pp. 149–50)

Confucius uses rhetorical questions in giving counsel; for example, in advising someone not to attack, he asks, "What reason can there be for attacking them?" *Analects* XVI.1 (ibid., p. 161).

He sometimes responds to a student's question with a question. This method of asking a rhetorical question and then answering it is common in Chinese classrooms as well as in Chinese textbooks. Students most often expect a teacher to answer her own questions, and it may feel like pulling teeth to get a student to answer a question unless he really believes it is an open question. Confucius is asked questions by his students and responds with wisdom. Rather than a midwife who helps give birth to a truth that lies within, he is a messenger who transmits the wisdom of the ancients. Instead of invoking an internal authority, he has been seen as providing his students with an external authority, though he frequently tells them to think for themselves.

Chen, in his study *Confucius as a Teacher* (1990), summarizes the teaching methods of Confucius as set down by the subsequent schools of Mencius and Hsun-tzu. The conception that human nature is fundamentally good is at the heart of the teachings and method of Mencius. Individual differences are the result of experience. The role of the teacher is to serve as a role model, to perfect virtue and assist in the development of talent, to answer questions, and to cultivate his own virtue and learning while encouraging students to do the same. Chen quotes Hsun-tzu on the methods of teaching:

Of all the methods of controlling the body and nourishing the mind (the chief purpose of education), there is none more direct than the rules of proper conduct (*Li*), none more important than getting a teacher, none more divine than to have but one desire. (Chen, 1990, p. 449)

In performing the rites, as well as listening and speaking, Hall and Ames point out, communication is central:

In fact, given the pragmatic, performative character of Confucius' language it would hardly be an exaggeration to say that it is music – that is, musical performance – that serves as the paradigm for correctly understanding the nature of language and communication. (Hall & Ames, p. 255)

The role of the teacher is to communicate with students. For both Socrates and Confucius, it involves listening and speaking, but, as we have seen, the goals of communication, the modes of questioning, and the stance toward tradition and written authority differ. They share the goal of education according to the Latin roots meaning "to evoke," as Socrates brings forth understanding that is new to him as well as to his students. However, as Hall and Ames assert,

[Confucius's] use of the second sense of evocation, however, is much stronger than that of Socrates. Platonic philosophy assumes the preexistence of the truths sought through the dialectical method. Such cannot be the case with Confucius. (Ibid., p. 303)

They emphasize the creative acts of the ancient sages that Confucius uses as models for his disciples without any preconceived idea about the truth of the matter. He appeals to his listeners to use their ingenuity to apply the models to their own situation. He works by analogy and allusion rather of than rational principle. It is not a matter of following precedent in already defined cases, but rather an intuitive grasp of a relevant model that may result in a different outcome. The constant reflection over consequences stems from the need to continually create responses to ever-changing situations. There is no established truth from which one can rationally deliberate in any given context.

Teacher and student roles can also be characterized in terms of the relationship of communicants to a text. Confucius frequently exhorts his disciples to study the *Odes,* while Socrates elevates to the status of philosopher those who do not rely on written text but are able to use spoken arguments to prove or defend propositions, as in the *Phaedrus:*

Socrates: And now the play is played out; and of rhetoric enough. Go and tell
Lysias that to the fountain and school of the Nymphs we were down,
and were bidden by them to convey a message to him and to other
composers of speeches – to Homer and other writers of poems,
whether set to music or not; and to Solon and others who have
composed writings in the form of political discourses which they
would term laws – to all of them we are to say that if their compositions are based on knowledge of the truth, and they can defend or
prove them, when they are put to the test, by spoken arguments,
which leave their writings poor in comparison of them, then they
are to be called, not only poets, orators, legislators, but are worthy
of a higher name, befitting the serious pursuit of their life.
Phaedrus: What name would you assign to them?
Socrates: Wise, I may not call them; for that is a great name which belongs to
God alone, – lovers of wisdom or philosophers is their modest and
befitting title.
Phaedrus: Very suitable.
Socrates: And he who cannot rise above his own compilations and compositions, which he has been long patching and piecing, adding some
and taking away some, may be justly called poet or speechmaker or
law-maker.

While Socratic discourse emphasizes what Goffman (1981) calls "fresh talk," in which the philosopher rises above even his own text, Confucian discourse is focused on classical text, though the student is expected to appropriate the text to his own circumstances. These differing orientations to text cause confusion among our students when they are given texts of which they are expected to be critical. While the Western teacher is likely to assign readings for which the teacher does not take responsibility, students often assume that readings are assigned because they have value for their own sake. Just as there is no straw man in Confucian discourse, texts are studied because they have stood the test of time.

Participation frameworks

Goffman has analyzed the communicative roles of speaker and hearer in terms of degree of responsibility and social engagement in what he calls "participation framework": "when a word is spoken, all those who happen to be in perceptual range of the event will have some sort of participation status relative to it" (1981, p. 3). Just as actors on a stage orient their movement and voice to an audience, and utter phrases they may or may not have authored, ordinary people in social situations can be cast as taking up certain speaking and listening roles, though there may be no curtains to mark the boundaries between onstage and offstage behavior.

I believe we can account for the differences described at the beginning of this chapter by applying Goffman's framework. When teacher and students meet together in a classroom, they agree to take up various positions, in terms of both physical location and participation in speaking. When someone speaks, generally there is another person who is ratified as a hearer; that is, at least two people agree that while one is speaking, the other will listen. Whether people become fully engaged in their roles cannot easily be determined. As Goffman says, "For plainly we might not be listening when indeed we have a ratified social place in the talk, and this in spite of normative expectations on the part of the speaker" (ibid., p. 132). This is especially true of many students in most classrooms at least some of the time. Goffman goes on to say, "The relation(s) among speaker, addressed recipient, and unaddressed recipient(s) are complicated, significant, and not much explored" (ibid., p. 133).

For our purposes here, we will be concerned only with the outward behavior of students in the Hong Kong tertiary classroom as they enact their roles as ratified listeners. In general, they display engagement in the discourse by both talking and listening. Students who are required to remain silent may sometimes seem withdrawn. There seems to be a marked difference between listening behavior depending on whether the lecturer is Western or Chinese. I would say that what Goffman calls "subordinated communication" is more tolerated by Chinese than by Western teachers. Much of the talk might be considered "'byplay': subordinated communication of a subset of ratified participants" (ibid., p. 134). Generally, no attempt is made to conceal this talk. A Western teacher may attempt to call attention to such byplay, to bring it into the central or official classroom discourse. This usually has the effect of silencing the students engaging in byplay. They may then conduct their byplay in a lowered volume, which may bring the suspicion of collusion. According to Goffman, "When an attempt is made to conceal subordinate communication, 'collusion' occurs" (ibid.). Students speaking in Cantonese, which is generally unintelligible to a foreign teacher, may easily lead to interpretations of sideplay, or students acting as bystanders rather than active participants, especially if they speak in hushed tones.

This is a fertile area for research, as Goffman has merely laid the groundwork. He says, "in our culture each of these three forms of apparently unchallenging communication [byplay, sideplay, crossplay] is managed through gestural markers that are distinctive and well standardized, and I assume that other gesture communities have their own sets of functional equivalents" (ibid.).

Whatever happens while a teacher is lecturing, the participation framework changes when a student asks a question. In the Western classroom, while one student becomes a ratified speaker, the other students retain the role of ratified listeners. In the Chinese classroom, on the other hand, students begin to engage in byplay, often acting like bystanders, who are ordinarily obliged to "enact a show of disinterest, by disattending and withdrawing ecologically to minimize our actual access to the talk" (ibid., p. 132). In other words, they move out of their previous role of ratified listeners, or resume talk on topics brought up earlier.

How are we to understand this behavior? It may help to recall that from the time of the early courts at Syracuse, members of the audience were ratified listeners responsible for judging cases of property disposition by listening to speakers establish the truth of the matter at hand, that is, the history of use of a particular piece of land. The lecture developed not long afterward in the academies of Athens. In China, however, the lecture is a recent phenomenon, and the court operates by different rules, as Hansen (1985) shows in describing a case in which the law the defendant was supposed to have broken was never mentioned, the crime being "failure to study." In the light of Confucian teaching and learning, if the criminal had studied the classics and considered his actions with reference to the appropriate allusions, he would not have disrupted the social order and been tried at court. According to Hansen's account of this trial, which took place in the People's Republic in the 1970s, there was no attempt to establish the truth of the matter, but only a concern with the consequences of failing to "conform to shared communist ideals" (p. 372). It was not because, as Socrates says, "philosophy is always true" (*Gorgias* [482]), but apparently because communist ideals were currently, if not eternally, right.

In Platonic terms, a juror in a court or a student in a classroom is a member of a set of interchangeable members, each of which is expected to hear everything that transpires. According to Hansen (1983), the contrast between a universal set and the collection of its members, the one to the many, is at the root of Western philosophy. We tend to think of abstract ideal types when we think of the universal set. For example, if we think of a bird, a prototypical bird comes to mind. We do not think of a penguin or a chicken, which, though members of the set of birds, do not fly. Nor are we likely to consider the ostrich. "Free as a bird" does not conjure up the image of a penguin or a chicken. We are more likely to think of a robin or a bluebird. The penguin, the ostrich, and the chicken belong to the set of creatures we call birds, but they do not fit the definition or ideal of a bird as an animal that has wings and can fly.

Similarly, the ideal student pays attention to everything that takes place in the classroom. Although we acknowledge that individual members of the set of students may diverge from the ideal, just as the penguin is not our ideal bird, we nevertheless behave as though we believe members of the collectivity of students should approach the level of our ideal student, just as we believe members of a jury should have the characteristic of an ideal, impartial judge. As a ratified hearer, each student is expected to pay attention.

In contrast to the set–member relationship, the one to the many, characteristic of Western philosophy, in Confucian thinking there is a concern for part–whole relationships, which Hansen (1983) ties to the nature of the classical Chinese verb. Although Hall and Ames (1987) disagree with some of Hansen's analysis, they agree that Confucius's concern is pragmatic rather than semantic; that is, consequences are more important than truth. Confucius's interest is in "tuning the language, the practical consequence of which is to increase harmonious activity" (p. 264). The Confucian emphasis on aesthetic, particularistic relationships among men is inimical to an abstract, rational order. I suggest that our students who opt out of the role of ratified listener when one of their classmates engages the teacher in interaction are seeking to facilitate and maintain a particularistic relationship between teacher and student. It is the same motive that produces similar bystander behavior in a teacher's office when the phone rings, when they actively show lack of involvement in the telephone conversation. The participation of everyone assumes theoretical thinking that "presupposes that one can be objective and dispassionate in the consideration of alternative modes of understanding and action" (ibid., p. 265). When thinking is assumed to be particularistic, the part–whole relationship or the teacher and student as a holistic system takes precedence over the set–member, one to many, objective system. In this view, what transpires between teacher and student is particular to that relationship. It does no good to overhear if there is no assumption of universal relevance.

Socratic and Confucian discourse in contact

In the early nineteenth century, Chinese began studying in mission schools in Connecticut and elsewhere. Yung Wing was the first Chinese to graduate from an American college, a member of the Yale Class of 1854 (McCunn, 1988, p. 17). Born in a village of Kwangtung, he had previously studied in a missionary school in Macau. After his graduation, he worked to give other Chinese youths the opportunity to study in America. Sun Yat-sen, the revolutionary, went to Honolulu to study in 1879. The same year, Ko Kun Hua went to Harvard to teach the Chinese language, dressing as a Chinese scholar and requiring of his students the respect due a teacher in China (ibid.). These early contacts of small numbers of Chinese abroad and small numbers of missionaries in China led eventually to the revolution and the May Fourth Movement or Chinese Renaissance. Instrumental in the latter was Hu Shih, who was influenced by the pragmatism of John Dewey with its emphasis on consequences. Both Sun and Hu are noted for questioning their teachers until they fully understood what they were being taught, unlike the majority of traditionally educated Chinese. Both saw the connection between Western education and Western-style government.

We get glimpses of the two systems in contact in the early days of the Republic. Two sources suggest a combination of Chinese and Western learning, with both traditional classics and modern science taught largely by Confucian methods, one in a family home and the other in a village schoolroom.

A Hong Kong woman describes her education early in the century. According to Chinese custom, it began with a formal ceremony for which a teacher is selected with particular care (Cheng, 1976). The child was carried with a silk cloth over his head to a schoolroom, where the cloth was removed and he was led to kowtow to a portrait of Confucius. He would then kowtow to his teacher and be taught passages from the beginning and ending of the *Three Character Classic,* repeating after the teacher several times and listening to his explanations. The teacher would also guide the student's hand in writing simple characters. The teacher used narratives of personal experience to teach traditional virtues, calling students in small groups to his desk to explain each lesson, beginning the *Analects* at an early stage, marking punctuation and tone and writing definitions, introducing two or three lines a day, and then reviewing longer passages. Each lesson was recited from memory before progressing to the next. Behavior was strictly monitored and errors pointed out.

Turner (1982) reports that teachers in a Kwangtung village in 1919 provided individual instruction in large classes, with the effect of "constant turmoil." Although the students all memorized the same classics, each advanced at his own pace. In this period of transition, modern science and history were taught by the "same old methods."

John Dewey, Hu Shih's mentor, was invited to China to lecture in 1919 and given an award, and has perhaps left a mark on education in China. English education in Hong Kong has continued up to the present. With the emigration of large numbers of Chinese, Western countries now encounter a Confucian legacy in the expectations of students and teachers in their classrooms. Their academic success attests to a degree of successful accommodation, yet problems of communication remain (Jin & Cortazzi, 1993, 1994).

Conclusion

I have shown that different participation structures in classrooms of Chinese students in Hong Kong can be related to differing philosophical assumptions concerning communication, teaching, and learning. Although participation frameworks have not been systematically investigated in the cross-cultural classroom, my observations suggest that Western and Chinese teachers and students have different ways of mutually negotiating roles within these frameworks. When the teacher is on stage, so to speak, Chinese students will assume the role of ratified hearer. When the teacher signals by movement – for example, walking away from the front of the classroom, sitting in a chair, packing up his or her briefcase – that the lecture is over, the students assume the role of bystander. Further research needs to be done to determine the precise gestures by which these roles are mutually negotiated. Definition of the situation as discussion, recitation, presentation, or private consultation by means not only of gesture but of topic and code may prove relevant to the exchange between teacher and students of speaking and listening roles.

Keeping in mind the primacy of consequences in Confucian thinking can help us think about the use of various participation frameworks. One obvious manifestation of Chinese students' concern for consequences is their seeming obsession with marks or grades. Great effort goes into preparing class presentations that will be evaluated, as well as into understanding what is required for written assignments and tests. By the same token, little effort goes into getting at the truth unless it is clear what the consequences will be. Teachers sometimes suspect that every little action is fed into a calculator to determine the possible effect on grades. I do not mean to imply that students always try to maximize their marks. In many cases they simply calculate what is required to maintain a C average. It is easy to see this as a modern phenomenon in a competitive world, but Derk Bodde points out that from before the Christian era Chinese thinkers have been interested in precise quantification, even of qualities that cannot be precisely measured (Bodde, 1991, p. 356).[2] Morality was quantified in the "Table of Ancient and Modern Men," compiled around CE 100, which placed each of 1,955 names under one of nine columns, ranging from "sage" down to "stupid man" (ibid., p. 357). A graduate of Providence University in Taiwan reports that even if she were to obtain a Ph.D. from Harvard or some other prestigious university, her chances of getting a good job would be limited because Providence ranks low in the hierarchy of Taiwan universities. Knowing that she is not likely to be able to move from one column to the next, she is hesitant to make the investment it takes to undertake work toward the Ph.D.

2 Bodde (1991, p. 357) cites this example from a Ch'in law of the third century BCE:
   [Question:] How many rat nests must there be in a granary to merit sentencing or
                reprimanding?
     [Answer:] According to judicial procedure, for three or more nests there is a fine of
                one shield, for two or less a reprimand. Three mouse nests are equivalent
                to one rat nest.

One result of taking into consideration the different expectations with regard to participation frameworks is to clearly distinguish between situations that require the attention of every student and those that do not. In the former, it may be best to lecture rather than try to elicit Socratic dialogue. When not lecturing, it may work best to accommodate to the expectation that a teacher will privatize communications. Another format that appeals to Chinese students is requiring them to prepare presentations. If given an opportunity to discuss problems in small groups, they are often active in reporting to the whole class what they have discussed. In large-group discussions, students often respond to being nominated to say something, though they may be reluctant to put themselves forward as volunteers.

Western teachers unaccustomed to a classroom full of Asian students all too frequently feel that their words are going to waste because they do not get the feedback they are accustomed to not only in terms of comments and questions but in head movement and facial expression. It is all too common in such a situation to fall into a downward spiral of lowering our expectations and simplifying our language, using more direct questions that tend to elicit simple yes/no answers and decrease the possibility of dialogic exchange. This has the effect of further lowering teacher expectations in a vicious circle that amounts to failure to speak to students in a way that is capable of fully benefiting them by providing the rich language environment they need in order to learn. In this we risk letting not only our students go to waste but ultimately our words.

I think we can avoid this downward spiral by understanding the contrasting traditions of Confucian and Socratic discourse and their convergence in the contemporary classroom.

2 Second culture acquisition
Cognitive considerations

James P. Lantolf

While research on the learning and teaching of second languages as codes has concerned itself with the internalization of the grammar of these languages and with questions such as universal grammar (UG) effects and ultimate attainment, work on culture learning and teaching has been more interested in attitudinal issues relating to learners' development of tolerance and understanding of other cultures as well as in the degree to which the study of other cultures enhances cultural self-awareness. It goes without saying that this work is important and needs to continue. To my knowledge, however, only a minimal amount of research has been carried out on the process and extent to which adults are able to acquire, in the sense of appropriate, another culture. The intent of this chapter is to consider what is entailed cognitively in appropriating a second culture as an adult and to explore what kind of evidence might indeed show that it is possible to appropriate a second culture (henceforth, SCA).

Robinson-Stuart and Nocon (1996, p. 435) make the following statement with regard to culture teaching and learning: "together, these elements reflect a current direction in language pedagogy, which is recognizing the importance of second culture acquisition." How are we to interpret "acquisition" when it comes to culture? Does it have the same meaning with respect to culture as it does in the case of linguistic development, or does it mean something different? Byram (1989, p. 42), for example, points out that the cultural experiences that teachers can provide for learners in the tutored setting are, at best, "vicarious" and argues that "it would be misguided to teach as if learners can acquire foreign cultural concepts, values and behaviors, as if they were a *tabula rasa* (Byram, 1991, p. 18). Kordes (1991, p. 288) reports that after 3 years of French study, including time in country, one third of 112 students in a sixth German *Oberstufe* remained monocultural, a small minority attained some intercultural understanding, and only six students reached the level of transculturation, in which they achieved some degree of identification with the foreign culture (p. 304).[1] Recognizing that cultural pro-

---

1 Transculturation is not SCA in the sense to be developed in this chapter. It is, however, recognition of the validity of different cultural viewpoints while remaining at ease with one's own culture (Byram & Morgan, 1994, p. 157).

ficiency may be more difficult to assess than linguistic proficiency, Kramsch (1991, p. 220) notes that even in the case of study-abroad experiences, the evidence pointing to the development of cross-cultural understanding or cross-cultural personality development is lacking (p. 234). According to Kramsch (1993b, p. 234), even individuals who immigrate to a new country and spend the remainder of their lives as active participants in the new cultural setting often report the feeling of not "really belonging to the host culture," but of being situated on its borders.

Robinson (1991, p. 115) suggests that the reason instructional programs in general fail to achieve their cultural goals is that we "have not looked at what it is that is acquired in the name of culture learning, how culture is acquired and modified, and by what processes." Byram (1991, p. 19), for one, believes that the goal of culture instruction cannot be to replicate the socialization process experienced by natives of the culture, but to develop intercultural understanding. Kordes (1991, p. 302) expresses a similar view in claiming that even though a foreign culture is less learnable than a foreign language, intercultural learning is feasible to at least some degree. Kramsch (1993a) proposes that in the classroom setting it is possible to foster the formation of what she calls a *third culture*, conceived of as the intersection of multiple discourses rather than as a reified body of information to be intellectualized and remembered. Robinson-Stuart and Nocon (1996) present the results of a classroom study that shows that it is possible for learners to develop positive attitudes toward the cultural perspective of members of different speech communities as a result of an instructional program that brings learners into meaningful interaction with members of the second culture (C2).[2]

Although it may be possible for people to develop an intellectual understanding and tolerance of other cultures, a more interesting question, perhaps, is if, and to what extent, it is possible for people to become cognitively like members of other cultures; that is, can adults learn to construct and see the world through culturally different eyes? At issue is not acculturation, that is, learning to function in a new culture without compromising one's own identity or worldview (Byram & Morgan, 1994, p. 25).

---

2 Although the findings of this study are encouraging to the extent that the students developed a greater degree of tolerance toward another culture and were also able to confront and begin to overcome some of their cultural prejudices and stereotypes, some of the learners' comments are troublesome, such as the following: "I learned that Mexicans are very much like we are and I also began to look at them coming into our country in a different way" (Robinson-Stuart & Nocon, 1996, p. 442). It is indeed a positive step that the student who produced this response goes on to say that Mexican people ought to be allowed to immigrate to the United States; however, I worry about the assumption that Mexicans "are very much like we are." Are Mexicans to be permitted to come to the United States only if we conclude that they are really like us after all and that cultural differences are not that important? If they were really not like us, would they then be prevented from coming?

It seems fairly uncontroversial that, given sufficient time and exposure to the C2 and the motivation to do so, adults can and do acculturate. The focus of the following discussion is precisely on trying to understand what needs to happen for someone to acquire (i.e., appropriate) a second culture. To do this, I will first consider the nature of the relationship between culture and mind, and then survey some existing research that I believe bears on the issue of second culture acquisition as a cognitive process. As a general theoretical framework for the discussion, I rely on the sociohistorical psychology of L. S. Vygotsky and his colleagues.

Culture and mind

Although the scholarly literature in the human disciplines, including anthropology, sociology, philosophy, literary theory, and psychology, and education reflects interesting discussion on precisely how culture is to be understood as a theoretical, and even a pedagogical, construct, the concern of this chapter is limited to only one of the ways of construing culture, and that is as a cerebral or cognitive category.[3] In this regard, perhaps the best-known definition of culture, and the one I rely on as the starting point for the discussion that follows, is provided by Geertz (1973, p. 89), who defines culture as a "historically transmitted semiotic network constructed by humans and which allows them to develop, communicate and perpetuate their knowledge, beliefs and attitudes about the world." This view of culture melds nicely with sociohistorical psychology, which conceives of culture and mind as semiotically organized functional systems and insists on an inherent dialectical relationship between the two (Vygotsky, 1978; Wertsch, 1985), such that during ontogenesis the biologically specified mental endowment of children is shaped in specific ways once it interfaces with cultural forces as children are apprenticed into their native culture (see Lave & Wenger, 1991).[4] Vygotsky captures this process in his genetic law of cultural development, which states that

any function in the child's cultural development appears twice, or on two planes. First it appears on the social plane, and then on the psychological plane. First it appears between people as an interpyschological category, and then within the child as an intrapsychological category. This is equally true with regard to voluntary attention, logical memory, the formation of concepts and the development of volition. (Vygotsky, 1981, p. 163)

3 Vygotsky was careful to avoid a reductivist stance by arguing that neither biological nor cultural forces alone are sufficient to account for mental development; rather, biology constrains what is possible and social forces organize the possibilities in accordance with the semiotic properties of the culture (Wertsch, 1985, p. 43).

4 Along somewhat different lines, Byram and Morgan (1994) propose an argument based on ingrained cultural schemata to explain the difficulty people have in moving between cultures.

Although all of the properties included in the scope of the law of genetic development are potentially relevant to SCA, in my view, the development of conceptual thinking may be the most important.[5] This is because concepts govern every facet of our daily activities and "structure what we perceive, how we get around in the world, and how we relate to other people" (Lakoff & Johnson, 1980, p. 3). Concepts can be thought of as networks of systematic beliefs about how the world is (Keil, 1989, p. 1).

Shore (1996, p. 47), in presenting a neo-Vygotskyan stance on concept formation, contends that concepts have their origins in two primary sources, personal mental models and cultural models. Cultural models are the conventionally constructed and shared cognitive resources of a community and are formed and transformed as a consequence of the endless negotiation that transpires as the members of a particular community go about the business of living. As Shore puts it, "to gain motivational force in a community, these models must be reinscribed each generation in the minds of its members. In this way conventional models become a personal cognitive resource for individuals" (ibid.). These models are constructed as mental representations and function as sociocultural constraints on what we as members of a culture attend to and as what we perceive as salient in our world. Personal mental models, on the other hand, are formed by individuals as a result of their unique experiences of life activity. The study of personal mental models has been the major focus of research within mainstream cognitive psychology, where they have been assumed to be representations of the physical world constructed by more or less isolated individuals (ibid., p. 49). Interest in cultural models has been confined largely to the domain inhabited by anthropologists. However, as Shore's research clearly and convincingly shows, personal and cultural models are dialectically interrelated, because the formation and transformation of personal models is heavily influenced by the cultural models appropriated during ontogenetic development. A full exposition of the nature of the interaction between personal and cultural models is well beyond the scope of this chapter. Instead, I would like to focus on one type of cultural model, and in so doing highlight what the appropriation of a second culture entails from a cognitive perspective.

Shore (ibid., p. 56) groups cultural models into two broad classifications: structural and functional. Functional models, which I will only mention in passing, are of three types – orientational, expressive, and task. Structural models incorporate linguistic as well as nonlinguistic submodels. Included among the linguistic models, and of concern for present purposes, are lexical and verbal submodels. The former consist of taxonomies, lists, and other linked items, and the latter are formed by

---

5 For a discussion of narrative models and their role in the acquisition of second cultures by adults, see Pavlenko and Lantolf (1997).

proverbs, sayings, prayers, tropes, metaphors, narratives, and the like. In what follows, I consider both the lexical and metaphorical aspects of concepts and their formation.

Lexical concepts and their formation

Space requires that I distill to their bare essentials Vygotsky's theoretical and empirical work on conceptual thinking and its ontogenesis.[6] The central player in concept formation for Vygotsky is the word, which serves to focus attention, select, analyze, and synthesize the distinctive features of the various phenomena in the social and objective world of humans.[7] According to Vygotsky (1986, pp. 106–107), "words and other signs are those means that direct our mental operations, control their course, and channel them toward the solution of the problem confronting us." In the early stages of ontogenesis, words for children are kinds of proper names for specific objects and nothing more. Eventually, words come to represent groups of objects, entities, or notions related to one another in a variety of ways. Importantly, the relationships signaled by words tend to be highly unstable. Vygotsky characterizes this type of variable thought process as thinking in complexes or loose collections or sets of complementary things anchored in the child's practical experiences in the world of objects (ibid., pp. 114–115). As Vygotsky's own experiments showed, children at the stage of complex thinking often begin by grouping things according to one feature – say color – and then move to grouping the same things by size, or shape. Thus, a word such as *blocks* might refer to a set of objects of the same color but of different shapes, or the reverse, or even to a mélange of things grouped by both color and shape.[8]

Eventually, children attain the stage of preconceptual thinking, in which they think in *pseudoconcepts* – a type of complex formed not on the basis of an abstraction, characteristic of mature adult thought, but on the basis of "concrete, visible likeness" (ibid., p. 119). The pseudoconcept provides the critical bridge between the complex-based thinking of chil-

6 Vygotsky's views on concepts and their formation have not gone unchallenged. Fodor (1972), for example, questions both Vygotsky's view of concepts and his claim that qualitative shifts occur in their organization during ontogenetic development. Keil (1989) presents an in-depth discussion of Fodor's criticisms, along with some criticisms of his own. In my view, however, both Fodor and Keil have misunderstood Vygotsky's writings in this area. In fact, it seems to me that Keil's interesting empirical research on concept formation fleshes out many of the areas Vygotsky's own work left undone.

7 According to Lakoff and Johnson (1980), our conceptual structure is largely organized on the basis of metaphor, which we can think of as a special kind of lexical manifestation.

8 Vygotsky found, for example, that children asked to group blocks of different geometrical shapes often put together things such as triangles and trapezoids because trapezoids reminded the child of triangles.

dren and the conceptual thinking of adults. Crucially, however, the bridge is formed as a result of the dialogue that arises between children and adults. In this dialogue, children have some freedom to spontaneously create new meanings, but this creative process is itself not completely unconstrained, because it is strongly influenced and shaped by the meanings of adults.[9] In other words, children have some room to maneuver, but in most cases they are compelled to appropriate the cultural models as presented to them by adults and older peers (ibid., p. 122). "Verbal communication with adults thus becomes a powerful factor in the development of the child's concepts" (ibid., p. 123).

Concept formation through analysis and synthesis requires one to abstract elements or properties from objects and to view these properties apart from the concrete experience from which they are originally contextualized. When a word such as *flower* first appears in children's speech, which, according to Vygotsky, is earlier than the name of particular flowers such as *rose,* it is applied to all flowers.[10] Even when the names of particular flowers begin to appear in the child's speech, one cannot claim that the concept *flower* has been formed, because for some time the word *flower* does not have a more general meaning than the words for specific flowers, despite the fact that *flower* may be more broadly applied than words such as *tulip* or *rose.* Only when *flower* becomes the superordinate term for the category and words such as *tulip* and *rose* are included as instantiations of the category has the child's mind moved to the level of conceptual thinking.[11]

It is clear that the organization of concepts, and hence conceptual thought, varies across cultures. The entities designated by the same word in one culture are not necessarily the entities labeled by a corresponding

9 The amount of creative freedom that children are assumed to have in developing lexical meaning is a controversial issue within neo-Vygotskyan theory. According to Newman and Holzman (1993, p. 87), learning in the zone of proximal development is the revolutionary activity of meaning making, undetermined by the symbolic tools offered to children by adults. Others, such as Wertsch (1985), seem to take a more conservative view of the ontogenetic development of meaning, arguing that children eventually appropriate the meanings and tools offered them by adults with less room for innovation and creativity than Newman and Holzman allow. The more radical view of Newman and Holzman is generally characterized as sociohistorical psychology and the more conservative perspective of Wertsch is usually referred to as sociocultural psychology. I cannot here explore these interesting and important differences further; however, the theoretical differences do not affect the fundamental argument on culture acquisition I am trying to make.

10 As Vygotsky (1986, p. 143) notes, even when a word such as *rose* predates *flower* in the child's lexicon, it takes on a general rather than a specific meaning and is thus used to refer to all flowers.

11 Vygotsky distinguishes between *spontaneous* concepts appropriated from everyday contextualized settings and *scientific* concepts learned in the school setting. Although the distinction is critical for his general theory of sociocultural thinking, it is not directly relevant to the discussion unfolding here, and I therefore will not pursue the issue further.

word (assuming a corresponding word even exists) in another culture. Hence, the Bororo people of Brazil include themselves within the concept *red parrot* (ibid., p. 128). In Hopi, no distinction is made between *spilling* (accidental act) and *pouring* (intentional act). Consequently, in an experiment related in Ratner (1991, p. 75), when asked to group any two of a set of three pictures together, Hopi subjects preferred grouping the picture of a man pouring fruit from a box by inverting it and that of a man spilling liquid while inattentively pouring it from a pitcher into a glass. Anglo-American subjects, on the other hand, grouped the picture showing the liquid spilling with one showing a coin falling from a man's pocket when he pulls out his handkerchief (ibid.). Similarly, Lucy (1996) reports on a series of cross-cultural experimental studies on object classification in which Americans preferred to classify objects according to shape, while Mayas opted for material-based classifications. Lucy attributes this finding to consistent lexical differences between Mayan and English. Nouns with concrete referents in Mayan refer to unformed substances; hence, when Mayan speakers wish to refer to a specific object, they must use a numeral classifier. For example, what in English is referred to as a "candle" in Mayan is called "one long thin wax" (ibid., p. 50).[12] Another relevant finding of Lucy's research is that Mayan children, like their American counterparts, prefer shape over material substance when classifying objects. At about the age of 8, he discovered a marked shift toward the adult classificatory pattern (ibid., p. 51).

The Wintu people of northern California, view *self* as not clearly demarcated from *other;* in addition, they conceive of the *self* as essentially coterminus with the body (Kearney, 1984, p. 150). The Anglo view of *self,* on the other hand, is sharply distinct from *other* and is smaller than one's entire body. For this reason, Anglos speak of "my body," "her face," and so on, which is not possible in Wintu (ibid.). Moreover, English, like other European languages, distinguishes "I go" from "We go," while Wintu uses the same word, *harada,* to mean "I go" or "we go" (ibid., p. 151). In U.S. culture, owing to the view of *self* and *other,* concepts of *individual rights* and *private property* are salient, while in Wintu culture the two concepts are virtually meaningless (ibid.).

Inner speech and cultural appropriation

In this section, I consider briefly the process through which individuals appropriate cultural concepts, and in so doing organize their minds in

---

12 English, of course, does have some nouns that pattern like Mayan nouns and thus may be used with a quantifier and a classifier, as in "one cube of sugar." The predominant pattern in English, however, and this is Lucy's point, is for concrete nouns to carry inherent shape, as in the "candle" example or in something like "box," which in Mayan would be rendered by something like "one cardboard."

culturally specific ways. The power of the mental organization set up during apprenticeship into one's native culture is extensively addressed in the writings of Bourdieu (1991). According to Bourdieu, individuals acquire a habitus very early in their cultural formation. The habitus is a shared body of dispositions, classificatory categories, and generative schemes that arise in collective history and is inculcated largely through the pedagogical practices of the family, which rely for their effectiveness on their thoughtlessness, nonreflectivity, and appearance of cultural neutrality (Jenkins, 1992, p. 80). For Bourdieu, it is the nonreflective nature of the dispositions of the habitus that leads to their immutability: "Once acquired it [the habitus] underlies and conditions all subsequent learning and social experience" (ibid., 79).[13] What is missing from Bourdieu's explication of the power of the habitus is a psychological account of the inculcation (or, in our terms, appropriation). It is here that the work of Vygotsky and other sociohistorical psychologists on *inner speech* is relevant.

As already mentioned, for Vygotsky, concepts and conceptual thinking are formed during the dialogic interactions that occur between children and adult (or older child) members of a culture. It is in dialogues that children appropriate the words of others through listening to others speak to them, and in so doing appropriate the organizational patterns (concepts) of the culture, including a concept of self (Ushakova, 1994, p. 138).[14] The research of Vygotsky and his colleagues traces the appropriation process from the outside in; that is, in sociohistorical theory, children initially deploy the speech of others in order to communicate with others in their sociocultural environment. Eventually, this social speech goes underground as *inner speech,* first passing through a stage of *egocentric* or *private speech* in which children produce language that looks social in form but is clearly mental in function. Private speech is speech directed at the self as interlocutor rather than at some other and it functions to organize and guide the child's own mental activity.[15] Eventually, private speech becomes completely covert as inner speech, but occasionally reemerges as private speech in the face of particularly difficult and complex mental tasks.[16]

13 Although dispositions are influenced by explicit pedagogical practices, such as those that occur in the schools, those formed within the family during the early years are the most important (Jenkins, 1992, p. 106). The difference, for Bourdieu, is that those acquired in the everyday world, as in the case of Vygotsky's spontaneous concepts, tend to be appropriated nonreflectively, whereas those learned in school generally entail a higher level of reflectiveness on the part of the student.

14 Bakhtin captures the process of appropriation in his notion of *ventriloquation,* the process through which one takes on the voices of others and makes them one's own (Wertsch, 1991, p. 53).

15 For a full discussion of private speech in ontogenesis, see Berk and Diaz (1992), and for its reemergence in the case of adult second language learners, see Frawley and Lantolf (1985).

16 Through a series of interesting experiments, using, among other techniques, electromyography, Sokolov (1972) was able to show a strong connection between problem-solving activity and often covert movements of the articulatory organs, including

The salient property of inner speech is its semantic content: "the contraction of inner speech means that its syntax and phonetics are reduced to a minimum, and word meaning acquires primary significance" (ibid.). As inner speech moves increasingly further from its social progenitor, it evolves into verbal thought or pure meaning. Vygotsky crucially distinguishes between conventional dictionary meaning (*znachenie* in Russian) present in social speech intended for others and sense (*smysl* in Russian) inherent in inner speech intended for the self. Sense, or *smysl,* is

a dynamic, fluid, complex whole, which has several zones of unequal stability. Meaning [*znachenie*] is only one of the zones of sense, the most stable and precise zone. A word acquires its sense from the context in which it appears; in different contexts, it changes its sense. Meaning remains stable throughout the changes of sense. The dictionary meaning of a word is no more than a stone in the edifice of sense, no more than a potentiality that finds diversified realization in speech. (Vygotsky, 1986, p. 245)

Thus, meaning, for Vygotsky, is conventional and culturally determined, while sense has a clear experiential patina. Furthermore, in inner speech "a single word is so saturated with sense that . . . it becomes a concentrate of sense" (ibid., p. 247).

An example of what Vygotsky intends by the difference between meaning and sense comes from Szalay (1984, p. 75), who, like Vygotsky, differentiates between a word's lexical, and hence fixed, meaning and its psychological, and therefore fluid, meaning. According to Szalay, the English word *drug* is conventionally defined as something like "a substance with medicinal effects," while its psychological meaning varies from person to person or from group to group depending on each one's respective experiences with the concept. Thus, to a Christian Scientist, *drug* may be infused with connotations of *hell,* owing to the word's common religious connotations, but for the addict, *drug* may well be saturated with meaning more closely affiliated with *heaven* and *pleasure* (p. 76).

The research of Ushakova, her colleagues, and her students indicates that "the base elements of inner speech do not remain isolated, but are integrated, joined together by multiple temporary connections, forming an extensive system of interrelated structures" (Ushakova, 1994, p. 145). The verbal network of inner speech consists of multiple connections cre-

---

digital impulses in the case of deaf individuals, and cerebral activation of the language areas of the brain even in the absence of overt verbal behavior. The more difficult and complex the mental activity, the more robust were the articulatory movements and the concomitant neurological patternings in the brain. Luria's (1973) research shows the neurological seat of inner speech to be situated in the frontal lobes. Luria discovered that when either the frontal lobe region of the brain or the neurological links between this region and other areas of the brain, such as the parietal and occipital regions undergo trauma, thinking is profoundly affected or destroyed altogether.

ated between verbal signals that in turn form the basis of the verbal concepts that appear as words (p. 146).

In a series of experiments on the learning of an artificially constructed second language conducted by Ushakova's research group, it was found that the way subjects grouped words in the L2 is determined by the "semantic foundation realized in the system of the earlier acquired (first) language" (ibid., p. 151). Moreover, it was found that the newly learned words were "classified according to the classification of the first language" (p. 152). Ushakova reasons that the principal driving force of first language ontogeny is inner self-development – a self organized on the basis of listening to, and appropriating, the words of others in the culture. Thus, inner speech structures laid down during ontogenesis are located at a very profound psychological level and tend to resist mutation, and so one can observe a clear parallel between Bourdieu's immutable habitus and inner speech.

Second language acquisition in adults, according to Ushakova, is not driven by the motive of self-construction but by a more externally directed motive of interacting with others who use the L2. This results in the "plugging in" of the new structures, including words, into the previously worked-out structures, or, as Ushakova metaphorically puts it: "second language is looking into the windows cut out by the first language" (p. 154). Similarly, John-Steiner (1985, p. 365) claims that learning a second language entails a "weaving" of new meanings into the fabric of verbal thought already existing in the first language. Although this view of second language learning may hold true in the case of classroom learners, as some of the evidence to be considered in this chapter seems to show under certain circumstances (i.e., cultural immersion), adults are capable of appropriating new cultural models and in so doing modifying their conceptual organization.

Research on lexical concepts in a second language

The data considered in this section comes from studies on word association experiments. Given that conceptual organization is semiotically based, patterns of word affiliations should provide insight into the conceptual organization of the individuals or groups that generate the affiliations (Szalay, 1984). Kolers (1963) and Ervin (1968) carried out two of the early word association studies among bilingual adults. Kolers, in his study of Spanish-English, German-English, and Thai-English bilinguals, reports that in the case of concrete stimulus words (e.g., *butterfly* and *tree*) subjects tended to generate similar responses in both their L1 and L2, but for abstract stimuli (e.g., *joy* and *rage*) subjects more often than not produced culture-specific responses. Kolers concludes that, in general, "experiences and memories of various kinds are not stored in common in some supralinguistic form but are tagged and stored separately in the language S[ubject] used to define the experience to himself" (Kolers, 1963, p. 300).

Ervin (1968) studied the Japanese wives of American servicemen residing in the United States during the post–World War II era. Similar to Kolers, she found differences in her subjects' responses to word associations depending on the stimulus language. Hence, for example, when *New Year's Day* was presented in English, subjects responded with words such as *party* and *holiday*. When presented with the Japanese equivalent of the same word, however, subjects responded with typical Japanese items such as *omochi* (rice cake) and *kimono*.

A more recent study of Japanese-English cross-cultural word association (Yoshida, 1990) reaches a different conclusion from that of Kolers and Ervin. The subjects for Yoshida's study were 35 Japanese college students who had lived in the United States for at least 2 years prior to entering a Japanese university. Yoshida gave his subjects stimulus words in Japanese and English and asked them to respond in the same language as the stimulus word. The Japanese and English versions of the association task were administered 1 week apart. Four categories of words were selected for presentation: nature (*haru*/spring, *hana*/flower), daily life (*oona*/woman, *sensei*/teacher), society and ideas (*jiyuu*/freedom, *nihon*/Japan, America), culture (*kurisumasu*/Christmas, *shougatsu*/New Year's Day).[17] Although some differences were noted between the bilingual's responses and those of the Japanese controls, the principal finding of Yoshida's study is that "the bilingual group's responses in both Japanese and English were quite similar to that of the Japanese control group, while differing greatly from that of the American control group" (ibid., p. 22). The one area in which Yoshida observed language-dependent differences is in the response patterns to the culture category, where he found the same kinds of patterns uncovered in Ervin's earlier study of Japanese women living in America. For the stimulus word *Japan*, however, the bilinguals, in both languages, patterned more like the Japanese than the American controls. Interestingly, for the stimulus *Christmas*, the bilinguals, again in both languages, generated *Christ* as one of their responses, while, as might be expected, the Japanese controls did not produce this response; on the other hand, the Americans also failed to manifest this association. This leads one to suspect, as mentioned above, that when a concept is unique to the C2 and perhaps known only at a conscious intellectual level in the C1, C2 learners may learn the concept, at least at the metalevel, because it is marked relative to their native culture. This

---

17 Yoshida also administered a social distance questionnaire to his subjects; however, since this portion of his work is not directly relevant to the present discussion, we will not consider these findings here.

possibility is bolstered by the fact that the most frequent response from the Japanese controls for *Christmas* was *Santa Claus,* a uniquely Western notion, which, by the way, was missing from the Americans' most frequent response tokens. Yoshida found similar results for the stimulus *New Year's Day* and *shogatsu.* Here, however, one of the frequent American responses, *football,* supposedly unique to this time of year in the United States, was missing from the bilinguals' response patterns. It seems then that even though culturally unique concepts generate evidence of cultural learning, it is not too surprising to find that if SCA is to happen at all, it would be in this domain.

As interesting as Yoshida's research is, it is not clear that real cultural acquisition, in the cognitive sense used in this chapter, has occurred. Yoshida notes, for instance, that the Japanese bilinguals, despite having spent a good deal of time in the United States and having developed a fairly high level of linguistic proficiency, "will never really be able to feel like an American, and that some may never even be able to behave in an American way. The most we can expect is that they will be able to understand and acknowledge the differences which exist between Japanese and Americans" (Yoshida, 1990, p. 25). It sounds as if Yoshida is describing a situation more akin to acculturation than to cognitive restructuring.

In the three previous studies, subjects were asked to respond with the first word (excluding a translation equivalent) that entered their mind immediately following presentation of the stimulus word. Thus, only one response word was generated per subject for any given stimulus word. According to the Associative Group Analysis (AGA) procedure developed and implemented in a series of studies by Lorand Szalay and his colleagues (1967, 1968, 1972, 1984), a more appropriate way of accessing a subject's or a group of subjects' conceptual organization is through the generation of sets of associative responses, usually elicited with little or no time pressure. According to Szalay, this procedure uses "the spontaneous free association produced by members of cultural samples to reconstruct their subjective images and meanings" (Szalay, 1984, p. 78). In AGA, subjects write free verbal associations to randomly presented stimulus words. Responses are then weighted according to their relative rankings across subjects, with earlier responses showing higher stability than later responses.

Szalay argues that one can gain access to the cultural beliefs of a group through analysis of the subjective meanings generated during AGA tasks. In short, it provides a way of getting a handle on the cognitive mappings of a culture (ibid., p. 74), or, in Shore's (1996) terms, a cultural model. In many ways, as mentioned earlier, Szalay's perspective is similar to Vygotsky's. He contends that the main representational units produced by subjects during AGA are not purely conventional lexical meanings but subjective psychological meanings (1984, p. 75) – in Vygotsky's terms, sense (*smysl*) rather than meaning (*znachenie*) – and for Shore (1996), these are personal mental models. These subjective meanings, however, are for Szalay clearly culturally linked, as indicated in the following commentary:

> beyond the development of conscious opinions which people can articulate in the form of judgements (e.g., I disapprove of the President's Middle East policy), they also develop their view or meanings. People are essentially unaware that these are dependent on their own frame of reference but assume that they represent plain and simple realities which exist independently of them. Only by comparing the perceptual/semantic representation developed by different culture groups do we discover how these representations vary from culture to culture, how they depend on our background, on our culture, and how people's behavior and their relationship to each other depends on these shared subjective representations. (Szalay, 1984, p. 74)

Szalay and Windle (1968) report the results of a comparative study of Korean and U.S. students residing in an American cultural setting. The Korean subjects responded to an AGA task in their L1 and in their L2, English. Their response patterns were then compared to the patterns generated by the U.S. subjects in their native language. The aim of the study was to determine if differences in AGA response patterns of groups from two different communities could be attributed mainly to language or to culture. The authors did uncover differences traceable to the milieu in which the language is learned, thus suggesting that different conditions of learning give rise to different conceptual organizations. Specifically, when language was held constant and the culture of the subjects varied (i.e., L1 and L2 English), the Korean subjects, who learned most of their English in the United States, did produce some affiliations that correlated with those produced by the American subjects. For the stimulus word *hungry*, for example, Koreans produced responses such as *food, eat, poor* (also common American clusters) more frequently in English than they did in Korean, where *cooked rice, people, pitiful* were favored. As might be expected when both language and culture varied (i.e., L1 English versus L1 Korean), the weakest correlations in intergroup responses were observed. However, when culture was held constant and only the language varied (i.e., L1 Korean versus L2 English), the highest correlations in response patterns were obtained. In other words, the Korean subjects generated a much higher incidence of intragroup associative patterns regardless of the response language than they did intergroup patterns when compared to Americans in English, thus indicating that culture is a stronger factor than the linguistic code.

In a follow-up study, Szalay, Lynse, and Bryson (1972) designed a task in which two American-born Korean social-science experts, who had lived in country for at least 6 years, were asked to write a set of descriptive sentences on the theme "hungry" as it related to people in the Korean context. They were provided with a set of sentences as a guide. The guide sentences were based on the response patterns of the Korean students in the previously discussed study as well as sentences that would be typical of the American context.[18] The experts were next asked to rank the sentences in a given category according to their relative cogency for the Korean subjects. The researchers then composed 54 sets of thematically organized sentences with each set consisting of three sentences – one based on a high scoring item from the original study, and the highest-ranking cogency sentence from each of the two experts. The sets were then given to a group of Korean students who were similar to the group in the earlier study. The subjects were asked to assign a number from one to three to each sentence in each set, according to how meaningful the sentence was to them. The results show that the Korean subjects assigned the highest cogency rating to the sentences derived from the original AGA task nearly twice as often as they did to the sentences drawn from the experts. This finding could very well suggest that if expert knowledge of the conceptual organization of a C2 in a second culture is inappropriate, it is unlikely that their own conceptual systems had reorganized to reflect a Korean worldview.

Grabois (1997) has extended Szalay's research paradigm to the comparative study of concept formation among natural and classroom second language learners. In his study, Grabois analyzes the lexical associations of 16 native speakers of English, 16 native speakers of Spanish, 16 natural and very advanced second language speakers of Spanish (L1 English), and 16 intermediate classroom second language learners of Spanish (L1 English) on a series of abstract concepts, including "power," "love," and "happiness." Grabois, not too surprisingly, found that the lexical associations of the native speakers of Spanish differed significantly from those of their English-speaking counterparts, taken as a group. Importantly, however, he reports that the networks of the very advanced natural learners of Spanish differ significantly from both the L1 speakers of English and the classroom L2 learners of Spanish, but they do not show a statistically significant difference when compared to the L1 Spanish speakers. Moreover, the classroom learners' networks were significantly different from both the advanced speakers of L2 Spanish and native Spanish speakers, but not from the native English speakers. An important conclusion of this research is that classroom learners, at least at the intermediate level, do not show evidence of reorganization of their native conceptual structure, while learners with an extensive immersion experience (the average length of residency in Spain of Grabois's advanced speakers was approximately 10 years) do indeed exhibit strong evidence of such reorganization,

18 An example of a Korean context sentence is "Hungry people are frequently farmers" and an example of an American context sentence is "Hungry people are frequently children."

and although it does not overlap completely with the conceptual structure of native members of the culture, it is not statistically different from theirs.[19]

Metaphors, cultural and mind

Metaphor and metaphorical thinking are an area closely related to associative networks that can also be fruitfully explored with regard to SCA in adulthood. According to Lakoff and Johnson (1980), metaphorical thought resides at the core of our everyday activity in the world. Danesi (1993, p. 495) states that metaphorical competence "is closely linked to the ways in which a culture organizes its world conceptually." Metaphorical thinking allows us to make sense of what happens to and around us, especially in the face of novel experiences, by linking such experiences to what is already known (Lakoff & Johnson, 1980, p. 190). Linguistic patterns, which at first glance may not appear to be metaphorical upon further analysis, reveal, perhaps in subtle ways, their metaphorical underpinnings. Hence, an utterance such as "Thanks for your time" reflects an underlying metaphorically organized concept (in American culture) that *time is money* (ibid., p. 8).

In the view of scholars such as Harris (1981), metaphorical thinking and metaphorical language are not marginal or exceptional processes; rather, they are at the very heart of everyday mental and linguistic activity. Winner (1982, p. 253) comments that without metaphor, human communication would be severely restricted if not terminated completely. Pollio, Barlow, Fine, and Pollio (1977) estimate that the ordinary native English speaker creates approximately three thousand metaphors per week. In fact, researchers have observed that even young children use metaphors regularly to express what they perceive as physical resemblances between objects (Danesi, 1986, p. 4).

A few scholars have begun to carry out research on metaphor comprehension and production by second language learners. Scollon (1993), for example, noticed that Cantonese-speaking learners of English clearly do not interpret American metaphors for *self* and *communication* in the same way as Americans, which often resulted in misunderstandings of their instructors' English utterances. In an attempt to locate the precise

19 Grabois reports a fair amount of individual variation within each of his four groups, with the classroom learners exhibiting the least heterogeneity. Such variation may well reflect personal mental models formed by the speakers as a result of their individual and unique experiences with Spanish culture, either as natives or as immigrants. Furthermore, Grabois speculates that a possible reason why the advanced speakers do not, as a group, look precisely like the native group is that their experience of the culture began as adults; hence, they missed, as it were, the experience of being children and teenagers in the Spanish cultural milieu.

source of the problem, Scollon compared the two metaphors in both cultures. For Americans, as suggested by Kearney (see discussion earlier in this chapter), *self* is conceptualized as a container and communication is a matter of packaging ideas that are *inside* of ourselves *into* language and sending it over to an interlocutor who unpackages the thoughts and inserts them into his or her self. Examples of utterances (cited in Scollon, 1993) that reveal the metaphor include, "He crammed the speech with subversive ideas," "I missed that idea in the sentence completely," "I am relatively self-contained." The Cantonese concept of self, not unlike the perspective of the Wintu, incorporates others in "intimate society and culture." Thus, for example, freedom for Chinese, according to Scollon, is freedom "to flock together," precisely the circumstance that Americans struggle so vigorously to liberate them*selves* from (ibid., p. 47).

Danesi (1993) reports on a series of classroom-based studies designed to determine if second language learners could develop what he refers to as "conceptual fluency" in a second language. According to Danesi (ibid., p. 490), students often develop a high level of speaking proficiency in a second language, but they continue to think "in terms of their native conceptual system: that is, students typically use target language words and structures as 'carriers' of their own native language concepts." In one study of elementary, intermediate, and advanced classroom learners of Italian at the University of Toronto, Danesi found that students performed poorly on a series of metaphor comprehension and translation tasks. In another study, this time with third- and fourth-year Spanish learners, at the same university, Danesi looked at the use of metaphorical expressions in short in-class essays on topics such as "What is friendship?" and "The presence of Canadian soldiers in the Gulf." In this study, Danesi determined the metaphorical density of each essay by calculating the number of sentences containing metaphors as a percentage of the total number of sentences produced. These were then compared to similar essays written by native speakers of Spanish. Not too surprisingly, Danesi reports a statistically significant difference between the metaphorical density of the native and nonnative writers, in favor of the natives. Crucially, however, it turns out that even when the learners did use metaphors, there was a strong tendency to rely on those that were similar in both languages. Hence, Danesi concludes that after 3 or 4 years of study, the students failed to learn how to think in conceptually different ways (ibid., p. 497).

In a cross-cultural study of the acquisition of conceptual metaphors by second language learners, Pavlenko (1997) provides evidence that parallels the findings of Grabois considered earlier. Pavlenko examines the metaphorical content of narrative protocols produced by native speakers of Russian, native speakers of English, Russian immigrants residing in the United States, classroom learners of Russian (L1 English) in the

United States, and classroom learners of English (L1 Russian) in Russia. Each participant was asked to relate the story depicted in a brief, non-verbal video constructed by Pavlenko for purposes of her research. Although Pavlenko used two videos, one based on a Russian conceptual metaphor and one based on an American conceptual metaphor, for present purposes I concentrate on the American video only. The American video was designed to depict what from the American perspective would be interpreted as the conceptual metaphor of "privacy" and the strong American view that individual privacy is sacred and is therefore to be profoundly respected. Pavlenko found, unremarkably, that monolingual Americans consistently interpreted the video as being about privacy and its violation, whereas monolingual Russians did not. The second language learners, on the other hand, interpreted the video according to the environment in which they learned their second language. Thus, Russian learners of English as a foreign language in Russian classrooms tended to interpret the video just as the Russian-speaking monolinguals had, but the Russian immigrants who had learned English in the United States setting, interpreted the video as the Americans had. They talked about it as depicting a scene about privacy and its potential violation. Interestingly, when Pavlenko asked Russian immigrants in the United States to recount the story not in English but in Russian, she discovered that many of them had a difficult time relating the story in their native Russian, because they viewed it as being about privacy and, according to Pavlenko, the conceptual metaphor does not exist in Russian culture.

In addition to the few studies on metaphorical concepts, L2 researchers have carried out a handful of studies on the learning and use of idioms (i.e., frozen metaphors) by second language learners. In a study of advanced Spanish L1 learners of English, Irujo (1986) reports that her learners were able to transfer idioms from their native language into the second language in those cases where they perceived a similarity between idioms (reminiscent of Danesi's study on metaphor). This occurred even in cases in which the respective forms of idioms were not exact, as in *tomarle el pelo* (to take one the hair) "to pull one's leg" or *consultarlo con la almohada* (to consult it with the pillow) "to sleep on it" (ibid., p. 297). In a later study, Irujo (1993) found that fluent bilinguals (L1 speakers of Spanish who had learned English as adults) who lived and worked as professionals in an English-speaking environment were able to produce, in a translation task, appropriate English idioms, including some that were quite colloquial and had no equivalent in Spanish. Despite this rather positive finding, Irujo (ibid., p. 211) wisely cautions that even though the speakers used the idioms in a translation task, "we cannot assume that these subjects would use idioms in normal conversation." Yorio (1989, p. 66), on the basis of a small-scale study of fairly advanced English L2 learners, concludes that even though learners may be able to recognize idioms in their second language, they either avoid using them or use them inappropriately when speaking extemporaneously.

Conclusion

In this chapter, I have proposed that the study of second culture acquisition need not be restricted to social and attitudinal considerations, but that it can be investigated from the cognitive perspective as well. From this perspective, SCA research presents some interesting questions for researchers to consider. The ultimate attainment question, for instance, which has been so controversial with respect to acquisition of second codes (see Coppieters, 1987; Birdsong, 1992; White & Genesee, 1996), becomes even more profound when dealing with cultural models, because what is at stake is the way minds, selves, and worlds are (re)organized and (re)constructed. Although the evidence is not overwhelming, it does seem to be possible for some adults under certain circumstances to restructure, to some extent at least, their conceptual organization, whereas for others, as in the case of classroom learners, reorganization does not seem to be a likely alternative.

A few words of caution are in order, however. First, this chapter has examined only two of the possible culturally constructed artifacts that people make use of to organize their mental lives – lexical networks and metaphors – but, as Shore (1996) notes, cultures make available to their members a wide variety of mediational tools, including gestures, image schemata, sound images, scripts, checklists, rituals, and more; these too need to be explored with regard to their cognitive consequences for second culture acquisition. Furthermore, to my knowledge, no work of the kind reported on by Lucy (1996) and Ratner (1991) has been conducted on second language learners. It is crucial to discover if Americans who have the opportunity to appropriate linguistically constructed Mayan cultural models of object classification learn to classify objects according to their substance instead of shape, and of course vice versa. Finally, the research reported on here is experimental in nature and consequently may not present the full picture (or may even present a distorted picture) of what happens when people appropriate other cultural models. Shore (1996) makes an important distinction between *observers'* (i.e., researchers) and *actors'* (i.e., members of a given community) cultural models. The former, according to Shore, "are adapted for the representation and social coordination of abstract general perspectives" and "tend to be organized more in terms of categories, permitting mutual rather than just personal orientation," while the latter are dynamic, graded, and ecological models that represent an "individual's changing relationships to any phenomenon" and govern ways in which actors negotiate the changing landscapes of life (p. 56). Cognitive anthropologists are only beginning to investigate how people construct and modify actors' models to either reactively or proactively deal with the ebb and flow of life activity. Clearly, C2 acquirers should be part of this research agenda. I would like to suggest that a potentially fruitful means of informing this work is provided by developments in Activity Theory research carried out by scholars such as Cole and Engestrom (1993), Engestrom (1995), and Zinchenko (1996), among others. A paper by Pavlenko and Lantolf (1997), in which the authors analyze the struggle of a single individual to reconstruct her self-identity in a second cultural setting, represents an initial attempt to explain the cognitive consequences of second culture acquisition from the perspective offered by Activity Theory. Clearly, however, much more research is required in this intriguing domain in order for us to understand more fully what the precise nature and consequences of appropriating a second culture are.

3 Developing nonnative speaker skills in interpreting conversational implicatures in English

Explicit teaching can ease the process

Lawrence F. Bouton

Conversational implicature (referred to from here on simply as *implicature*) is a type of indirect communication, first described by Grice (1975). It is based on what Grice calls the *Cooperative Principle* – an assumption that people taking part in a conversation will make what they say appropriate to the mutually accepted purpose of the conversation and to the direction it is taking at the moment. At the very least, Grice says, people are expected, and expect each other, to follow four basic maxims, which can be paraphrased as *"Be sufficiently informative to meet your interlocutor's needs," "Be truthful," "Make what you say relevant,"* and *"Be clear."* When the literal meaning of what someone says does not seem to provide *enough information* or to be *true* or *relevant* or *clear*, people assume that the speaker is being cooperative and that it is their understanding of what the speaker has said that is flawed, not the utterance itself – and they look for another message that might have been intended that would be appropriate to the conversational context at that moment. Messages arrived at indirectly in this way are said to be derived through the use of implicature (Grice, 1975, 1981).[1]

As an example of how implicature is used as a means of indirect communication, imagine the following situation:

(1) As Hank is walking along Green Street, a car slows down beside him and the driver, a stranger, rolls down the window and speaks to him.
     Stranger: Excuse me. Could you help me? *I'm almost out of gas.*
     Hank: Sure. *There's a gas station about 3 blocks on down the street on your right.*

Two different implicatures are actually used here, one by each of the speakers. The first occurs when the stranger asks for help but does not

---

1 Throughout this chapter, we will use the term *implicature* to refer both to the process of drawing context-based inferences such as these and to the inferences themselves. Grice avoided this ambiguous use of the term by using the term *implicature* to name the process by which the inferred messages are derived, while calling the inferred message itself an *implicatum*. General practice has ignored the latter rather ponderous term, however. An interesting example of how writers have extended the meaning of *implicature* in this way can be seen in Green (1989, p. 91).

state directly what it is that he wants. Instead, he simply describes his problem – that he is out of gas – and leaves it to Hank to infer what type of help he is asking for under the circumstances. Hank's response about the existence of a gas station is also expressed indirectly. What the stranger has to infer from what Hank says is that the gas station is open and that he will be able to buy gas there. In both of these cases, the addressee has to use implicature to understand what the other person has said because in neither case did the speaker say everything that he meant. Only by asking oneself why the other person made the statement – what its relevance was in that particular context – could each of these individuals understand what the other meant by what was said.

But the indirect meaning expressed in both comments in (1) is fairly obvious. Perhaps the impact of the context of what is said on its meaning would be easier to see if we considered an utterance in different contexts and noted how its meaning changed depending on the context in which it appeared at the moment. For instance, notice how the meaning of the question "Hungry?" changes somewhat in each of the following. It retains its literal meaning as a yes/no question in all three cases, but the function it serves is different in each.

(2-a)   It is noon, and a friend comes by your desk, putting on his coat and says, "Hungry?"
(2-b)   It is the middle of the afternoon, when someone walks into the room holding out a box of chocolates and asks the same question.
(2-c)   You and a friend have just started a new diet this morning. It is late afternoon when the phone rings. When you pick it up, you hear your friend's voice at the other end of the line. "Hungry?" she asks.

In all three instances, the syntax and intonation patterns associated with "Hungry?" lead us to recognize it as a simple question: in each case the speaker is asking the addressee if he or she is hungry, and the answer is relevant to the immediate context. But, in each case, there is more to the speaker's message than a simple request for information. In (2-a), the question is most likely an *indirect invitation* – a suggestion that he and the addressee have lunch together. In (2-b), the addressee is being *offered* candy. In (2-c), the question might amount to a *lament* or some gentle *teasing*, but it will definitely be understood as an indirect expression of the bond between the two suffering friends. In all three of these cases, the intended function performed by the question is different from its function in the other two, and comes from the interaction of "Hungry?" with the context in which it occurred. Meaning derived in this way is what Grice labeled *implicature*. Examples such as these, together with the dozens that occur around us every day, give credence to Green's (1989) comment that "Conversational implicature is an absolutely unremarkable and ordinary conversational strategy" and, therefore, a part of any native speaker's communicative competence (p. 92).

The impact of culture on interpretations of implicature

Commonplace as implicatures are within a given language community, a question arises when we think of implicature as a conversational strategy in *cross-cultural* interaction. In discussing how people are able to communicate with one another through implicature, Grice (1975) indicated that the strategy could only be successful to the extent that speakers and their audiences have a common understanding of four factors integral to it:

1. the literal meaning of the utterance in question;
2. the roles and expectations associated with each of the participants in a conversation;
3. the situation in which the conversation is taking place and the nature of the conversation itself; and
4. the world around them as it relates to the occasion.

At the same time, several authors (e.g., Keenan, 1976; Tannen, 1986; Spencer-Oatey, 1993; Huang, 1996) have demonstrated that people from different cultural backgrounds may see conversational roles or the context of a conversation, or the world itself as it pertains to that conversation, quite differently. If that is true, then to the extent that differences such as these do exist, the people involved might very well derive different messages from the same utterance in the same context; and when this happens, the value of implicature as a conversational strategy in cross-cultural interaction would be reduced.

But is it true? Do people from different cultural backgrounds infer different messages from the same utterance in the same context?

Keenan (1976) provided one example suggesting that they do, when she compared the implementation of Grice's first maxim, "Be sufficiently informative," within the Malagasy society on Madagascar among Western Europeans. Her conclusion: "The expectation that [Malagasy] speakers will satisfy informational needs is not a basic norm" and applies less consistently with them than among the people of Western Europe (p. 70). In fact, she suggests, if members of these two cultures were involved in a conversation, the difference in the extent to which they follow Grice's first maxim could easily lead them to misunderstand each other.

But Keenan's findings were related only to Grice's first maxim, and only to the Malagasy. If Grice's other maxims were investigated, and among people from other cultures, would we find the same thing, that is, that the use of implicature in cross-cultural interaction was a potential barrier to communication in those situations as well? The question is an empirical one, so in 1986, we began a longitudinal study to gather data with which to answer it.

The ability of nonnative English-speaking international students to interpret implicatures in English as American native speakers do. At the time that this study began, the accuracy of Grice's Cooperative Principle and its maxims had never been tested empirically over a reasonably large number of subjects – not even in Grice's own native English-speaking community – and so, at that time, two questions needed to be explored. First, if confronted with an utterance in a particular context, would native English speakers from the United States agree as to whether or not they should use implicature in interpreting that utterance and, if they did use it, would they tend to derive the same message? Second, to what extent would the nonnative English-speaking students from cultures other than that of the United States derive the same message from an implicature expressed in American English as did the Americans?

The first step in investigating these issues was to give a set of open-ended questions to 70 undergraduate American native English speakers at a small Midwestern college (Bouton, 1988). Each item on the questionnaire contained a dialogue in which at least one utterance expressed its message through the use of implicature. Also, the dialogue was embedded in a brief context sufficient to permit the subjects to derive the intended message. The undergraduates were then asked to write in their own words what they thought the message was. The degree of consensus among these 70 American individuals was surprising and suggests that one group of Americans at least – namely, American college students – tends to interpret a great many implicatures in the same way.[2] At the same time, the same questionnaire was administered to 60 nonnative English-speaking university students who had just arrived in the United States and whose answers were often quite different from those of the Americans. Once this data had been gathered, it was used to generate a multiple-choice questionnaire using the most common response by the American native speakers as the expected answer and the most common responses by the nonnative speakers that differed from those of the Americans as the distractors.[3] When the multiple-choice version of the instrument was ready, it was checked by giving it to 28 more native speakers.

2 Overall the native speaker (NS) concurrence as to the interpretation of the items on this test was quite high: 100% of them agreed as to the message conveyed by 9 of the items; at least 90% agreed on another 8; and at least 79% agreed on 6 more. Taken together, at least 79% of the Americans agreed on the interpretation of 23 of the 28 items. Of the remaining 5, 4 had exceptionally high reliability quotients, and a comparison of the mean scores for the NSs and nonnative speakers (NNSs) for these 5 items shows the NNSs deriving the expected message only 80% as often as the Americans.

3 In addition to the multiple-choice items developed in this way, a few were drawn from examples of implicature found in Levinson (1983), Richards (1980), and Grice (1975, 1978), in which the interpretation suggested by the particular author was accepted as the norm and distractors were derived by piloting the items among other small groups of NNSs.

When this proved successful, the test was administered to 36 international students entering the university who had just arrived in the United States. The English proficiency of these students was represented by TOEFL scores of from 467 to 672, with 95 of them between 500 and 600, the average being 554.

The results of this testing showed quite vividly the impact of a person's cultural background on the messages that he or she draws from an implicature. For one thing, the NNSs derived the same message as the Americans from the various items only 79.5% of the time overall. For another, the use of a one-way ANOVA showed that the performance of the subjects on the overall test was significantly affected by their cultural background $(F [6,323]) = 23.83, p < .0001$). And when the six different culture groups were compared with each other, the Bonferonni T test found statistically significant differences $(p < .05)$ between the groups in 13 of the 21 possible pairings. A person's cultural background not only is important when comparing NSs and NNSs, then, but it also distinguishes the message derived by one culturally defined group of NNS from that of another. When the scores of the six groups in this study were charted, a continuum resulted, stretching from the Americans at one pole to the People's Republic of China (PRC) on the other, with the middle positions being filled by the Germans, Latin Americans, Taiwan Chinese, Koreans, and Japanese, in that order. Furthermore, when an expanded version of this study was carried out in 1990 using a revised and shortened form of the test instrument, a comparison of the results achieved by subjects from different cultural backgrounds provided a similar pattern[4] (Bouton, 1992a).

On the basis of these results, there seems to be no question that people from different cultural backgrounds interpret at least some implicatures differently. The fact that the NNS international students arrived at the same message that the Americans did only 79.5% of the time when using implicature does seem to pose a potential obstacle to cross-cultural communication between those students and the Americans with whom they interact. But the subjects we have been discussing had only recently arrived in the United States, and so one wonders how quickly their ability to handle implicatures in English would improve when they were immersed as students in the culture of an American university.

4 The culture groups added were from France and Malaysia/Indonesia, and the number of subjects in each of the original groups was increased. Even so, the groups continued to spread themselves over a continuum with the Americans and students from the PRC at the poles and the mean scores of all NNS groups differing significantly from that of the Americans (p < .05). The only exception to this latter result was the enlarged German group, whose mean score rose so that it was no longer significantly different from that of the American NSs. It should also be noted that the enlarged study included two other groups of native English speakers – British and Canadian – and that their scores were *not* significantly different from those of the Americans.

TABLE 1. COMPARISON OF THE MEAN SCORES OF NONNATIVE AND NATIVE
SPEAKERS IN THE 4½-YEAR STUDY

NNSs/NSs	NNSs	NNSs	NSs
Date given	Aug 86	Jan 91	Aug 86
Number of items	28	28	28
Mean score	19.97	22.97	25.11
N	30	30	28
% choosing expected message	71.3%	82.0%	89.7%
Ratio – Mean$_{nns}$/Mean$_{ns}$	79.5%	91.5%	—

Acquiring implicature interpretation skills without explicit instruction

The speed of the acquisition of implicature interpretation skills by international, nonnative English-speaking university students. Two studies provide at least a partial picture of the relatively slow progress made by NNS international students toward acquiring a mastery of the skills needed to interpret implicatures in English.

The first (Bouton, 1992a) was carried out with subjects who had been on the campus of the same American university for 54 months and showed that considerable progress had been made overall by the end of that period. Although these subjects had had no explicit instruction designed to help them interpret implicatures in American English, by the end of the 54 months they were able to derive the same message as the Americans did 91% of the time – up from the original 79.5% (see Table 1).[5] What is more, only 8 of the 23 implicatures that had caused them trouble when they first arrived still did so; and most important, the only type of implicature that was still systematically difficult was irony.[6] Yet, 8 of the 28 implicatures on which they were tested remained troublesome, and the difference in the performance of the Americans and that of the internationals after 54 months on campus was statistically significant (p < 0.019).

A second and more detailed study (Bouton, 1994) was carried out using the newly revised 22-item multiple-choice instrument that was shorter and represented a more balanced assortment of implicatures. This new

5 Originally, as reported in Bouton (1988), the test used in 1986 included 33 items and, based on those 33 items, the NNSs interpreted the implicature as expected only 75% as often as the NSs. Over the years, however, 5 of the original 33 were shown to be invalid or unreliable and were omitted from subsequent analyses of the initial testing and all subsequent uses of the 1986 test. All results reported in this chapter are based on the 28 items that proved to be both valid and reliable.

6 The various types of implicature that we have been investigating in this study will be described and illustrated in more detail later in this chapter.

TABLE 2. PERCENTAGE OF NATIVE SPEAKERS AND NEWLY ARRIVED (1990)
NONNATIVE SPEAKERS DERIVING THE EXPECTED MESSAGE

The easy dozen					The tough 10				
Item	NSs	NNSs	Diff	Type	Item	NSs	NNSs	Diff	Type
16	100	99	1	Relevance	17	100	79	21	POPE Q
19	100	98	2	Relevance	23	95	75	20	Relevance
10	100	94	6	Relevance	24	70	74	(4)	Scalar
4	97	92	5	Relevance	2	99	65	34	Ind. crit.
5	100	89	11	Relevance	11	91	65	26	Sequence
7	99	88	11	POPE Q	15	100	60	40	Ind. crit.
12	81	87	(6)	Min. Req.	22	64	52	12	Ind. crit.
13	97	86	11	Relevance	6	84	51	33	Irony
21	96	83	13	Relevance	1	86	48	38	POPE Q
20	81	82	(1)	Min. Req.	18	75	47	28	Irony
8	91	80	11	Ind. crit.					
25	88	78	10	Relevance					

instrument was normed using 77 native English-speaking undergraduate Americans and then administered to 375 internationals who, as before, had just arrived in the United States. From the beginning, the items were categorized in terms both of the type of implicature they represented and of the difficulty that each caused for the international students when they first arrived (see Table 2). An implicature was termed *difficult* if the difference in the percentages for NSs and NNSs interpreting it as expected was 20 percentage points or more, or if no more than 76 of the NNS derived the expected message. This categorization of the implicatures into the *Easy Dozen* and the *Tough 10* will be useful when we compare the performance of those students who acquired their implicature skills through simple immersion with that of those who received explicit instruction designed to assist them with the task. For instance, those types of implicature classified in Table 2 as the Tough 10 proved difficult to learn without explicit instruction even over an extended period of time. On the other hand, they were the extremely easy to teach. Three interesting points can be derived from Table 2:

1. The 5 easiest items for the NNSs on first arriving in the United States all involved relevance-based implicatures such as that in example (3), and in examples (1) and (2) earlier. In fact, 8 of the 12 items found in the *Easy Dozen* in Table 2 were this type. Of the 4 remaining easy items, 2 were based on the Minimum Requirement Rule [Levinson, 1983; Bouton, 1989; see example (4) and 2 were aberrant members of more difficult types [see examples (3) and (4)]. At the same time, only 1 relevance implicature and none based on the Minimum Requirement Rule fell into the *Tough 10*.

(3) **Relevance:**
   A: How about going for a walk?
   B: *Isn't it raining out?*

(4) **Minimum Requirement Rule – Two golfers are talking about their chances in the local university golf tournament.**
   Fred: What do you think it will take to make the cut tomorrow, Brad?
   Brad: Oh, a 75 ought to do it. *Did you have a 75?*[7] I didn't.
   Fred: *Yeah, I did.*

2. Eight of the *Tough 10* for the NNSs when they first arrived were from 1 of 4 types of implicature that proved consistently troublesome for them (and occasionally for the NSs as well): the POPE Q, (5) and (9); indirect criticism, (6); sequence-based implicatures, (7); and irony (8).

The *POPE Q* implicature answers one question with another. For the implicature to work, the person asking the first question must realize that the answer to that question is the same as the answer to the second one and just as easy. This implicature is highly formulaic and is named for the prototype response, *Is the pope Catholic?*

(5) **The POPE Q implicature:**
   A: Does Dr. Walker always give a test the day before vacation?
   B: *Does the sun come up in the East?*

The *Indirect Criticism* implicature often follows a request for an evaluation of something. When expressed using this implicature, the evaluation is negative. That effect is achieved by praising some unimportant feature of the item being evaluated, thus implying that there is nothing more flattering that can be said.

(6) **Indirect criticism:**
   A: Have you seen *Robin Hood?*
   B: Yeah. I went last night.
   A: What did you think of it?
   B: The *cinematography* was great.
   A: Oh, that bad, huh?

Sequence-based implicatures are based on the assumption that unless there are indications to the contrary, events being described occur in the

---

7 This question can also be interpreted as involving the Minimum Requirement Implicature in that after stating the minimum score that it will take to make the cut in the tournament, Brad is clearly not asking Fred whether his score was exactly 75, but whether he made the cut; and his own remark that he did not must be interpreted within the same frame, that is, that he himself did not make the cut. At the end of the dialogue, we still do not know what score either of the two men shot.

order in which they are expressed. The effect of this assumption is easily seen in the difference in the sequence of events implied by sentences such as those in (7).[8]

(7) **Sequence-based implicature:**
Jack drove to Chicago and had dinner.
Jack had dinner and drove to Chicago.

(8) **Irony:** Bill and Peter work together in the same office. They sometimes are sent on business trips together and are becoming good friends. They often have lunch together and Peter has even invited Bill to have dinner with him and his wife at their home several times. Now Peter's friends have told him that they saw Bill out dancing with Peter's wife recently while Peter was out of town on a business trip. On hearing this, Peter's comment was . . .
Peter: *Bill knows how to be a really good friend, doesn't he?*

3. As mentioned earlier, only two other types of implicature besides Relevance and the Minimum Requirement Rule implicatures were among the 12 easier items – and one of these, the POPE Q implicature in item (9), was successfully treated as a relevance-based implicature by many of the NNSs because of the way the item was written. Instead of using the POPE Q features of the item, they realized from the rest of the conversation that Rob is angry and selected the right answer because that is what they thought an angry man would say, thus avoiding the normally *difficult* POPE Q implicature format altogether.

(9) Randy and Rob are talking about some men they had played cards with the night before.
Rob: I really lost money in that card game last night. I don't think I will play with those guys again.
Randy: Yeah. They sure were good, weren't they?
Rob: Good? You mean they were awfully lucky, don't you?
Randy: Lucky? What's the matter? Don't you trust them?
Rob: *Is the sky green?*

Each of these four types of implicature proved difficult for NNS international students newly arrived in the United States and account for all but 2 of the 10 items with which they had the most difficulty. The ninth item was an exception to the fact that relevance implicatures were normally easy for the NNSs, and the tenth item was built around the

8 Although the relationship between the order in which events are narrated and the order in which they occurred is obvious to native English speakers, it was not obvious to a great many NNSs. Of the students from China, Japan, and Taiwan, fewer than half recognized and used the relationship to interpret the item involved, and both the Koreans and the French also had considerable difficulty with it.

scalar implicature[9] and may have produced somewhat less reliable results. Because it proved difficult for NNSs and NSs alike, and because the item analysis done when the NSs took the test showed the item to be only moderately reliable, it may have been the item and not the scalar implicature itself that proved difficult. In any case, the relative difficulty of the implicatures for the incoming international students seems to have been as it appears in Table 2. This provides us with a framework within which to take a detailed look at the progress the international students made toward interpreting implicatures effectively over periods of 17 and 33 months and from 4 to 7 years.

The 17- and 33-month immersion groups. Seventeen and 33 months after their arrival on campus, two groups of randomly selected international students, NNSs who had been initially tested in the fall of 1990, were tested again. As might be expected after being immersed for that length of time in an English-speaking academic community, the mean score for both groups for the test as a whole showed statistically significant improvement ($p < 0.0001$), with the ratio of the mean score of the immersion groups to that of the NSs rising to 90.6% for the 17-month group and 94.1% for the 33-month group. In spite of that, there was still a statistically significant difference between their scores and those of the Americans, just as there had been in the case of the 54-month group discussed earlier. Finally, when these two immersion groups were compared with each other, there was no statistically significant difference between the scores, suggesting that overall growth in the ability of NNSs to interpret American English implicatures was rather slow after the first 17 months.

But in spite of progress made by both the 17- and the 33-month groups over the periods of their immersion, the data displayed in Tables 3 and 4 shows that, to a considerable extent, the implicatures that were easier for the NNSs on arrival in 1990 remained easier, while those that tended to be difficult at the outset remained relatively difficult. There were just two exceptions, one negative and one positive: (1) among the easier set, the 17-month group performed less well than the entire group of 375 NNSs

---

9 *Scalar* implicatures occur when someone makes an assertion using a term that can be located along a scale (Levinson, 1983, pp. 132–133). For instance, the terms *ok, good,* and *great,* or *few, a few, some, quite a few,* and *a lot,* form continuas of *goodness* and *amount,* respectively. The scalar implicature says that when speakers use any term from scales such as these to describe someone or something, the audience infers that no stronger statement can be made. In other words, if someone says that *a few people were angry about your decision,* then you can infer that that is the strongest statement that person can make, that is, that there were not enough to be referred to as quite a *few* – or even as *some.* We use this implicature regularly and understand it easily; it is hard to know why constructing a test item to demonstrate the commonality of this implicature is so difficult, but to this point we have been unable to come up with any that have not proved to be difficult for NNSs and NSs alike.

TABLE 3. IMPLICATURES LISTED IN TABLE 2 AS RELATIVELY EASY
FOR NONNATIVE SPEAKERS

	Arrival	NNS immersion group			NSs	
Item	375 NNSs	After 17 mo	After 3 mo	After 4–7 yr		Type
19	98	94	100	100	100	Relevance
16	99	100	100	100	100	Relevance
4	92	100	100	100	97	Relevance
10	94	97	94	94	100	Relevance
5	89	85	91	97	100	Relevance
13	86	91	94	94	97	Relevance
21	83	82	94	82	96	Relevance
25	78	88	89	91	94	Relevance
12	87	74	89	85	81	Min. Req.
20	82	82	82	83	82	Min. Req.
7	88	97	94	82	99	POPE Q
8	80	91	91	99	91	Ind. crit.
Mean	88.0	90.1	93.1	91.8	94.8	

Note: All results are expressed as the percentage of the group selecting the expected interpretation.

TABLE 4. IMPLICATURES LISTED IN TABLE 2 AS DIFFICULT
FOR NONNATIVE SPEAKERS

	Arrival	NNS immersion group			NSs	
Item	375 NNSs	After 17 mo	After 3 mo	After 4–7 yr		Type
23	75	88	89	94	95	Relevance
2	65	82	94	94	99	Ind. crit.
5	60	76	71	76	100	Ind. crit.
22	52	52	68	91	64	Ind. crit.
11	65	76	86	65	91	Sequence
17	79	82	86	92	100	POPE Q
1	48	62	71	53	86	POPE Q
18	47	53	60	56	75	Irony
6	51	53	57	76	84	Irony
24	74	74	74	86	70	Scalar
Mean	61.9	73.8	79.3	78.5	89.1	

Note: All results are expressed as the percentage of the group selecting the expected interpretation.

had originally (in 1990) on two relevance implicatures (items 5 and 21) and on one item based on the Minimum Requirement Rule (item 12); and (2) both immersion groups were able to interpret easily the one relevance-based item (item 23) that had given them trouble earlier.

To show the relative progress of each of the groups in dealing with the various types of implicatures in Tables 3 and 4, we have left the implicatures in the same two categories, the *Easy Dozen* and the *Tough 10*. However, we have then set an arbitrary goal for the NNSs of being able to come within 10 percentage points of the American NSs for each implicature. Those cases where this is not achieved are in bold print. This gives us a quick way of checking on the progress of each group. The one with the best performance overall will be the one with the *fewest* figures in bold print on the two tables.

In reviewing the data from these tables, we notice that the performance of the 17-month group shows 12 of the 22 items are in bold and have remained difficult for them – especially the 8 items from Table 4 involving *indirect criticism, sequence,* and *POPE Q,* implicatures and *irony,* for each of which the entire implicature type seems to be a problem. For those 8 items, the 17-month group derived the intended message an average of 16% less often than the NSs did. In addition, and rounding out the 12 that were difficult for this group, there were the three items from Table 3. In short, although the members of this group did improve considerably in their ability to interpret implicatures in American English over their 17 months of immersion in American university life, they had not yet mastered any of the more difficult types in Table 4.

As for the 33-month group, in spite of the fact that there was no statistically significant difference between them and the 17-month group, they did seem to have slightly better skills in certain specific ways. For example, of the 22 implicatures the subjects were asked to interpret, the 33-month group had trouble with only 7, or just half as many as proved difficult for the 17-month group. Also, 79.3% of the 33-month group answered the implicatures in Table 4 as expected, compared to only 73.8% of those that had been on campus only 17 months. In addition, the 33-month group interpreted the sequence implicature effectively and 2 of the 4 items involving indirect criticism; both of these had proved more difficult for the 17-month group. However, the 33-month group was still unable to handle POPE Q implicatures, those involving irony, and the other two suggesting indirect criticism; and its inability to interpret these three types of implicature is what made its performance and that of the NS significantly different ($p < 0.0001$).

The 4–7-year group. Although there is no initial test against which to compare the performance of the subjects in Tables 3 and 4 who had been on campus from 4 to 7 years, the similarity of their results to those of the other two groups lends credibility to all three. None of the results attained by any one of these three groups – the 17- and 33-month groups

TABLE 5. TYPES OF IMPLICATURES REMAINING DIFFICULT
FOR IMMERSION GROUPS

17 months	*33 months*	*4–7 years*	*54 months*
Ind. crit.	Ind. crit. (?)		
Sequence			
POPE Q	POPE Q		
Irony	Irony	Irony	Irony
Scalar	Scalar	Scalar	NA

or the 4–7-year group – differs from the others with any statistical significance, and the ratio of the scores of the 33-month and the 4–7-year
groups was nearly identical.

A subtle distinction can be drawn between these latter two groups,
though, one that is very similar to the difference between the 17- and 33-
month groups: the longer the international students were in the United
States, the fewer the number of implicature types that were systematically problematic for them. The 17-month group had trouble with 3 of
the *Easy Dozen;* in addition, as indicated in Table 5, they were consistently bothered by 4 different implicature types (not including the scalar);
the 33-month group was bothered by 2 types and had trouble with half
of the indirect criticism group; and the 4–7-year group stumbled only
over *irony.* Furthermore, if we look again at the 54-month group described earlier, we see that they, too, are bothered only by the irony-based
implicatures. Thus, in spite of the fact that there is no statistically significant difference in the overall scores of these 17-month, 33-month, and
4–7-year immersion groups, there does seem to be a slowly increasing
mastery of the more difficult implicature types as time passes, with each
successive group demonstrating a greater skill than the one at the stage
immediately preceding it.

But progress was slow. Thirty-three or 54 months is a long time to
wait to gain competence in a facet of English that is "an absolutely and
unremarkable conversational strategy" used innumerable times every day
(Green, 1989). Therefore, one wonders, can anything be done in the ESL
classroom to speed up the process? It was to answer this question that
we undertook the study described in the next section.

Developing NNS skill at interpreting implicatures in American English through explicit classroom instruction

In this study, four sections from the university's regular ESL program
were used as the experimental group. These sections consisted of a total
of 55 international graduate students and were taught by four different

instructors, two of whom were familiar with the different types of implicatures and how they work prior to their taking part in this study and two of whom were not. The first of these classes was taught in the spring of 1993 as a pilot study to see if it could be done, and the other three were taught in the fall. The rest of the sections of the same course from both spring and fall, a total of 109 students, received no instruction regarding the use of implicature and constituted a control group. The actual instruction related to the interpretation of implicatures took place over a 6-week period during the particular semester and both the experimental and the control groups were tested at the beginning and end of that period. The same instrument was used as both a pre- and a posttest. Furthermore, it was the same instrument that had been used in the second longitudinal study so that comparisons between the experimental and the immersion groups could be drawn.

It should be emphasized that the classes in which these students were enrolled were sections of a regular university ESL course. The time and materials oriented toward the development of the students' skill in interpreting implicature were made a part of the regular syllabus for the experimental sections for the semesters involved. Because of this, the total time available for formal lessons devoted to the development of that skill was only 6 hours, 1 for each of the different types of implicature to be covered. Of course, once a particular implicature type had been introduced, teachers sometimes dealt with it informally and briefly as the opportunity arose, but this happened no more and no less than one might return to any other facet of the course that had been taken up earlier simply to keep it fresh in the students' minds.

Developing the skills and understandings necessary for the effective interpretation of implicatures in English

The teaching materials. The teaching materials used in the experiment were developed in the form of handouts, one for each of six different types of implicature: the POPE Q, indirect criticism, relevance-based, sequence of events, scalar, and Minimum Requirement Rule implicatures and those involving irony. (Samples can be found in Appendixes A and B.)

Because they give examples of the implicatures in question and then ask questions that help students focus on the intended interpretation, these handouts formed the starting point for all four teachers. Students read the examples, answered the questions, and tried to develop some generalizations about how the implicature works. Some of the points that were covered during the discussions were (1) how implicature functions as a tool of indirect communication, (2) how specific implicatures work, (3) when the different types of implicature are appropriate, and (4) comparable implicatures from the students' own languages if any exist. In most cases, the pattern of the discussion was inductive, though when the implicature lesson was somewhat hurried because of other things that had to be taken up, a more deductive approach was sometimes used. But in no instance did the teachers discuss the actual implicatures from the test.

A key feature of implicatures that was highlighted in the handouts was that they result from the interplay between an utterance and its context. One way of demonstrating this point to the class was to use the same utterance in two or more contexts and watch how the meaning of the utterance changed – much as was done at the outset of this chapter in examples (1) and (2).

The handouts were not the only focal point of the formal lessons, however; all four teachers adapted, revised, and supplemented the handouts as necessary to match their own teaching styles. One excellent source of additional samples of implicatures was such regular cartoon strips as *Calvin and Hobbes* or *The Born Loser* from the pages of the daily newspaper. The students enjoyed finding and describing the implicatures contained in such strips. Political cartoons were also a good source, although these sometimes unintentionally turned the attention of the students away from implicatures to politically oriented discussions of the issues on which the cartoon focused.

Finally, and most important, we turned to a variety of texts to find examples of the different implicatures that we planned to teach. What we found was that although there were several examples that could be used, none of them were highlighted and only rarely was the type of indirect communication found in implicature dealt with in any way, explicit or implicit. Some of the examples we found we used in the handouts; some we introduced as additional examples during class. That these were available for us to find and use is important because it means that teachers can probably find at least some examples of implicatures in texts that they are already using. All that is necessary is that they focus on these examples and develop questions and activities that will help the students infer the indirect message that is suggested, while becoming aware of the process they are learning to use.

For example, consider the following dialogue from *Say It Naturally* (Wall, 1987, p. 249):

Pat is in the drugstore, looking around, confused.
Clerk: May I help you?
　Pat: Yes, please. *I'd like to buy some toothpaste.*
Clerk: It's over there by the back entrance – on your right. . . .

Pat's statement here is an example of a relevance implicature and means more than it says explicitly. This is made obvious for the students by the clerk's response, that is, giving directions to where Pat can find the

TABLE 6. COMPARISON OF PERFORMANCE OF EXPERIMENTAL AND CONTROL
GROUPS WITH THAT OF IMMERSION GROUPS AT END OF LEARNING PERIODS

	Control		*Experimental*		*Immersion Groups*			*NS*
	Pre	*Post*	*Pre*	*Post*	*17 mo*	*33 mo*	*4–7 yr*	
Items	22	22	22	22	22	22	22	22
Mean	16.61	17.07	16.00	18.73	18.06	18.80	18.74	19.92
Std. Dev.	2.62	2.32	2.56	1.98	3.11	1.62	2.68	1.54
N	109	109	55	55	34	35	34	77
Ratio of means (NS/NNS)	83.4	85.7	80.3	94.0	90.7	94.4	94.1	

toothpaste. That response is not relevant to what Pat has said if one takes it at face value. Only if one interprets it in light of the context and understands it to be a request for information does the clerk's remark make sense. To use this dialogue as an illustration of conversational implicature, one could ask, "What does Pat mean by the comment 'I'd like to buy some toothpaste'?" and "How does the clerk know that is what he means?" In addition, we can also ask, "If we had overheard this conversation and had taken what Pat said literally, that is, simply as a statement of why he was in the store, how could we tell from the conversation itself that he meant more than that?" This last question draws the students' attention to the many opportunities they will have to see how others use and interpret implicatures by simply watching participants in conversations that go on around them.[10]

The results of the pedagogical study

The initial testing at the beginning of the instruction period showed no statistically significant difference between the mean scores of the experimental and the control groups or between either of them and the entire group of 375 NNSs who were tested when they first arrived in 1990. At the end of the 6-week period of instruction, however, the situation had changed dramatically, as Table 6 indicates. While the control group made only minimal progress, progress that could be the result of being tested

10 Although the author of *Say It Naturally* (Wall, 1987) asks some excellent questions about the dialogue (which is longer than this extract), the implicature focused on here is not discussed. The distinction between idiosyncratic and formulaic implicatures does not seem to explain why the Minimum Requirement Rule could not be taught – or why only 80% of the NSs interpret it as expected. This is a question that needs further investigation.

TABLE 7. COMPARISON OF INCREASE IN ABILITY OF EXPERIMENTAL AND
CONTROL GROUPS TO INTERPRET AMERICAN ENGLISH IMPLICATURES
(PERCENTAGE OF EACH GROUP ANSWERING AS EXPECTED)

Generally easy to learn; otherwise hard to teach

Item	$Cont_1$	$Cont_2$	C_2-C_1	Exp_1	Exp_2	E_2-E_1	Type
4	82	96	+4	87	93	+6	Relevance
5	90	91	+1	89	85	—	Relevance
10	92	95	+3	95	95	—	Relevance
13	89	88	−1	89	89	—	Relevance
16	94	97	+3	100	100	—	Relevance
19	96	97	+1	98	98	—	Relevance
21	78	77	−1	84	76	−8	Relevance
23	75	77	−2	76	73	−3	Relevance
25	82	76	−6	71	78	+7	Relevance
12	83	90	+7	84	91	+7	Min. Req.
20	83	80	−3	84	78	−6	Min. Req.
24	76	72	−4	75	76	+1	Scalar
Avg	84.9	85.1	0.5	86.0	86.0	0.0	

Hard to learn; easy to teach

Item	$Cont_1$	$Cont_2$	C_2-C_1	Exp_1	Exp_2	E_2-E_1	Type
1	51	65	+14	55	85	+30	POPE Q
7	94	94	—	76	96	+20	POPE Q
17	81	81	—	80	95	+15	POPE Q
2	67	76	+9	53	96	+43	Ind. crit.
8	81	84	+3	67	93	+26	Ind. crit.
15	52	49	−3	42	78	+36	Ind. crit.
22	61	70	+9	53	84	+31	Ind. crit.
11	61	62	+1	58	80	+22	Sequence
6	44	44	—	36	69	+33	Irony
18	50	57	—	49	64	+15	Irony
Avg	64.2	68.1	+3.3	58.5	83.3	+27.1	—

using the same instrument twice within 6 weeks, the experimental group moved ahead to the point at which there was no statistically significant difference between its mean score and that of any of the immersion groups.

But if the overall performance as represented by the mean scores of the experimental and immersion groups was essentially the same, their skill in interpreting specific kinds of implicature was not. We can see this from Tables 7 and 8, in which the items are grouped according to their type, with those types that have shown themselves to be relatively easy being in the top half of each table and the more difficult ones in the bottom half. As before, the scores on individual items that show 10 percentage points fewer NNSs than NSs deriving the intended message are in bold type.

One of the things that we notice first when looking at Table 6 is something that we have seen before, namely, that a high percentage of the NNSs handled most of the relevance-based implicatures fairly easily by the time they arrived in the United States and that this was also true of both the experimental and the control groups during the pretest at the outset of the instruction period. But the instruction itself made no difference. At the end of the 6 weeks, neither the experimental nor the control group had made any real progress in relation to these implicatures. No more subjects were able to interpret these implicatures appropriately on the posttest than had been able to at the beginning. In fact, on several items, the percentage of both groups actually went down slightly.

The reason for this may reside in the fact that the three-way relationship between the relevance implicature and the utterance and context from which it comes is largely idiosyncratic. As a result, it is difficult for teachers and students alike to generalize from one instance of this type of implicature to another. Moreover, because it is impossible to teach all of the background information that NNSs need to learn in order to handle each and every relevance implicature with which they will routinely come in contact, probably all the teacher can do is to raise the students' awareness of such implicatures and to encourage them to learn what they can about them as time passes. In fact, as Table 8 indicates, time seems to be the only factor that correlates with an overall improvement in understanding relevance implicatures.

Implicatures based on the Minimum Requirement Rule were another type that was relatively easy for the NNSs from the start but that was unaffected by formal instruction. In fact, there was no meaningful increase in the ability of either the experimental group or the immersion group to deal effectively with these implicatures at any point in this study. We have no idea why this should be so, but it may be relevant that these implicatures proved somewhat difficult for NS to recognize and interpret as well. What is important for us at this moment is that no implicature from the *Easy Dozen* was positively affected by explicit instruction.

With regard to those implicatures in the *Tough 10*, however, the result of our teaching was much more dramatic. At the end of the 6-week instruction period, the percentage of those in the experimental group who had learned to interpret the four types of implicatures represented in the bottom half of Table 7 rose an average of 27% per item; on one item, 43% more subjects were able to interpret it effectively at the end of the instruction period; and none of these items saw an increase of less than 15%.

Obviously, with these implicatures, the instruction worked: at the beginning of the 6 weeks, only 56.9% of the experimental group could interpret these implicatures as expected; at the end, that number had risen to 84%. During that same period, as Table 6 indicates, the percentage of the control group answering as expected rose only 4% from 64.2% to

TABLE 8. COMPARISON OF PERCENTAGE OF EXPERIMENTAL AND IMMERSION
GROUPS AND NATIVE SPEAKERS ANSWERING AS EXPECTED ON VARIOUS
IMPLICATURE SETS

Generally easy to learn; otherwise hard to teach

Item	On arrival Aug 1990	Experimental Exp	Exp	Immersion 17 mo	33 mo	4–7 yrs	NSs	Type
4	92	87	93	100	100	94	97	Relevance
5	89	89	85	85	91	97	100	Relevance
10	94	95	95	97	94	94	100	Relevance
13	86	89	89	91	94	94	97	Relevance
16	99	100	100	100	100	100	100	Relevance
19	98	98	98	94	100	100	100	Relevance
21	83	76	73	82	94	82	96	Relevance
23	75	71	78	88	89	94	95	Relevance
25	78	84	76	88	89	91	88	Relevance
12	87	84	91	74	89	85	81	Min. Req.
20	82	84	78	82	83	82	81	Min. Req.
24	74	75	76	74	86	68	79	Scalar
Avg	87.5	87.0	86	89.2	93.0	92.1	94.1	

Hard to learn; easy to teach

Item	On arrival Aug 1990	Experimental Exp	Exp	Immersion 17 mo	33 mo	4–7 yrs	NSs	Type
1	48	55	85	62	71	53	86	POPE Q
7	88	76	96	97	94	82	99	POPE Q
17	79	80	95	82	86	91	100	POPE Q
2	65	53	96	82	94	94	94	Ind. crit.
8	78	67	93	91	91	99	91	Ind. crit.
15	60	42	78	76	71	76	100	Ind. crit.
22	52	53	84	76	76	91	64	Ind. crit.
11	65	58	80	76	86	65	91	Sequence
6	51	36	69	53	57	76	84	Irony
18	47	49	64	53	60	56	75	Irony
Avg	64.3	58.5	83.3	74.7	79.3	77.4	86	

68.2%. When we compare the performance of the experimental group
on these four types of items with that of the different immersion groups
that we have discussed, we find that the percentage of the experimental
group handling these four types of implicature at the end of the instruction period was 5% higher than that of any of the immersion groups (see
Table 8). With an expenditure of very little time or effort, the competence
of the experimental group had matched that of those who had been living in an American university environment many times longer than the
experimental group had, but who had had no explicit instruction related
to these particular skills.

Why these four types of implicature are more easily taught may well be related to their formulaic nature. With each, there are structural or semantic clues that form part of a pattern typical of that implicature type. Some clues, such as those found in the POPE Q and sequence implicatures, are essentially structural. Some, such as those in indirect criticism and irony, are semantic. But whichever they are, the clues form a pattern that is there to be taught – and subsequently to be recognized and used. The presence of this pattern is what differentiates these highly teachable, formulaic implicatures from the essentially idiosyncratic relevance implicatures discussed earlier, which seem impervious to our teaching efforts.

Conclusion

We have argued that if NNSs are to be able to communicate effectively with American NSs, they must be able to derive the same messages from implicatures that the American NSs do. At the same time, we have shown that on arrival in the United States, NNSs do this about 79% to 84% of the time. This means that at that time implicatures pose an obstacle to cross-cultural communication about 16% to 21% of the time they are used.

But this overall score glosses over a dramatic difference in the success that NNSs have with two subsets of these implicatures that we have referred to as *idiosyncratic* and *formulaic,* respectively. Among the clearly idiosyncratic are what we have called relevance-based implicatures. With most of these, the NNSs in this study derived essentially the same messages as the NSs from the time they first arrived in the United States. The more formulaic types of implicature, on the other hand – the POPE Q and sequence implicatures and those involving indirect criticism and irony – proved much more difficult for most NNSs to interpret at the outset and, for the immersion groups, relatively hard to learn.

Fortunately, however, these formulaic implicatures are amenable to explicit, focused instruction in the ESL classroom. With no more than 6 hours of formal instruction plus moments of informal follow-up over a 6-week period, NNSs reached a proficiency in interpreting formulaic implicatures that surpassed to a considerable degree the level of those who had been immersed in the campus community for from 17 months to 7 years, and they came very close to the competence level demonstrated by the American NSs on the same items.

At the same time, it is somewhat ironic that the more idiosyncratic relevance-based type of implicature, which was generally easier for the NNSs initially, seemed also to be more resistant to direct instruction than did the formulaic in those instances in which such instruction seemed necessary. This may have resulted from the fact that for each of these implicatures the message to be derived seemed to be uniquely related to its own utterance and context and not part of a more general pattern that could be learned and applied to other similar instances of this type of implicature. There also was a bonus that came about with the formal instruction given the experimental group, namely, the interest that it generated among the students in implicature as a tool of indirect communication – and a determination to understand and master its use in English.

Finally, we have shown that it is possible to develop new materials, and to adapt old ones, for use in the teaching of implicatures. In many cases, one needs only to search out and highlight the examples of different types of implicatures that are already present in dialogues in well-known textbooks.

Given the pervasiveness of implicature as a conversational strategy and the difficulty that NNSs seem to have interpreting a number of different kinds of implicatures in English, therefore, it seems apparent that they pose an obstacle to cross-cultural communication. At the same time, those implicatures that are most difficult for the NNSs arriving in the United States and the slowest to be mastered by those left to learn them on their own have also proved to be the most amenable to explicit instruction over very little time. All of this suggests that at least the more formulaic implicatures ought to become a part of the ESL curriculum and that research should be devoted to expanding the set of implicatures to which the label *formulaic* can be applied.

Appendix A

Sample materials developed as handouts
for teaching implicature

LESSON I: INTRODUCTION AND POPE Q FORMULA

Introduction: In many languages, including English, people often do not say exactly what they intend to communicate. Sometimes in English we imply information and expect others to figure out what we really mean. One kind of indirect speech is called conversational implicature. Conversational implicatures take different forms, but they are always a result of the interaction between language and context. The examples below illustrate one kind of conversational implicature.

Instructions: Read the following examples and answer the question following each example.
Example 1: Paul and Georgette are discussing a mutual acquaintance who is always running late.

    Paul: Do you expect Sheila to be late for the party tonight?
Georgette: *Is the pope Catholic?*

What is the answer to Georgette's question? What do you think she means?

Example 2: Celia and Ron are discussing their boss, who is very unpleasant.

Celia: So, do you think Mr. Stinguy will give me a raise?
 Ron: *Do cows fly?*

What does Ron mean?

Example 3: Larry and Charlene are talking about a test they recently took.

Charlene: Do you think you got an "A" on the test?
  Larry: *Do chickens have lips?*

What does Larry mean?

Discussion: In each of the examples above, the second person answers the first person with another question, so we have the formula Question 1 + Question 2 = Answer. In each case, the obvious answer to Question 2 becomes the answer to Question 1 also. For example, in the first case Paul asks, "Do you expect Sheila to be late for the party tonight?" (Question 1). Georgette answers, "Is the pope Catholic?" (Question 2). Because the obvious answer to Question 2 is "yes" (the pope is the leader of the Catholics), Georgette's answer to Paul is also "yes."

Activity (5 minutes): Do you have examples of this kind of formula in your own language? Try to think of some examples to share with the class.

LESSON 2: UNDERSTATED CRITICISM

Instructions: Read the following examples and answer the questions underneath each example.
Example 1:

 Lee: How do you like my new sweater?
Sandy: *It's an interesting color.* (Mendelsohn, Laufer, & Seskus, 1984, p. 25)

What does Sandy think of Lee's sweater? How do you know?

Example 2: Laura has spent a lot of money on a new suit and she asks her roommate Brenda about it.

 Laura: You haven't said a word about my new suit, Brenda. Don't you like it?
Brenda: I'm sorry I didn't say anything about it sooner. *It certainly is unique. I
    don't think I have seen anything like it before.* (Wall, 1987, p. 205)

Does Brenda like the new suit? What makes you think so?

Example 3: George and Sheila are looking for a house to buy. Sheila just went to look at a house in their price range and is reporting back to George.

George: So, what did you think of the house?
 Sheila: *Well, it had a nice mailbox.*
George: Are there any other houses we can visit?

What does Sheila think about the house? Why does George ask about visiting other houses?

Now, consider the sentence in italics from Example 2 in a different context.

Hernando: Can I see your watch for a minute, Sara? Wow! That's nice! Did you get it here?
 Sara: No, I got it in Switzerland when I was there last year.
Hernando: Well, I really like it! I *don't think I have seen anything like it before.*
 Sara: Thanks, I like it a lot, too.

This is the same comment that Brenda made, but does it mean the same thing? What is the difference?

Discussion: In examples 1–3, Sandy, Brenda, and Sheila are indirectly criticizing the things being discussed. They do not directly say, "I don't like that sweater/suit/house," but they imply their dislike by praising a quality of each item that is relatively minor. For example, when Sheila says that the house has a nice mailbox, she is implying that more important aspects of the house are not so nice. There is an idiom to describe this implicature: if one uses this implicature, one is "damning something with faint praise."

Activity (5 minutes): Can you think of an example of this kind of implicature in your language? Try to write out an example to share with the rest of the class.

Appendix B

*Conversational implicatures from the students
from other cultures*

POPE Q

Puerto Rico: Are there poinsettias at Christmas?
Sri Lanka: Does a monkey build a house? Can you get feathers from a tortoise?
Taiwan (China, Kyrgyzstan, Japan): Does the sun rise in the West?
Taiwan: Can a man become a turtle?

> Kyrgyzstan: Can a pig fly?
> Venezuela: Does a frog have hair?
> Malay: Do cats grow horns on their noses? Do fish walk?

Interestingly, most of the POPE Q samples generated by the students were frozen, not creative, and had to do with natural phenomena, and this also seems to be true of at least some of the POPE Q implicatures in English as well – for example, the prototype, *Is the pope Catholic?* Also, all of the examples given during the classes were negative; in English, POPE Q implicatures can be used to say either "yes" or "no."

INDIRECT (UNDERSTATED) CRITICISM

Most of the examples of this type of implicature had a misogynistic slant. For example:

> Q: Do you think this girl is beautiful?
> Taiwan: She is very kind.
>   She is very safe.
> Korea: She wears nice clothes.
>   She is nice.
> Sri Lanka: She has a nice makeup set.

Note: The students giving these examples were all imagining a situation in which their parents had arranged for them to meet a woman with the possibility that marriage might result. After the meeting had occurred, the parents wanted to know the son's opinion and so asked the question to which the son was imagined to have made one of the replies given. Other classes has similar examples but in different contexts.

> (Taiwan) Wife: Am I beautiful today?
>   Husband: Yes, your clothes are very beautiful.
> (Turkey)   A: Do you like my new car?
>   B: The tires are nice.
>   A: Would you like to go to a movie?
>   B: I hear there's a sale at the mall.

PART II:
CULTURE AND SECOND
LANGUAGE WRITING

The chapters in Part II examine the influence of culture on writing and learning to write in a second language. The three chapters approach textual paradigms in writing as representations of social and cultural values that differ among communities of language speakers and language learners. Robert Kaplan's work in the 1960s gave rise to the domain of studies that has since become known as contrastive rhetoric. Kaplan first proposed that the writing of nonnative speakers of American and British English may differ from that of native speakers in systematic and identifiable ways. He also claimed that rhetorical organization of text and its progression are often determined by the thought patterns of members of a particular culture. Although this facet of Kaplan's original studies has not been widely recognized, the thrust of his argument has remained influential: Rhetorical patterns in writing often reflect culturally determined concepts that find other manifestations within a particular culture.

Since Kaplan's original publication, researchers have come to recognize that the structure of written text and rhetorical paradigms is based on cultural frameworks, derived from different stylistic, religious, ethical, and social notions, all of which comprise written discourse conventions. Rhetorical constructs are often determined by the conceptualizations of the purpose of writing, the text's audience, and notions of what represents good writing. All these are bound up with the culture of the writer and the audience for which a text is created. What represents a logical progression of text and how the text should be constructed to communicate the writer's purpose relies on concepts that are not necessarily shared by members of different cultures. However, the quality of writing and the ideas expressed in it often become important issues in communication between members of different cultures. The chapters in Part II were selected to reflect the main issues that deal with the influence of culture on second language writing and the outcomes of learning to write in a second language.

The authors of the three chapters in Part II demonstrate that in the Anglo-American culture the purpose of writing is usually associated with promulgation or acquisition of knowledge. In academic writing, the expectations and the analyses of second language writing are also subject to ideologies widely accepted in the realm of educational institutions. In addition to the cultural constructs inextricably intertwined with rhetorical paradigms, power relations between nonnative speakers, who often remain outside the mainstream, and native speakers, who occupy positions of control in the academy, appear to have a great deal of impact on the research and second language pedagogy associated with second language writing. The chapters in Part II indicate that native-like proficiency in writing may not be easily attainable for learners of a second language and a second culture and question whether an ability to produce native-like writing is truly necessary.

In Chapter 4, Yamuna Kachru focuses on the pedagogical aims of the contrastive rhetoric hypothesis originally developed by Kaplan. Studies in contrastive rhetoric seek to analyze rhetorical paradigms accepted in various cultures and specify the differences among them. Kachru questions whether the findings of applied linguistics and contrastive rhetoric research should be employed in the teaching of nonnative speakers and whether these research findings are misused in the ideological structure of the Anglo-American academy. She explains that the stated goal of comparisons of texts written in languages such as Hindi to those written in English often represents an attempt to understand how nonnative speakers construct written text and thereby facilitate the teaching of second language writing. However, she points out that English language pedagogy also operates on the assumption that nonnative speakers have to be taught to write according to the Anglo-American rhetorical paradigms because of the power structure in the academy. Pedagogical goals of teaching nonnative speakers to write in accordance with the expectations in Anglo-American educational institutions imply that nonnative speakers of British or American English have a restricted access to the promulgation of knowledge. In addition, the academic expectations that writing follow Aristotelian logic and argumentation patterns implicitly (and sometimes overtly) exclude members of cultures who belong in the communities other than Anglo-American.

In Chapter 5, Eli Hinkel employs a quantitative approach to written text analysis to determine how native and nonnative speakers construct a rhetorical stance of objectivity and credibility in academic writing in English. According to the rhetorical paradigm prevalent in the Anglo-American academy, writers are often expected to present their views objectively and approach a topic from a balanced perspective. However, not all rhetorical traditions and cultures share these expectations or interpret them in the same way, and even after many years of language learning and exposure to L2 texts, nonnative writers do not always follow the rhetorical paradigms and objectivity conventions frequently expected of them in educational institutions. The findings of her study demonstrate that the writing of trained nonnative speakers from cultures that do not follow the Aristotelian notions of persuasion and argumentation differs significantly from that of native speakers of English. Hinkel concludes that many years of language learning may not necessarily enable members of cultures other than the Anglo-American to write according to the rhetorical paradigms expected in the Anglo-American academy.

In Chapter 6, Linda Harklau's ethnographic exploration discusses the ways in which culture is dealt with in ESL writing classrooms and examines L2 writing instruction as a representation of culture. She investigates the case of students who are long-term residents in the United States and whose presence among traditional ESL students raises fundamental issues in the teaching of writing in a second language and a second culture. She addresses the issues of linguistic proficiency and the acquisition of a second culture by immigrant learners. She asks when long-term residents in a second language community should be seen as proficient second language writers, even if their command of the linguistic and rhetorical features exhibits idiosyncrasies and fossilization that may not be readily subject to change. In Harklau's view, in ESL writing instruction, the issues of culture often bring forth the need to reexamine the normative expectations of rhetorical values and course contents. The implicit assumptions about culture and its membership, which are common in mainstream writing instruction, appear to problematize teaching of nonnative speakers and create a divisive effect. The ideology and power structure in educational institutions are rarely acknowledged in U.S. instructional practices. On the other hand, they seem to be closely tied up with educational politics and the identity of the L2 writer. Harklau concludes that the social context of writing and writing instruction shapes the ways in which culture is represented in the classroom. She proposes that second language education and the many aspects of culture closely intertwined with writing can provide an opportunity to construct and redefine cultural membership.

4 Culture, context, and writing

Yamuna Kachru

Language neither drives culture nor is driven by it; the old question about which determines which can be set aside as irrelevant, because the relation is not one of cause and effect but rather (as Firth saw it, though not in these words) one of realization: that is, culture and language co-evolve in the same relationship as that in which, within language, meaning and expression co-evolve. Thus, above and beyond the random, local variation between languages that was the subject matter of earlier topological studies, we may expect to find nonrandom variation realizing different construals of reality across major alterations in the human condition. But given that language and culture evolve together in this kind of relationship, it is inevitable that language will take on an ideological role. (Halliday, 1993, p. 11)

In this chapter, I am concerned with one aspect of the relationship between language and culture: the interaction of cultural meaning and rhetorical style in the written mode across languages and traditions of literacy. The context in the title refers to the context of acquisition of language and literacy. The focus is on what has come to be known as the research area of contrastive rhetoric (henceforth, CR).

This area of research developed out of pedagogical concerns related to writing by international students in English as a second or foreign language (ESL/EFL; see Kaplan, 1966/1980; more recent works in this tradition include Carson and Leki, 1993; Connor, 1996; Kroll, 1990). With the growing body of research on various conventions of writing, the concern is no longer purely pedagogical (Kaplan, 1966, 1988); the interpretations and the resultant claims of Kaplan's 1966 study have been questioned and modified by several researchers, including Kaplan himself.

Nevertheless, the contrastive rhetoric hypothesis (henceforth, CRH) has inspired a great deal of research on writing across cultures, and on the teaching of writing in English to speakers of other languages (Leki, 1991). Writing in several languages has been compared with writing in English, for example, Choi (1988), Clyne (1983, 1987), Connor (1987), Eggington (1987), Hinds (1980, 1983a, 1983b, 1987), Johnstone-Koch (1983), Y. Kachru (1983, 1988, 1996), Kaplan (1988), Katchen (1982), Ostler (1987), Pandharipande (1983), Reynolds (1993), Tsao (1983), among others. The claims and assumptions made in these and other studies have been attracting a great deal of attention. There is, therefore, a need to

take a look at CR research closely and examine its theoretical foundations and methodological approaches. A beginning has already been made
in this direction (see, e.g., Y. Kachru, 1983, 1988, 1995a and b; Martin,
1992), but, no coherent theory has yet emerged to guide all aspects of this
area of research.

The major theoretical claim of the CRH is that different speech communities have different ways of organizing ideas in writing. A related
claim is that, unlike the native speakers of English, who expect expository prose to be developed as a sequence of claims and (direct) Aristotelian
proofs, nonnative users of English employ rhetorical progressions of text
that are incongruous with the expectations of the Anglo-American reader
(Kaplan, 1972; Reid, 1989; Scollon & Scollon, 1981). Hence, their writing is often assigned labels such as "basic," "inexperienced," or even
"developmental," and the writers themselves are considered "unskilled"
(Johnson & Roen, 1989, p. 6). It is, therefore, both necessary and desirable for the nonnative users of English to learn to construct text according to paradigms commonly found in Anglo-American writing (Swales
& Feak, 1994; Johns, 1997) if they wish to participate in and contribute
to the pool of scientific and technological knowledge. Programs of English education (and ESL training) have been designed with the purpose
of helping nonnative speakers to achieve this goal.

This chapter focuses on issues relevant to CR and English education,
particularly from the point of view of users of English in the Outer Circle
(B. Kachru, 1985).[1] The theoretical perspective in this discussion is that
of "socially realistic linguistics" (Labov, 1972, p. xiii), as represented by
Halliday (1978), Hymes (1974), B. Kachru (1981), and Labov (1988),
among others. This perspective is used in looking at the writing in the
Outer Circle of English, in that the discussion exploits the notion of
"meaning potential" (Halliday, 1973) of rhetorical styles in different literacy traditions. Subsequently, I look at the ideology of CR research,
adopting the perspective of "critical linguistics."[2] Finally, I suggest an
alternative orientation to English education around the world. The suggested alternative aims at enriching the writing experience of all users of

1 B. Kachru (1985) divides the English-using world into three concentric circles: the Inner Circle consists of the native English-speaking countries (Australia, Canada, New
   Zealand, the United Kingdom, and the United States). The Outer Circle consists of
   the former colonies or spheres of influence of the UK and the United States, (e.g., India, Kenya, Nigeria, the Philippines, and Singapore). In these countries, nativized varieties of English have achieved the status either of an official language or of a language widely used in education, administration, the legal system, and so on. The
   Expanding Circle consists of countries where English is fast becoming a dominant
   second language in the domains of education, science, and technology (e.g., China,
   Japan, Taiwan, Thailand, and the countries of Europe).
2 Fowler (1988) and Kress (1994) are good introductions to this approach. For a more
   comprehensive list of references, see Balk (1995).

English, native and nonnative, and is in consonance with the findings of research in related fields of literacy and language socialization.

Cultural meaning

It may be helpful at this stage to clarify what I mean by "cultural meaning." The term *culture* has been defined in various ways in different disciplines. By culture, I mean "the pattern of meanings embodied in symbolic forms, including actions, utterances and meaningful objects of various kinds, by virtue of which individuals communicate with one another and share their experiences, conceptions and beliefs" (Thompson, 1990, p. 132). Culture is not static; it evolves as people conduct their daily lives. Nevertheless, culture also denotes a body of shared knowledge, that is, what people "must know in order to *act* as they do, make the things they make, and *interpret* their experience in the distinctive way they do" (Quinn & Holland, 1987, p. 4; emphasis added). "Act" in this sense includes verbal acts – whether in the spoken or the written mode. The shared knowledge in verbal behavior refers to the familiar conventions followed in using language, which make it easier for us to "interpret" or "make sense" of one another's utterances and actions. Everyone readily recognizes the fact that only very restricted communication is possible without a shared language. However, the realization that, even with a shared language, successful communication may depend on sociocultural factors, which include conventions of language use, is just beginning to dawn. This understanding has led to renewed interest in investigating the interface of language and culture in many fields of linguistics. One such area of investigation, obviously, is CR.

Writing in English in the Outer Circle

The concept of "meaning potential" referred to earlier is relevant to all symbolic systems, including linguistic structures and rhetorical patterns. According to Halliday (1985), language is not a set of isolated sentences; rather, it is an interrelated set of texts in which meaning potential is actualized: People express meanings to realize some social goal. Evaluation of texts rests on interpretation of the context of situation and the context of culture.

That cultural considerations play a role in the development of linguistic structures and rhetorical patterns is corroborated from the history of writing in English in the Outer Circle. It has been shown in several studies that the institutionalized varieties of English used in the countries of the Outer Circle have developed their own grammatical and textual forms to express their contexts of culture (e.g., Dissanayake, 1985, 1990; B. Kachru, 1982, 1987, 1992; Y. Kachru, 1987, 1988, 1992, 1996; Nelson, 1991; Smith, 1987; Thumboo, 1985, 1990; Valentine, 1988, 1991, 1995). For instance, in Indian English, the categorization of verbs in terms of stative versus dynamic is not significant; instead, verbs are categorized in terms of volitionality, as is done in Indian languages such as Hindi, Marathi, and Kashmiri.[3] In texts, it has been suggested that Indian English manifests stylistic features that re-create the Sanskritic noetics (Y. Kachru, 1992). It has been emphasized in studies on world varieties of English (e.g., Dissanayake, 1985, 1990; B. Kachru, 1987, 1992; Thumboo, 1985, 1990) that users of these varieties are bilinguals or even multilinguals; English is one code in their code repertoire. The lexicogrammar and discoursal patterns they use represent their "ways of saying and meaning," to use Halliday's terms.

A critical look at CR

At the present state of CR research, several facts have not been clearly established. First, in order to have meaningful contrastive research, there have to be comparable data. As Vähäpassi (1988) has pointed out, it is not easy to establish the congruency of writing tasks in empirical research. It is equally difficult to determine comparability of registers (Halliday & Hasan, 1976) and genres (Bhatia, 1993) across languages. I will confine my discussion to genre, because that is of immediate relevance to this chapter. Establishing comparability of genre is important because (1) there may be genres in one or more languages and cultures that have no counterparts in other languages and cultures, (2) there may be different rhetorical patterns associated with different genres, and (3) similar, or even identical, speech situations may call for different genres across cultures.

One or two examples may make the first point clearer. It is well known that literary genres do not "match" across languages and cultures (e.g., English ballads and lyrics versus Hindi *pada* and *geet* [short poems meant to be sung, not just read and recited]). Turning to nonliterary genres, in the traditional Indian context no need was felt for written directions for accomplishing various tasks, so that recipes for cooking, patterns for knitting, or weaving mats and carpets, and so on, did not exist. Even now the intricate designs one sees in rugs, silk materials, and so on, are orally recited or sung out as several weavers work on a piece. The genres of recipe, instructions for operating appliances, and so forth, have been borrowed from English and "nativized" in Indian languages such as Hindi.

3 The fact that the distinction between stative and dynamic verbs is not significant in Indian English explains why utterances such as "You must be knowing that S," and "Yes, Yes, I am hearing you" are acceptable in this variety.

One social event in the Anglo-American tradition in which a special genre has a definite function is that of a wedding. A wedding calls for a written invitation in Inner Circle Englishes. In the context of Indian languages, the genre has been borrowed from English, but has not replaced the traditional methods of extending an invitation. Therefore, in these languages, including Indian English, a written invitation has to be preceded by an oral face-to-face invitation, or where great distances are involved, a personal letter apologizing for extending invitation through the written medium only. As regards the genre of wedding invitation, Indian conventions regarding who extends the invitation differ from the Inner Circle conventions. In the Indian context, both the bride's and the groom's families issue invitations. It is the head of the household, usually the grandparents of the bride and groom, who extend the invitations, and generally all the siblings of the grandparents and parents of the bride and groom (and their spouses) are included as signatories as well. These two differing conventions follow from the goal of wedding invitations in the two sociocultural settings. The purpose of the Indian invitation is to identify the family unit and reinforce family solidarity for internal as well as external acknowledgment. Weddings are between families, not between individuals, and it is a social event for reaffirming the families' position within their social network. The genre of invitation, nativized to reflect these values of Indian culture, thus differs from the Inner Circle genre in crucial respects.

In academic writing, much research effort has been devoted to argumentative and/or persuasive text structure in Inner Circle Englishes, and contrasting such texts across languages and cultures (e.g., Connor, 1987; Connor & Lauer, 1985; Mao, 1991; Teo, 1995; Tirkkonen-Condit, 1985). According to a standard textbook on grammar and composition published by the National Council of Educational Training and Research, India (Vyas, Tiwari, & Srivastava, 1972, p. 209), argumentative essay is not a distinct genre in Hindi. The section on composition mentions the following categories of essay:[4] descriptive (*vərnənātmək*), narrative (*vivərənātmək*, deliberative (*vičārātmək*), explanatory (*vyākyātmək*), and imaginative (*kəlpənātmək*), and further reduces it to three groups: descriptive (including narrative), deliberative (including explanatory), and imaginative. Argumentation is one subtype of deliberation or explanation; it is not a distinct category.

Additionally, an argumentative text in American and British English is defined by its problem–solution structure, and its purpose to convince the readers of the superiority of the solution provided in the text (Teo, 1995). A deliberative text in Hindi, on the other hand, is defined by its

4 The Hindi term for "essay," *nibandh*, comes from the Sanskrit root meaning "to tie down." The term *nibandh*, it has been suggested, was used in Sanskrit in the context of philosophical treatises where arguments were tied down in composition or writing.

raising of one (or more related) issue(s), and discussing it (them) by providing either just the writer's opinions and prescribing solutions, or several opinions and solutions, including those of the writer, so that the readers can arrive at the desired solution. There is no rigidly prescribed form for the text, either. Vyas, Tiwari, and Srivastava (1972, pp. 210–211) mention three parts of an essay: introduction, elaboration, and conclusion. They list the following seven types of introduction:

1. quotation from a poet, author, orator, or some discipline (*śāstra*)
2. a brief summary of an event or a story
3. a demonstration of the importance of the topic
4. a definition of the topic
5. a presentation of the antithesis
6. a proverb or a saying
7. a direct thesis statement

It is worth noting that the direct thesis statement is listed at the end, as the last choice among a number of choices.

As regards the elaboration, the advice given to students in Vyas, Tiwari, and Srivastava (1972, p. 211) is as follows: "[F]or elaboration (*prəsār*) [i.e., the body of the essay], material should be categorized carefully to facilitate the sequential presentation of points. Everything that is said must be proved (*prəmānit*) by arguments (*tərk*), facts (*təthy*), events (*ghətnā*) or quotation (*udahərən*) [citing authority: YK] and they should be arranged in such a form that *readers can easily arrive at the conclusion desired by the writer*" (emphasis added). The purpose is not just to *convince*, but also to *prescribe*, or *lead* the readers to find the solution.[5]

The conclusion is said to be as important as the introduction and is said to be of the following types (Vyas, Tiwari, & Srivastava, 1972, p. 211):

1. some propitious sayings related to the topic;
2. some quotation;
3. a proverb;
4. a summary of the essay; and
5. the future unfolding of the topic.

Again, it is worth noting that a recapitulation of the main thrust of the essay is not the first choice for concluding the essay.

---

5 There was a practice of oral debates (*sha-stra-rtha*) in the Indian tradition whereby philosophers could prove their systems to be superior to other competing systems. In this domain, argumentation claiming one's position to be true as opposed to the others' false positions was permissible. Shankara, the great philosopher of eighth century, has been credited with establishing the supremacy of his Vedantic Monistic philosophy as compared to other competing systems, including Buddhist philosophy, by engaging in such debates all over India. I am not aware of any account of the nature and conduct of these debates; the topic awaits further research.

An example of a deliberative essay given in Vyas, Tiwari, and Srivastava (1972) is cited in translation in Appendix A, which poses a problem, analyzes its causes, and prescribes solutions.[6] The textbook does not give an example of an essay that follows the steps (i.e., presentation of arguments, and facts, events, and quotations to support the arguments) suggested in the quote above. An example of argumentative writing in Indian English, which follows to a large extent the pattern prescribed above, is given in Appendix B.[7]

An instance of specific rhetorical patterns associated with particular genres in Hindi and Indian English is the preference for circular or spiral rhetorical pattern of expository prose, as compared to the straight linear pattern of scientific-technical writing (Y. Kachru, 1988, 1996).[8] Writing in the Indian tradition contains traces of the oral tradition, because there is an intimate interaction between the oral and the written traditions throughout Indian history beginning with Sankrit and continuing in the contemporary literatures. The rhetorical styles in essays may thus reflect the oral tradition of exposition. More research is needed in the Sanskrit tradition of written argumentation and oral tradition of debate and exposition in India before any definite conclusions can be drawn.[9]

In addition to the criteria of comparability, the framework of CR needs to be based on a theoretical model that takes into account the social meaning and the intertextuality of texts, because texts derive their meaning from the social context, and from other texts in the tradition. The concepts needed for such a model are already available as a result of research in pragmatics, sociolinguistics, ethnomethodology, and ethnography of speaking. Research in pragmatics and ethnomethodology has yielded valuable insights into how we use language to express our intents and get other people to act for the realization of our own or mutually desirable goals. Research in sociolinguistics and ethnography of speaking has demonstrated the relevance of variables pertaining to sociocultural situations, events, participants, purposes, norms of interaction, and language varieties. All these need to be exploited in proposing a framework for research in CR. This must be done in addition to the theory of textuality

6 The claim here is not that the category of argumentative prose in Inner Circle varieties of English excludes such an essay. I am sure that the raising of an undesirable state of affairs, listing its causes, and prescribing a series of solutions is attested in, say, newspaper editorials and other instances of argumentative/persuasive writing in Inner Circle varieties, too. The difference is one of the conceptualization of what argumentative writing is supposed to achieve in the Indian context.
7 I have presented only the schematic analysis of the data that I have analyzed and presented elsewhere (especially in Y. Kachru, 1997). A complete presentation of data and analysis would require a great deal more space than has been allotted here.
8 The latter style may or may not be the result of India's colonial experience, as suggested in Leki (1991). It may be based on the style followed in the genres of philosophical debate, and prose texts on scientific and technical topics in Sanskrit.
9 A step in this direction has already been taken in Y. Kachru (1997).

aimed at in Martin (1992), if CR is to achieve explanatory and predictive power.

Intertextuality of texts is important in order to account for differences in genres across cultures. Quoting from authority is a legitimate way of validating one's opinion in the Indian deliberative text. It may not be so in the Inner Circle English argumentative texts. Furthermore, intertextuality of texts is important in that the authority referred to would differ from culture to culture. For instance, in the Indian context linguistic topics involve references to Panini (seventh century BCE) and Patanjali (second century CE), topics on literary criticism to Anandavardhana (ninth century), and legal literature to Manu's treatise (second century CE?) or the shariyat (Islamic law). These will not be the expected references in the relevant Inner Circle texts. Popular texts in Indian languages, including Indian English, contain many references to and quotations from the epics and folk literature, and make allusions to Indian mythology, historical events, and folk literary figures.

"Fact" and "truth" and ideology

There is often a misunderstanding of oral traditions and the nature of "fact" and "truth" in observations such as the following (Kaplan, 1987):

In societies in which information is held in living memory, simply because information is variably retrieved (depending on the condition of the owner of memory and the nature of the audience for whom retrieval is accomplished), fact is inevitably somewhat flexible and truth mutable. But once the capacity to fix information in invariable form exists, and once the capacity to retrieve information invariably across time and space exists, the nature of fact and truth changes, fact becoming invariable as the form in which it is stored and truth becoming invariable. These features make possible the whole structure of science – an activity absolutely dependent upon invariable, easily retrieved information.

The developments in scientific inquiry in the Indian oral tradition and the changing nature of "facts" and "truth" in the contemporary American and West European literate societies question the claim in this quote. The following observation of Foucault (1980, pp. 131–132) approaches "truth" from another perspective:

Truth is a thing of this world: it is produced only by virtue of multiple forms of constraint. And it induces regular effects of power. Each society has its regime of truth, its "general politics" truth: that is, the types of discourse which it accepts and makes function as true; the mechanisms and instances which enable one to distinguish true and false statements, the means by which each is sanctioned; the techniques and procedures accorded value in the acquisition of truth; the status of those who are charged with saying what counts as true.

In societies like ours, the "political economy" of truth is characterized by five important traits. "Truth" is centered on the form of scientific discourse and the institutions which produce it; it is subject to constant economic and political incitement (the demand for truth, as much for economic production as for political power); it is the object, under diverse forms, of immense diffusion and consumption (circulating through apparatuses of education and information whose extent is relatively broad in the social body, notwithstanding certain strict limitations); it is produced and transmitted under control, dominant if not exclusive, of a few great political and economic apparatuses (university, army, writing, media); lastly, it is the issue of a whole political debate and social confrontation ("ideological" struggles).

The following quote from Cameron, Frazer, Harvey, Rampton, and Richardson (1992, p. 2) in the context of current social-science research, questions Kaplan's claim about the nature of "fact" in literate societies:

[C]itizens of modern democracies are controlled less by naked violence or the economic power of the boss and the landlord than by the pronouncements of expert discourse, organized in what he [Foucault: YK] calls "regimes of truth" – sets of understanding which legitimate particular social attitudes and practices. In studying and presenting the "facts" about these phenomena, they have both helped to construct particular people ("criminals," "deviants," "teenage mothers") as targets for social control and influenced the form the control itself will take.

The characterization of non-Anglo-American writing as indicative of flawed logic and idiosyncratic reasoning presents nonnative users of English as incapable of contributing to the growth of relevant knowledge. The emphasis on rigid paradigms of text and writing perpetuates the prevailing regime of truth and results in excluding researchers from several traditions from contributing to the pool of human knowledge. It is sobering to speculate on the loss to knowledge if the "ornate" and "metaphorical" style of Sanskrit had interfered with the Arab scholars' appreciation of Indian traditions of mathematical and scientific inquiry; if the parallelism and repetition of Arabic had discouraged European scholars from interacting with Arab scholars and mathematical and scientific texts in that tradition; and, in more recent ages, if the nonlinear pattern of German writing (Clyne, 1983, 1987) had prevented the rest of the world from appreciating the writings of German philosophers, or, closer to the linguistic sciences, the neogrammarians' work.

Educational implications

Most studies that deal with educational implications of CR studies suggest that it is desirable for all users of English to learn the preferred rhetorical mode(s) of English (e.g., papers by Connor, Eggington, Hinds, and Kaplan in Connor & Kaplan, 1987). This is because the "tendency to treat demographic markers in writing as sources of interference is predicated on the notion that communicative success and positive evaluation requires 'unmarkedness' in discourse styles . . . [v]oiceless, gender-less, identity-less prose is the most desirable" (Rubin, 1995, p. 5). Besides, an awareness of the wider perspective of the use of English as relevant to the Outer Circle has so far been totally absent. If we take the wider perspective, an alternative view of what the needs are of the field of English education relevant to the Outer and Expanding Circles becomes obvious. While it is perfectly legitimate to raise the consciousness of all writers regarding the rhetorical patterns preferred in the varieties of Inner Circle, it is equally legitimate and desirable to raise the consciousness of English educators regarding the different rhetorical conventions of learners of English. Just as no language is more or less logical than another, no rhetorical pattern is more or less logical (Y. Kachru, 1995a and b).

The suggestion to foster an awareness of different rhetorical styles among English educators is motivated by two major considerations. First, in view of the findings of the research on socialization through language, it is not possible to train the entire English-using population of the world to the way of thinking and writing in American, British, or any other variety of English. As Halliday (1978, p. 113) observes, even the "mode," the rhetorical channel with its associated strategies, though more immediately reflected in linguistic patterns, has its origin in the social structure; it is the social structure that generates the semiotic tensions and the rhetorical styles and genres that express them. Obviously, not all the English-using world can become identical to the Anglo-American society; nevertheless, it would be a pity to deny large numbers of people of the Western and non-Western worlds the opportunity to participate in and contribute to the development of knowledge in all fields, including science and technology. A narrow view of what constitutes good writing may shut out a large number of original studies from publication and dissemination, because most information technology is controlled in the Inner Circle. Any view of rhetoric that keeps a majority of people from contributing to the world's knowledge base, and legitimizes such exclusion on the basis of writing conventions, shortchanges not only those who are excluded, but also those who would benefit from such contributions. The historical connections between Indian-Arabic-European scholarship mentioned in the previous section is worth remembering.

Furthermore, the teaching of rhetoric – an American institution not shared by all native English-speaking countries – seems to reflect an idealized notion of what an ideal English paragraph or composition is. Most real texts, even within the American culture, exhibit variation from the idealized pattern(s). The repetitions of Arabic and the circularity of Indian writing occur in English writing as well (Y. Kachru, 1995a and b). It has also been demonstrated that writing across Inner Circle Englishes does not follow identical conventions (see, e.g., Connor & Lauer, 1985). If academic writing in general is not to become exclusionary, formula-oriented activity, we have to encourage individual creativity in writing. It is the tension between received conventions and the innovative spirit of the individual that produces good writing in academic disciplines, as well as in creative literature.

My arguments in support of widening the rhetorical horizons of writers and readers does not mean, however, that I am advocating neglecting the readers and their expectations. According to Barthes (1977, p. 148), "The reader is the space on which all the quotations that make up a writing are inscribed without any of them being lost; a text's unity lies not in its origin but its destination." Because conventions differ across cultures and we all have to live together, it is as desirable to educate the readers of texts produced by international users of English as it is to educate the international writers to be sensitive to the expectations of the Inner Circle readers. Instead of putting all the responsibility on the writers from the wider English-using world, it is desirable that the readers from the Inner Circle be willing to share the responsibility of making meaning. Human history is witness to the fact that neither the Chinese nor the Arabs were intimidated by the Sanskrit tradition of scholarship. Similarly, the Indians were not intimidated by the Greek, Perso-Arabic, or, more recently, West European traditions of scholarship. An openness to other traditions enriches the available and acceptable range of linguistic structures and rhetorical modes, as is obvious from the development of American English, to name just one outstanding result of cultural contact. After all, it is already happening in creative literature: A large number of the major literary prizes in recent years have been awarded to multilingual, multicultural writers (e.g., the Booker Prize of Britain to the Maori writer Keri Hulme in 1985, the Neustadt Prize of the United States to the Indian writer Raja Rao in 1988, and the Nobel Prize to the Nigerian writer Wole Soyinka in 1987 and to the Trinidadian writer Derek Walcott in 1992).

Conclusion

The CRH, as currently conceived, is not compatible with the pluricentricity of languages of wider communication, especially English. Contrasting rhetorical patterns is as legitimate an activity as contrasting linguistic structures, but such contrasts should aim at arriving at a set of universals of rhetorical patterns. Contrasting rhetoric with the aim of changing the behavior of nonnative users of English is a form of behaviorism no longer acceptable in linguistic research or language education. In view of the history and societal traditions of literacy, it is doubtful that

any such effort will succeed. Language and rhetorical styles are too inti-
mately bound with cultural identity to be dictated from the outside. Contrasting rhetorical styles to discover the meaning potential realized in
texts is a legitimate activity for fostering cross-cultural understanding via
an appreciation of cultural differences. Teacher education programs in
the Inner and Outer Circle universities are ideally situated to take the lead
in this venture.

Appendix A

Students and indiscipline

There is an enormous dearth of discipline in the world of students these
days. Whether it is in a train or a bus, in a cinema theater, a classroom,
or family home, everywhere one has the bitter experience of students de-
parting from discipline. The major problem before the teachers is whether
to utilize their energy in teaching or in establishing discipline. One hears
of some lack of discipline in other corners of the world, too, but the form
of indiscipline that one sees among Indian students is unprecedented. It
is hard to believe that the New India waking up from its slumber is heir
to the same India that was redolent with the penance and self-control of
sages such as Kapil, and where sanctuary was sought in yoga to rein in
one's inclinations. The question arises: If such indiscipline was not in our
blood, where did it come from? Actually, one does not have to go far to
seek its causes. Almost all the germs of this disease exist in the present
and recent past.

Toward the last quarter of the past century, we were being influenced
by Western thought. As a result we developed a political awareness and
slowly began our battle for independence. Students were a group who,
being relatively free [from job and family responsibilities], could participate in this struggle easily. To realize this potential, it was necessary to
keep the students who were truly the future citizens and who had to bear
the burden of the future, aware of and attached to the political developments in the country. For these reasons, between 1900 and 1947 all our
leaders, major or minor, taught the students to be rebels. The students
started to learn to be mutinous in all aspects of life for political, economic,
religious, and social freedom. This disposition to insurgency is what today's students have inherited from the earlier generation. Now that foreign
rule has ended, this proclivity is manifesting itself in other domains,
which results in indiscipline. This is definitely the main reason for indiscipline, but it is not the only reason. There are other reasons, too, which
are worth taking note of.

The different political parties also have a hand in today's indiscipline.

Before independence, the parties incited the students against British rule, and today they incite them sometimes for truth, at other times for their own vested interests. The appalling results of this have been apparent at the universities of Varanasi, Lucknow, Allahabad, etc. It is amazing that the so-called leaders of the country are destroying the nation by manipulating future India in this manner for their self-interest.

This is an age of conflict between the old and the new. To some extent, the germs of the disease exist in this conflict, too. Besides, education today is not such that upon completion it can free contemporary students from their worries about, at the minimum, [their need for] food and clothing. Naturally, this state of affairs has reduced the students' confidence in education. The lack of confidence surely is responsible to some extent for the indiscipline.

The relationship between teacher and pupil is very significant, but that is also lacking now as compared to earlier times. Teachers are averse to such a bond and so are the students. The root cause of this is perhaps the large number of students in each class. Be that as it may, the lack of connection also contributes to indiscipline.

All the above reasons are external; some internal reasons can also be deemed responsible for the indiscipline, though the internal is not totally unrelated to the external. Two points are worth mentioning in this connection: One is the greater than needed development of the sense of [individual] self in the student, and the other, his or her greater focus on rights rather than duties. A sense of self can not be called altogether wrong. It is a part of personhood and is necessary to some extent. But it has developed to such an extent in today's students that they have totally lost qualities like moral conduct, humility, and civility. Opposition to elders in all matters, unbridled behavior, and lack of restraint are becoming major characteristics of their personality. They are very conscious of their rights; they even hold what is not their right to be so. Rights and duties are mutually dependent. The only healthy situation is where the two are in balance. Today, since the students are more aware of their rights, they are less alert about their duties. Crossing [the barrier of] one constraint has repercussions on other constraints, too.

These have been some of the reasons for indiscipline.

Because of this indiscipline, the students' interests are suffering. They are neither able to develop their personality well, nor are they able to concentrate on getting a good education. Teachers are also not able to pay as much attention to educating students as is desirable. There are two reasons for this: First, they lose their enthusiasm when they see the students' lack of interest, and secondly, they have to spend most of their time and energy in disciplining the students. Thus, because of indiscipline, both the aims of student life – character development and acquisition of education – remain unfulfilled.

The question of how to release the new generation from indiscipline is becoming increasingly serious. This disease is surely not to be cured by any one agency. In order to release future India from the clutches of this epidemic, teachers, students, parents, administrators, and leaders of political parties all have to be battle-ready. Students must realize the situation and resolve to free themselves of this tendency [to indiscipline]. Teachers must realize their responsibilities and fulfill their duties, thus making themselves into real *ācārya* [spiritual guide or teacher] so that students consider their conduct worthy of emulation. Needless to say, indiscipline has increased because of teachers who are unqualified and indifferent toward their responsibilities. [Moreover,] it is necessary to reform education so that it is responsive to life's needs and attractive to students. In this matter, the administration should help by providing for larger funding, etc. Parents often spoil children by excessive affection and indulgence and this, too, results in indiscipline. In the previous generation, as compared to the present one, the relationship between parents and children was different. This does not imply that parents should not demonstrate their love for their children; what is implied is that parents should not shower so much affection that as a result children devalue good behavior and humility and become unrestrained. Similarly, political leaders should give up exploiting the students by encouraging their undisciplined behavior. If all the categories of people identified above behave as suggested, there is no reason why we could not change the present situation. Freedom from indiscipline is essential for our student body to become, in the real sense of the term, *vidyā* + *ərthī* [seeker of knowledge] and make progress in all directions.

From Vyas, Tiwari, and Srivastava, 1972, pp. 221–224

Appendix B

1. Outline of the paper by Garapati, Umamaheshwar Rao (1991), "Subgrouping of the Gondi Dialects," published in B. Lakshmi Bai & B. Ramakrishna Reddy (Eds.), *Studies in Dravidian and General Linguistics: A Festschrift for Bh. Krishnamurti* (pp. 73–90). Hyderabad: Osmania University Publications in Linguistics.

- Introduction (p. 73): The study of Gondi dialectology began in 1942 with at least three main dialects of Gondi. . . ."
- Previous works
- Nomenclature
  Various attempts at subgrouping Gondi dialects were largely unsatisfactory because of the limitations inherent in the nature of data considered, and of the methodological approaches. . . . To overcome some

of these shortcomings the controlled data is collected from a number of locations scattered over the area where Gondi is spoken.

- Innovations and subgrouping of the Gondi dialects
- A note on the phonological innovations
- Morphological innovations
- Lexical differences
- Subgroups of Gondi
- Therefore, ten major dialects can be identified in Gondi, and they can be divided into two major groups.

2. Analysis of the paper

The paper is by a linguist and argues for a subgrouping of Gondi dialects different from the accepted subgrouping at the time. A number of features of the paper are noteworthy. The Introduction, for example, does not provide any clue to the purpose of the paper; it does not explicitly state what the author proposes to do. It starts by citing the authoritative works relevant to the beginnings of the history of Gondi dialectology and various names given to the dialects, and proceeds to a discussion of previous works in the second section. The third section points out the problems with names of dialects based on Shukla ethnic names and lists 10 different names based on geographical distribution. The author does not state that these are the names he is proposing based on his research or that he will argue subsequently that these labels represent better groupings. At the end of the section occur the sentences quoted above, again, with no reference to the names proposed for the dialects. The subsections on personal pronouns (Section 5) and lexical isoglosses (Section 6) list forms that belong to the 10 different dialects, but the reader has to wait until the concluding section where it becomes clear that the author is proposing these groupings on the basis of the phonological, morphological, and lexical features that he has identified. Thus, the paper does present facts and arguments systematically, and lists references to relevant authorities, but it does not follow the prescribed linear generic structure of Anglo-American academic writing (Bhatia, 1993). Another paper devoted to the same topic and appearing in the same volume by L. Smith, a British linguist, follows the prescribed generic structure of academic writing and makes the difference between Anglo-American and Indian writing very clear.

It is noteworthy that out of the 15 papers written by Indian scholars in this volume, only one introduction explicitly states what the paper is arguing about, eight others make the purpose of the paper clear, but six introductions do not provide any information on the topic at all. It is interesting to note that two of the papers written by American authors for the same volume, though argumentative in nature, do not explicitly state their thesis either.

5 Objectivity and credibility in L1 and L2 academic writing

Eli Hinkel

Introduction

In composition writing in American colleges and universities, students are often expected to present their views objectively, approach a topic from a balanced perspective, and support their views with appropriate information to lend these views credibility. Students are usually instructed that the reader needs to be convinced of the validity of the writer's position and that the onus of persuading the reader is on the writer (Leki, 1995; Smoke, 1992).

Research has demonstrated that in academic settings the writing of NNSs frequently does not present balanced argumentation and can be generalization-prone and subjective to a greater extent than that of NS writers (Scarcella, 1984; Scarcella & Lee, 1989). Carlson (1988) indicated that the L2 writing of Chinese students was more vague and less objective than that of NSs with similar educational levels and training. She commented that, overall, the essays of Chinese L2 writers tend to be scored significantly lower than those of NSs because they contain fewer justification, credibility, persuasion, and reasoning devices. Scarcella (1984) noted that NNS writers – in particular, speakers of Chinese – relied more heavily on historical allusions and direct assertions than did NSs with a similar educational background. In her view, in L2 academic settings, instructors found NNS writers' assertions distracting and even occasionally inappropriate. Similarly, Hvitfeldt (1992), who compared NS and NNS argumentation essays, stated that NNS writing can be highly personalized because in many writing traditions other than the Anglo-American, one's "idea of truth is the result of everyday experience" (p. 33). She further indicated that the tendency to give a one-sided presentation rather than a balanced argument can be an outcome of L1 discourse traditions, conventions, and rhetorical value systems.

Since the early 1980s, research into L2 learning and acquisition has

An earlier draft of this chapter was presented at the Ninth International Conference on Pragmatics and Language Learning, University of Illinois, Urbana-Champaign, Illinois, March 1995.

established that NNSs frequently transfer their knowledge of L1 rhetorical and discourse paradigms and conventions to L2 writing. Many experienced ESL teachers of writing and composition have come to expect that essays written by NNSs contain fewer devices and markers of rhetorical objectivity than they consider necessary. The purpose of this study is to examine and compare the use of objectivity conventions in the compositions of NSs and trained NNSs in light of the current instructional methodologies for L2 composition writing. Specifically, this study examines the use of rhetorical objectivity devices and syntactic and referential markers in NS compositions and in the essays of advanced and training NNSs in order to identify the specific discourse features that make L2 writing appear less objective and balanced than that of NSs.

Objectivity in Anglo-American academic writing and composition

Academic writing as a genre (Swales, 1990) has been analyzed from various perspectives. Swales approaches academic writing as a "sociorhetorical" discourse (p. 24) accepted in a community of writers and readers who function within a framework of communicative goals, conventions, socialization processes, and solidarity moves. Atkinson (1991) points out that "the superordinate notion of 'scientific objectivity,' at least partly conventional in origin" (p. 65), can be reflected in how the author approaches and develops a topic, follows written discourse paradigms, and employs syntactic and referential markers. Atkinson contends that these and many other conventions of the academic discourse community have achieved a level of "normativity" that can be hard for "outsiders" to learn (p. 62). In his analysis of rhetorical and syntactic features associated with objectivity in written discourse, he points out that at the rhetorical level, academic norms prescribe "establish[ing] the territory" (p. 66) by means of introductions and employing the "scientific passive" (p. 65) and appropriate pronouns, for example, "*we* and *us* as alternatives to I and me" (p. 68).

Other researchers have identified additional specific characteristics of "objective" academic written discourse that conforms to the discourse community norms and the expected conventions. Connor and Lauer (1988) note that in academic composition in Anglo-American educational environments, "credibility appeals include the writer's personal experience, knowledge of the subject, and awareness of the audience's values" and rhetorical argumentation needs to be based on "the structure of reality" (p. 146), that is, examples, illustrations, analogies, and metaphors.

However, what represents rhetorical objectivity devices and markers is not clear-cut. Dialect and cultural variations have been identified even among the rhetorical conventions accepted in English-speaking societies. Connor and Lauer (1988) compared the use of objectivity and credibility devices in the persuasive academic writing of American, British, and New Zealand students. They found that significantly fewer credibility strategies were used in the writing of American students, compared to the compositions of students in England and New Zealand. Although the authors attributed some of the differences to the lack of adequate training of American students, they concluded that additional divergencies in the use of objectivity strategies may come from different cross-cultural views on the author's objectivity and credibility.

Smith (1987) indicates that the norms of a discourse community underlie the expectations regarding the effective structure and presentation of information and that "using a common linguistic medium (English) does not mean that discourse strategies are shared" (p. 5).

Objectivity and credibility in some other rhetorical traditions

Written communicative paradigms represent a convergence of different stylistic, cultural, religious, ethical, and social notions, all of which comprise written discourse notions and frameworks. Kachru (1988, p. 112) asserts that "different language-speaking communities have developed different 'conventions'" of writing. Experts on the Chinese rhetorical tradition have observed that, according to the Confucian, Taoist, and Buddhist precepts associated with writing, the writer is presumed to be the champion of the truth that he or she announces to the reader (Oliver, 1971; Matalene, 1985). From this perspective, the writer does not need to prove to be knowledgeable because, by virtue of writing the text, the author is assumed to have authority, credibility, and knowledge. Scollon (1994) comments that in Anglo-American academic writing the rhetoric of objective fact occupies a prominent place, but in the Chinese writing tradition it is assumed that what is presented as fact is inseparable from who said it. In the communities that embrace Confucian, Taoist, and Buddhist philosophical precepts, the Anglo-American need for rhetorical objectivity and persuasion is often perceived to be artificial, cumbersome, and unnecessary (Bloom, 1981; Kincaid, 1987; Scollon, 1994).

Hwang (1987) and Yum (1987) indicated that in the Korean rhetorical tradition, based on Confucian and Buddhist assumptions, factual objectivity and persuasion have little value because the writer is expected to achieve a mutual understanding with the reader and avoid overt persuasion. According to Lee (1987), in the Korean rhetorical paradigm, historical allusions, references to common wisdom, direct personal appeals, and advice take the place of objectivity. Tsujimura (1987) also asserts that the influence of Confucianism and Buddhism on Japanese culture pervades many aspects of Japanese discourse and rhetorical tradition and that Japanese strive to attain "higher perceptions of the truth" derived not from words but "from mind to mind" (pp. 117–118). Hirokawa (1987) and Hinds (1983b) demonstrated that objectivity and proof are rarely expected in Japanese writing, in which ambiguity and vagueness have a considerable rhetorical value. The Indonesian rhetorical tradition is also closely bound to its Confucian and Buddhist historical and cultural origins, in which the notions of harmony and understanding between the reader and the writer represent one of the fundamental values, and factual objectivity is not usually expected (Prentice, 1987).

Strevens (1987) asserts that the need for (Aristotelian) rhetorical objectivity and justification may present a formidable obstacle for L2 learners if they are "absent in the learner's culture" (p. 171). He specifically refers to the Chinese rhetorical paradigm in which persuasion in the Western sense is not necessary or expected and indicates that Chinese L2 learners may be faced with a different reality when writing in English, where the author's credibility represents the key to objective writing.

Objectivity and credibility in L2 writing research and pedagogy

Strategies for conveying objectivity and credibility, as reflected in Anglo-American academic writing, are emphasized in the teaching of L2 writing. L2 instructional methodologies often incorporate the notions of rhetorical objectivity, proof in persuasion, and supported argumentation (Connor, 1987). Leki (1995) devotes several sections of her textbook to using, gathering, arranging, and presenting "objective pieces of evidence" (p. 106) and establishing the writer's credibility in order to convince the reader. She also states that a writer must persuade the reader of the validity of his or her assertions by providing demonstrations of how a generalization applies to a typical case, analogies to explain ideas, "facts . . . that bring objective evidence to prove a point," and "references to recognized authority or experts on the subject" (ibid.). Similarly, Raimes (1992) and Smoke (1992) call for the use of facts, statistics, analogies, balanced arguments, and references to authoritative sources to convince the reader and establish the author's objectivity.

In addition to these rhetorical and discourse features, Carlson (1988) also stipulates that the writer's credibility can be conveyed through the use of such rhetorical strategies as justified claims, generalizations, and qualifications and structural markers, that is, the passive voice and existential constructions. She also notes that the usage of "vague words" (p. 252) and subjective adjectives tends to diminish the author's credibility in academic writing.

Arnaudet and Barrett (1984) specifically address the issue of the author's objectivity in L2 academic writing. In their text for advanced NNSs, they focus on descriptive and factual information as a means for establishing rhetorical objectivity. They also present and discuss syntactic structures that serve to promote the author's objective and balanced position in argumentation – that is, the use of passive constructions, citations of relevant sources, hedging devices, and concessive clauses. Swales and Feak (1994), who also assert that NNS writers need to maintain objectivity in their writing, focus on the appropriate use of pronouns, impersonal passive, and hedged claims.

The study

The devices and markers of objectivity outlined in this study are largely based on those identified in, primarily, L2 composition research and methodologies and, secondarily, the characteristics of the Anglo-American published academic genre. To determine rhetorical and syntactic and referential constructs for inclusion in this study, instructional texts and research on L1 and L2 writing and composition were surveyed, with the goal of defining the array of features stressed in current ESL composition pedagogy. The examination of these texts resulted in 12 rhetorical and syntactic and referential dimensions commonly addressed and recommended as means for producing relatively objective and credible L2 compositions and rhetorical argumentation. In addition, such inclusive categories as *Slot Fillers* (nonreferential *it* and existential *there*) (Jacobs, 1995), *Pronouns,* and *Modal Verbs* were subdivided into additional subclasses, yielding a total of 18 rhetorical devices and syntactic markers. Each of these devices and markers is discussed in conjunction with the results of the study.

Rhetorical devices

The following rhetorical devices were identified in the texts and tallied for examination: *Proverbs and Sayings, Direct Personal Appeals, Contradictions and Juxtapositions, General Rules, Rhetorical Questions,* and *Analogies.*

Syntactic and referential markers

In addition to the rhetorical devices, the following syntactic and referential markers were identified and analyzed: *Concessives, the Passive Voice, Slot Fillers, Amplifiers and Emphatics, Pronouns,* and *Modal Verbs.*

The data

The data from the study came from essays written by 30 NSs and 120 NNSs. Among the NNSs, 30 were speakers of Chinese, 30 of Korean, 30 of Japanese, and 30 of Indonesian. Each of these language groups represents a culture heavily influenced by Confucian, Taoist, and/or Buddhist philosophy, cultural values, and written discourse traditions (Cushman & Kincaid, 1987; Yum, 1987). The NNSs had achieved a relatively high English-language proficiency with TOEFL scores ranging from 567 to 623 (a mean of 580). All NNSs had been admitted to graduate and undergraduate university programs and pursued studies toward their degrees. The NNSs whose writing was analyzed were selected on the basis of their relatively high linguistic proficiency, as established by TOEFL scores and their length of residence in the United States. The NNSs had completed the required composition courses designed especially for NNSs and, subsequently, all the composition courses required for NSs in an American university. All had received extensive instruction in ESL and L2 reading and writing for a period of 4 to 20 years, with a mean of 13.1 years. Their residence in the United States typically fell within 1.5 to 3.1 years, with a mean of 2.1 years. Therefore, it follows that NNSs had had a relatively extensive exposure to L2 reading and writing in L2 academic environments.

Both NSs and NNSs wrote the essays during 1-hour required placement tests written in response to two prompts (see Appendix for topics). The compositions analyzed in this study were randomly selected in sets of 15 per prompt (two prompts for NSs and two for NNSs) from each group of students (NSs, Chinese, Korean, Japanese, and Indonesian) for a total of 30 from each group. The essays were written in response to prompts that were modeled on the Test of Written English, administered by the Educational Testing Service (ETS) and Michigan Test of English Language Proficiency Composition prompts, as well as those commonly found in ESL and L1 writing/composition textbooks. All essays were written in the rhetorical mode of argument/exposition with the purpose of convincing/informing an unspecified general audience (Connor & Lauer, 1988; Park, 1988). The objectivity devices and markers employed in the NNS texts were compared to those in essays written by NSs of American English.

Data analysis

To determine whether NSs and NNSs similarly used objectivity devices and constructions, the number of words in each of the 150 essays was counted, followed by a count of the occurrences of each of the rhetorical markers and syntactic/referential markers in that essay. For example, NS essay 1 consisted of 250 words and included one occurrence of a concessive, and three instances of the slot filler *it*. To ascertain the percentage of usage of these markers in the essay, a computation was performed for concessives (1/250 = .4%), and then repeated for the three occurrences of it (3/250 = 1.2%). The computations were performed separately for each of the rhetorical objectivity devices and syntactic markers and for each of 30 NS and NNS essays per group.

Nonparametric statistical comparisons of NS and NNS data based on rank orders were employed because the majority of percentage rates did not show a normal distribution; a large number of essays did not contain all types of objectivity devices and markers. The measure used to establish differences between NS and NNS uses of a particular objectivity device was the Mann-Whitney U Test. The medians, ranges, and results of statistical tests are presented in Table 1. In cases where the reported median is 0, at least half of the sample essays written on the topic did not contain a particular objectivity marker. The ranges are reported to reflect the frequency of use for each objectivity device.

Results and discussion

The findings indicate that NS and NNS usage of objectivity markers differed to varying degrees but was also similar in some respects (see Table 1).

Rhetorical devices and constructs

PROVERBS/SAYINGS

Identified by the words *proverb* or *saying*, and the phrases *people/many say, I/we heard it said*, as in *There is a proverb in my country . . . , as the saying goes . . .* , and *there is a (common) saying. . . .* For example: (1) *There is a saying in my country that people are never satisfied with what they've got*; (2) *People in my country say, "Consider your choices more than once."*

Proverbs and sayings were used in the essays of NNSs significantly more frequently than in those of NSs, although NSs also occasionally included them. Smoke (1992) instructs that the writer can cite external sources of support in order to "persuade readers of the credibility or believability of the piece of writing" (p. 198). However, it is not always clear what represents an appropriate source of information to lend credence to arguments in student compositions (Scollon, 1994).

Although the use of proverbs and sayings does not represent a rhetorical strategy commonly accepted in Anglo-American composition and academic writing (Leki, 1995), it is often found in Chinese, Japanese,

TABLE I. RHETORICAL DEVICES AND MARKERS OF OBJECTIVITY IN NS AND NNS
ESSAYS (MEDIAN %)

Devices/markers		NSs	Chinese	Korean	Japanese	Indonesian
Rhetorical devices and constructs						
Proverbs/Sayings		[.00	.14]*	.57]*	.40]*	.27]*
	Range	.17	.93	2.08	2.14	1.93
Direct personal appeals		[.00	.39]*	.74]*	.00]*	.43]*
	Range	1.11	1.92	1.91	3.68	2.79
Contradictions		[.00	.78]*	.00]*	.09]*	.46]*
	Range	.00	2.21	3.09	2.14	2.38
General rules		[.17	3.36]*	1.25]*	.96]*	1.05]*
	Range	3.18	5.95	4.93	3.33	4.55
Rhetorical questions/tags		[.00	.38]*	.42]*	.41]*	.44]*
	Range	.63	1.94	2.72	1.94	3.43
Analogies		.00	.00	.00	.00	.00
	Range	.92	1.11	1.42	.00	.33
Syntactic and referential markers						
Concessives		[.40	.84]*	.82]*	.89]*	.75]*
	Range	1.58	4.09	2.72	2.19	2.84
Passive		[.00	.83]*	.81]*	.42]*	.79]*
	Range	1.61	2.75	1.48	1.00	1.56
Slot fillers						
Nonreferential *it*		[.70	.29]*	.33]*	.00]*	.63]*
	Range	1.82	1.45	2.72	1.65	2.82
Existential *there*		[.00	.00	.41]*	.33]*	.00
	Range	.92	1.23	2.22	2.30	.60
Amplifiers/emphatic		[.40	.82]*	.70]*	.67	.32
	Range	2.50	2.79	2.52	4.29	1.24
Personal pronouns						
I (1st p. sg)		[1.29	.54]*	.46]*	.34]*	.46]*
	Range	3.79	8.33	6.28	7.22	6.28
we (1st p. pl)		[.00	.82]*	.56]*	.61]*	.58]*
	Range	2.93	5.77	6.06	5.36	5.68
you (2d p. sg/pl)		[.00	.57]*	.69]*	.68]*	.49]*
	Range	3.57	3.11	8.92	6.67	6.58
he/she (3d p. g, 0-it)		.00	.00	.00	.00	.00
	Range	1.72	3.30	3.93	4.46	2.29
they (3d p. pl)		[.00	.71]*	.73]*	.83]*	1.04]*
	Range	3.08	3.52	5.80	4.29	5.08
Modal verbs						
Possibility		[.26	1.08]*	.92]*	.68]*	.69]*
	Range	3.75	3.88	5.20	2.38	2.67
Necessity		[.24	.63]*	1.03]*	1.05]*	.70]*
	Range	1.74	2.20	2.55	2.62	2.86
Predictives		.51	.85	.50	.82	.62
	Range	2.73	4.88	2.78	2.51	5.07

*2-tailed *p* ≤ .05. *Note:* All comparisons are relative to English speakers.

Korean, and Indonesian texts when authors feel that they need to strengthen their position by referring to the assumed common knowledge embodied in proverbs (Scarcella, 1994; Hwang, 1987). Ohta (1991) reports that, in Japanese, attributing an utterance to someone else and employing direct or indirect quotations from an external authority are accepted in discourse as a way of avoiding responsibility for the truth-value of the proposition. Scollon (1991, 1994) identifies proverbs and sayings as a ubiquitous rhetorical device of support and objectivity in the English compositions of Chinese students. In Matalene's (1985) view, educated Chinese often cite proverbs, maxims, and pieces of folklore to establish their credibility with the reader and demonstrate their familiarity with classical sources. Sayings extracted from the work of prominent Chinese philosophers and writers often represent unquestioned support for assertion and display respect for the traditional rhetorical practice.

DIRECT PERSONAL APPEALS

Distinguished by the generic usage of *you* and imperatives. For example: (1) *You want to graduate and get a job, so you can have your own life;* (2) *Don't wait until the decision what to major in comes to you. Decide and stick with your answer.*

Significantly more NNSs than NSs employed a device of direct personal appeals. In general, personal appeals and addressing the reader directly, as in the case of imperatives, are among the strategies to avoid in Anglo-American composition and academic writing (Latulippe, 1992) because they are viewed as devoid of rhetorical objectivity. Swales and Feak (1994) suggest that NNS writers not address the reader directly and that approaching the audience in this way is rarely considered appropriate; instead, the author is expected to make objective facts speak for themselves. On the other hand, Oliver (1971) and Bloom (1981) indicated that direct personal appeals to the text's audience represent a rhetorical strategy common in classical Chinese writing tradition, where communicating with the reader directly has the goal of achieving mutual understanding and solidarity, and objective facts cannot be established (Scollon, 1994). Wong (1990) further explained that in Chinese classical rhetoric, personal appeals are often intended to give force to argumentation and are, therefore, seen as a mark of the author's conviction. She indicates that the rhetorical approach of appealing to the reader is derived from ancient Chinese models and exhibits the writer's authoritative stance and increased credibility.

CONTRADICTIONS (AND JUXTAPOSITIONS)

Setting up opposing positions, making a statement, and then confuting it, as in *Some people believe xxx, and others think yyy; I have some friends who do xxx, but I also have friends who do yyy.* For example: (1) *In Ko-*

rea, some think that they are powerless to change the government, but others think that the government has to be changed through education; (2) Some students study hard when their parents are watching them every minute, and others study because they really want to learn what the teacher is teaching.

Pedagogical composition texts for NNSs often indicate that the writer's argumentation must be presented as balanced, that is, the author is expected to discuss both pros and cons of his or her views (Smoke, 1992; Swales & Feak, 1994). To add balance to their argumentation, NSs did not use sentence-level contradictions or juxtapositions (such as those exemplified above), but rather presented brief descriptions of positions and arguments counter to their own. These were comparatively longer and more detailed than those mentioned by NNSs and usually were a paragraph or two to three sentences long. Leki (1995, p. 262) encourages students to "set aside at least one section of your paper to honestly discuss arguments against your position." On the other hand, Scarcella (1994, p. 266) simply states that "the position about which you can argue . . . must have two sides, one for and one against something," without indicating the appropriate amount of elaboration to accord the opposing point of view.

NNSs commonly employed a sentence or a phrase to acknowledge counterarguments and did not elaborate on their reasons. Bickner and Peyasantiwong (1988) and Bloom (1981) reported, however, that NNS writers often briefly mention the point of view opposing the thrust of their argument and may perceive the elaboration of counterarguments to be purpose-defeating. Oliver (1971) further stated that in the classical Chinese writing tradition the writer's position is expected to be subjective, and accounting for the opposing point of view is not among his or her responsibilities. As the data in Table 1 shows, NNSs in all groups used a substantial number of sentence-level contradictions/juxtapositions to make their arguments appear balanced.

GENERAL RULES (AND GENERALIZATIONS)

Statements indicating a wide application of the proposition, marked by the following constructions: *in (today's/our) life/history/society/world, in our lives, man/people/humans/the human, today/these days/nowadays, in America/the United States, in my country, in our/the human life, we/(Chinese)/(Americans), people in (a certain) country.* For example: (1) *The best way for a man to learn about life is to get experience;* (2) *In today's world, parents build their lives around their children.*

NNSs employed significantly more general rules and generalizations in their essays. ESL instructional texts (Arnaudet & Barrett, 1984; Latulippe, 1992; Raimes, 1992; Smoke, 1992) caution NNSs writers about using generalizations, which must be carefully supported by factual information or authoritative sources. However, Bickner and Peyasanti-wong (1988) found that Thai students relied on general rules and large-scope generalizations to maintain a neutral and impersonal tone in their English essays. According to Ohta (1991), Scarcella and Lee (1989), and Scollon (1991), in the Confucian, Taoist, and Buddhist discourse traditions, generalized claims in writing and speech have the goal of projecting the writer's responsibility for the truth and accuracy of a proposition that can apply to most audiences and most events. Maynard (1993) shows that the speaker/writer in Japanese is assumed to be subjective and the need to support a generalization may not apply.

RHETORICAL QUESTIONS AND TAGS

For example: (1) *Do you know what the most important thing in the world is? What can people do to help their country?* (2) *Can any person meet this goal?*

The number of direct and tag questions was also significantly greater in NNS than NS essays. In general, direct and tag questions are discouraged in Anglo-American academic writing because they are viewed as excessively personal and subjective (Swales & Feak, 1994; Wong, 1990). Leki (1995) and Raimes (1992) noted that questions can be used for invention, and Smoke (1992) discussed the acceptability of direct questions as essay leads if the writer chooses to select a "journalistic approach" (p. 72). Tadros (1994) reported that in formal discourse, questions mark detachment from the proposition, but their use should be limited because, as Myers (1989, p. 27) notes, they can be viewed as "obviously personal." On the other hand, Hwang (1987) and Ohta (1991) stipulate that in Confucian and Taoist discourse, questions are frequently employed to show hesitation and uncertainty of facts that may be compared to the use of hedging in English. Wong (1990) similarly observes that in Chinese, rhetorical questions perform various functions, such as hinting about the purpose of the text to the reader, thereby replacing the thesis statement without a direct assertion. She further stipulates that in the classical Chinese rhetorical tradition, questions assume audience participation and involvement and the reader's understanding of the writer's position. Furthermore, Biq (1990) specifies that question words often perform the role of hedges in Chinese discourse and can be employed to demonstrate the writer's authoritative and objective stance.

ANALOGIES

Comparisons of the unfamiliar to the familiar in order to explain what is meant, marked by comparatives *as (. . . as), like, similar (to), the same (as), and compare(-ed/-ing) (to)*. For example: (1) *Doing the routine tasks every day is like doing laundry by hand: You spend a lot of time but don't get anything new;* (2) *When you think about it, studying in America is the same as having a job because you do what you can to survive.*

Although analogies are frequently encouraged in L2 composition texts (Leki, 1995; Raimes, 1992) as an explication device, neither NSs nor NNSs included analogies to any great extent in their essays. While Atkinson (1991) finds that analogies are particularly difficult for NNSs to use appropriately, Leki (1995) and Latulippe (1992) recommend them for the purpose of clarification. They also caution NNS writers against false analogies and instruct that the compared issues and objects need to be similar in "important" ways.

Syntactic and referential markers

CONCESSIVES (CLAUSES AND PHRASES)

Although, though, even though. For example: (1) *Although helping my country is important to me, my first duty is to my parents;* (2) *I studied for another year after I failed on the entrance examinations, even though I didn't think I would make it into the university I wanted to enter.*

Although the syntactic structure in NNS compositions is frequently considered simplistic, it appears that the writing of advanced NNSs contained a significantly higher rate of concessives than did that of NSs. Concessive clauses can be used to introduce background information (Quirk, Greenbaum, Leech, & Sartvik, 1985; Biber, 1988) or present a balanced argument, which accounts for opposing views (see Contradictions above). Jacobs (1995) stated that concessive clauses can be used to contrast ideas and that the information included in the subordinate structures is usually less crucial than that in the independent clause. Leki (1995) suggested a "formula" using although (p. 129) for creating a balanced thesis statement and presenting the writer's position objectively.

PASSIVE (+ BY-PHRASE)

For example: (1) *What he studies was decided by his family and mostly, his father;* (2) *All that Asians want is to be treated fairly, equally, and justly.*

NNSs used passive constructions significantly more frequently than did NSs. Carlson (1988) observed that the use of the passive in NNS compositions appears to be topic- and subject matter-dependent. The passive voice often serves as one of the more typical markers of academic writing and the detached style that is intended to convey objectivity and un-involvement (Biber, 1988; Chafe, 1985; Myers, 1989). In fact, Atkinson (1991) stipulates that the use of the passive voice is closely associated with conventionalized rhetorical constructs specific to Anglo-American academic writing. In addition, agentless passive can also be employed to front thematic information or remove the agent from the prominent sentence position (Jacobs, 1995). In reaction to this academic convention, however, many NS writing teachers and texts discourage the use of passive voice (Memering & O'Hare, 1983; Winkler & McCuen, 1984; Williams, 1985). On the other hand, Ohta (1991) observed that in Japanese the passive is often used to convey group belonging and solidarity by avoiding pronoun referentials. In Korean writing, the passive is also employed to convey the author's respect for the audience (Hwang, 1987).

The complexity of using the passive voice appropriately, however, appears to be great because of its contextual, lexical, and semantic constraints. Master (1991) devoted his study to contexts in which passive verbs are used in academic writing in English and observes that they can function as hedges. Although he provides detailed descriptions of types of academic discourse when the passive voice is more appropriate than the active voice, Owen (1993) shows that the use of the passive in English is lexically constrained and frequently idiomatic, and therefore not necessarily learned from demonstrations and textbooks. He asserts that many uses of the passive can be pragmatic or discoursal and, in some cases, unacceptability of the passive is subjectively gradient, ranging from nonidiomatic to idiomatic.

SLOT FILLERS

It (nonreferential, clause-subject position) and existential *there*. For example: (1) *It is necessary to improve the environment in Taiwan because air pollution is getting worse;* (2) *There are many people in my country who work all day for pennies.*

NNSs used fewer occurrences of nonreferential *it* than did NSs. The use rate of existential *there* was significantly lower in the compositions of NSs than in those of Koreans and Japanese, but did not differ considerably from those of Chinese and Indonesians. The function of nonreferential clause subjects in academic writing in English is discussed in Biber (1988) and in Quirk et al. (1985), who state that *it* has little lexical content. In the view of McCarthy (1994), nonreferential *it* can be contextually ambiguous and, thus, project detachment and refer to whole segments of the preceding text that can be assigned a functional label of *evidence,* as a semantic and rhetorical unit. Hence, the increased evidentiality supports the writer's objective position in academic discourse and lends implicit authority to the text's claim.

Huebler (1983) classifies *it* as a complex syntactic hedging device that removes the main proposition to the secondary clausal position. Myers (1989) comments that, in academic writing in English, the filler *it* (Jacobs, 1995) serves to depersonalize text and create a sense of hedged objectivity, particularly when accompanied by private and perception verbs that mark evidentiality (e.g., *seem/appear*). In Scollon's (1994) view, the use of *it* marks a convention accepted in academic and "scientific" writing in English. According to Quirk et al. (1985) and Jacobs (1995), the discourse function of *there* can be similar to that of nonreferential *it* in that it contributes to the depersonalization of text and increases the overall impression of textual objectivity.

AMPLIFIERS/EMPHATICS

Absolutely, a lot, altogether, completely, definitely, entirely, extremely, for sure, fully, greatly, highly, just, more, most, perfectly, real(ly), strongly, thoroughly, totally, very. For example: (1) *I spent a lot of time and money learning theory and found out that I couldn't do anything;* (2) *I strongly support the opinion that some people need to mature to decide what to major in and cannot make this decision when they are sixteen or seventeen.*

The essays of NSs contained significantly fewer amplifiers and emphatics than those of Chinese and Koreans, but there was not a significant difference in the quantity of amplifiers and emphatics used by NS and Japanese and Indonesians. Amplifiers and emphatics mark certainty and a high degree of conviction, have the effect of increasing the reliability of propositions and claims (Biber, 1988), and diminish the writer's objectivity (Quirk et al., 1985). They are often found in student compositions (Smoke, 1992) and tend to make text appear colloquial and less academic. In addition to conveying certainty, amplifiers and emphatics can be used to mark solidarity with the reader and may not be appropriate in propositional contexts (Holmes, 1984). Huebler (1983) and Myers (1989) noted that amplifiers and emphatics are rarely found in written published texts and/or academic genre. ESL composition texts (Smoke, 1992; Raimes, 1992) often advise against their use because they may decrease the author's projected objectivity and credibility.

PERSONAL PRONOUNS (AND CONTRACTIONS)

First person singular (*I, me, my, myself*)
First person plural (*we, us, our, ourselves*)
Second person singular and plural (*you, your, yourself, yourselves*)
Third person singular (*he, she, him, her, his, her[s]*, referential *it*), and plural (*they, them, their[s], themselves*)

For example: (1) *The better university I graduate from, the more chance I will get to find a good job, but how can I be accepted in a famous university?* (2) *We often believe that our first opinion is correct;* (3) *Only having experienced achievements and frustrations, you can learn knowledge, and the classes and exams will not be the power to lead you to learn;* (4) *He can set employment criteria in different periods, depending on the company needs, and he will determine whom he hires during the year;*

(5) *If students have talent or potential to learn, they can build up their confidence to devote themselves to study.*

The use of pronouns in NS and NNS writing differed significantly; however, the differences were congruent with the Anglo-American and Confucian, Taoist, and Buddhist rhetorical traditions and textual constructs.

First person singular.   In accordance with the findings of Ohta (1991), Scollon (1991), and Myers (1989), NSs employed noticeably more first person singular pronouns in their compositions. Scollon (1994) and Ohta (1991) observed that use of the first person singular pronoun is considered largely unacceptable in the Confucian, Taoist, and Buddhist writing traditions because it is associated with the individual, rather than the collective, identity. Maynard (1993) commented that when *I* is used in Japanese, it often stands for the group instead of the individual opinion. Furthermore, these authors specify that in Confucian, Taoist, and Buddhist rhetoric, using *I* to stand for the individual would undesirably increase the individual's responsibility for the truth-value of the proposition and diminish solidarity and group belonging.

Advice on the use of first person singular in academic writing appears to be divided. Swales and Feak (1994) and Raimes (1992) explicitly stated that NNSs should not use first person singular pronouns in writing because their use diminishes the objective tone in writing. Arnaudet and Barrett (1984) also recommended that the use of *I* be avoided in order to project objectivity and lend credibility to writing. However, Biber (1988) and other researchers (Chafe, 1985; Poole, 1991) stated that the use of *I* is often associated with ego involvement in text, and Myers (1989) reported that first person singular pronouns can be used to present claims that everyone shares or that the author assumes that everyone can potentially share.

First person plural.   Similarly, the occurrences of first person plural pronouns (*we* and its other forms) in the essays of NSs differed significantly from those in the writing of Chinese, Koreans, Japanese, and Indonesians. Myers (1989) states that first person plural pronouns can be used to stress solidarity with readers. Conversely, Swales and Feak (1994) advise against it. Atkinson (1991) observes that *we* and *us,* as opposed to *I* and *me,* mark formal, yet interactive, contexts and attributes the use of this pronoun to conventionalized forms in academic writing in English. In Johnson's (1995) view, the pronoun *we,* as opposed to *they,* serves to construct group identification in formal discourse and may be used to create group boundaries.

Second person singular and plural.   All groups of NNSs employed significantly more second person pronouns, thus, possibly making writing appear more personal than that of NSs and than is common in American compositions. According to Swales and Feak (1994), writers should not address "the reader as 'you' (except, of course, if you are writing a textbook)" (p. 19). Smoke (1992) stated that "[w]e rarely use second person for essay writing" (p. 106). Nonetheless, Hwang (1987), Ohta (1991), and Matalene (1985) stipulated that in Confucian, Taoist, and Buddhist rhetorical frameworks, *you* is employed to elicit the reader's involvement and thereby contribute to group solidarity (Hinds, 1976, 1983; Tsujimura, 1987).

Third person singular (and referential it) *and plural.*   The differences in the use of third person singular pronouns and referential *it* were not significant. However, NNSs used the third person plural *they* at a significantly higher rate than NSs did. Biber (1988) defined third person pronouns as markers of inexact reference to persons and objects outside the immediately accessible scope of the writer's view. He further noted that these pronouns are often encountered in narratives and exposition and usually accompanied by the past tense. In composition writing, third person pronouns are commonly perceived to impart formality and objectivity to writing (Smoke, 1992). McCarthy (1994) cited several composition studies that recommend the use of *it* in essays as *it* helps create and maintain a referential frame in a piece of writing.

Scollon (1993) and Johnson (1995) specified that use of the third person pronouns serves to identify the boundaries of group belonging and to define those who remain outsiders. The distinction between third person singular and third person plural pronouns extends to the differentiation between the outsider individual or group and thus determines the degree of the outsider influence. Referential *it* is a syntactically flexible pronoun that can refer to inanimate objects, animate beings, abstract concepts, and clauses. Similar to other third person pronouns, *it* is relatively inexplicit and rare in published academic genre (Biber, 1988; McCarthy, 1994).

MODAL VERBS

Possibility and ability (*can, may, might, could* [and contractions]); Necessity (*ought, should, must, have to, need to* [and contractions]); Predictives (*will, would* [and contractions]).

For example: (1) *We can find and create ourselves, and we don't need to worry about losing it;* (2) *They have to accept strict training from childhood, if they want to succeed in their chosen field of study;* (3) *If I finish my degree here, I will help my people to have a better future.*

Following the seminal studies by Coates (1983), Hermeren (1978), and Quirk et al. (1985), Biber (1988) divides modals into three functional classes: (1) permission, possibility, and ability, (2) obligation and necessity, and (3) volition and/or prediction. Although the uses of the modals of possibility and necessity in the NNSs' writing was significantly (and expectably) more frequent than it was in the NSs' essays (Coates, 1983; Atkinson, 1991; Hinkel, 1995), the occurrences of predictives were not (Tadros, 1994). Possible implications of these findings are that NNSs employed modal verbs of possibility to hedge their propositions and claims to a greater degree than NSs did. On the other hand, the use of predictives in NS and NNS essays may reflect the meanings of *will* and *would* in spoken and informal discourse, in which the hedges *maybe, probably,* and *possibly* are frequently omitted (Tadros, 1994).

According to Smoke (1992) and Raimes (1992), in composition writing, the line between the meanings of the modals of possibility, necessity, and prediction is often unclear. Swales and Feak (1994) observed that authors need to demonstrate "good judgment" (p. 87) to be credible, and to demonstrate good judgment writers need to use modals appropriately so as to moderate claims and avoid strong predictives and implications of certainty. In Chafe's (1985) view, the modals of possibility and ability can also perform the role of evidentials. Similarly, Maynard (1993) and Hwang (1987) noted that these modals can function as evidentials in Japanese and Korean, respectively. In his extensive study of predictives in English formal prose, Tadros (1994) recommends that both NS and NNS students be trained in using predictives as textual cues to signal topic shifts to the reader.

Modal verb usage in student essays is, however, a complex issue. Coates (1983) commented that modal verb uses and meanings "conform" (p. 27) to the conceptual structure and reality of NSs of English and are heavily dependent on notions of factuality and truth. The use of modals of obligation and necessity in NNS student essays has been identified as culturally dependent because they often reflect notions not ordinarily found in NS compositions (Hinkel, 1995). Collins (1991), who investigated the corpora of published texts in American, Australian, and British English, indicated that the meanings of these modals are indeterminate, frequently culturally stereotyped, and convey normative and referential relationships that differ even across the dialects and societal structures in English-speaking communities.

Conclusions and methodological implications

The findings of this study demonstrate that although NSs and NNSs used analogies, third person singular pronouns, and predictive modals at similar rates, NNS writing differed from that of NSs in the use of the other 17 devices and markers of rhetorical objectivity. In general, it appears that advanced and trained L2 learners from cultures influenced by Confucian, Taoist, and Buddhist precepts employed the rhetorical objectivity devices and markers common to the Confucian, Taoist, and Buddhist writing traditions rather than those expected in Anglo-American academic compositions. These L2 learners may not interpret the notion of rhetorical objectivity similarly to NSs and may implement the textual constructs that are meant to project it differently in their writing. If this is the case, it seems that despite their relatively high linguistic proficiency and extensive training in L2 composition, the rhetorical devices and syntactic and referential markers associated with Anglo-American notions of objectivity writing remain inaccessible to them. It may be that the composition instruction in ESL and NS classes has accomplished its purpose only to a limited extent.

Conventions of Anglo-American composition require rational (Aristotelian) argumentation, objectivity in the writer's position and views, and factuality in justification and proof. These concepts and rhetorical frameworks are not commonly accepted in many other writing traditions. Scollon (1994) states that "because . . . the academic authorial self is taken to have characteristics of individuality, rationality, and autonomy, it represents an ideological position which is likely to be in conflict with the culturally constructed selves of non-native speaking students of English" (p. 17). Rhetorical objectivity is only one facet of this ideological position (Atkinson, 1991; Strevens, 1987). Presenting students with techniques for conveying an objective position and formulas for writing balanced thesis statements is unlikely to accomplish its stated goal of making L2 learners good writers in English.

The issue of differences and similarities between the English writing of NSs and that of NNSs has been surrounded by controversy. Some researchers found few differences in the rhetorical frameworks and constructs between published scientific articles written in English by NNSs and those written by NSs of English (Mohan & Lo, 1985; Taylor & Chen, 1991). On the other hand, others have found important differences between the English compositions of NNSs and those written by NS students (Bickner & Peyasantiwong, 1988; Scarcella & Lee, 1989).

Although Anglo-American academic writing has been reasonably well researched, it appears that the characteristics of student compositions are less specific. As Biber (1988) notes, the differences between NNS and poor NS texts have been difficult to identify. In addition, as Biber (1988) and McCarthy (1994) report, different rhetorical paradigms and textual constructs are employed in the Anglo-American composition writing and published academic genres. Biber (1988) indicates that student essays written for required composition classes "are unlike any of the published genres of English" (p. 204). In his view, although many surface forms of Anglo-American academic writing are maintained in essays written for composition courses, their information content is relatively low, and their persuasive form is very high. Among the many outcomes of this disparity, it seems that composition writing does not have well-defined discourse and community norms and that students' performance is often rated according to the institutional, task, sociocultural, and literacy norms expected and accepted in a particular academic environment. It is possible that the writing of NNS, as well as NS, students could more readily be improved by placing more emphasis on the rationale that underlies them and the contrast between the conventions accepted in different discoursal societies and writing traditions.

Many methodologies for teaching the Anglo-American conventions and norms for writing college composition focus on the pedagogy associated with discrete skills and techniques. Even if a methodology for teaching L2 writing devotes several sections to the explanation of the reader's expectations and the writer's responsibility to explain the ideas to the reader, in L2 composition training, it appears that the writer also needs to be convinced (Hinkel, 1994). The teaching of Anglo-American rhetorical conventions and notions and their main precepts, such as objectivity, factuality, and textual support, in contrast to the conventions accepted in different writing traditions, may need to be the starting point for L2 composition instruction, eventually leading to instruction in the discrete skills and techniques for writing.

Appendix

Prompts for NS and NNS essays

NSS

1. What is your major? Describe your values and characteristics that caused you to make this choice.
2. Describe how you or your chosen career can benefit our country.

NNSS

1. What job or profession are you preparing for? What are your personal views and qualities that made you choose this field of study?
2. Discuss how you or your training in your major can contribute to the development of your country. Use detailed reasons and examples.

6 Representing culture in the ESL writing classroom

Linda Harklau

By tradition and necessity, second language instruction often addresses cultural issues. As ESL teachers, we are often called upon to explain English-speaking cultures and cultural differences, and to help students adjust to the target culture. Yet, interpreting culture is a perilous enterprise that is neither clear-cut nor simple. This chapter illustrates some of the difficulties teachers face in discussing culture with their students. It shows how cultural representation is made more complex when participants in ESL writing classrooms include long-term residents whose experiences with and orientations toward American culture may be quite different from that of newcomers. It demonstrates how, in this context, views of culture that are implicitly conveyed by instructors and the curriculum may be met with resistance from students holding contending views. Furthermore, it shows how taking long-term residents' perspectives can shed light on both the potentials and the pitfalls inherent in addressing cultural issues in ESL writing instruction.

Language is inextricably bound up with culture. Cultural values are both reflected by and carried through language. It is perhaps inevitable, then, that representation of culture implicitly and explicitly enters into second language teaching. This chapter is about ESL college writing classrooms. How is culture typically dealt with in these classrooms – what elements or ideas do they emphasize? Perhaps the most-examined and best-documented aspect of culture in ESL writing pedagogy pertains to norms for writing and how these norms are manifested in the linguistic and rhetorical features of texts. Research has demonstrated that differing expectations for prose structure across cultures manifest themselves in rhetorical style, purpose, task, topic, and audience (see Connor & Kaplan, 1987; Hinkel, this volume; Kachru, this volume; Leki, 1991; Purves, 1988). Many of these expectations appear to be transferred when writing in a nonnative language. Thus, ESL writing instruction addresses cultural issues most explicitly in efforts to socialize L2 learners into expected cultural norms for academic texts in the target language.

Less examined, but perhaps equally pervasive, is another way in which the teaching and learning of culture enters into second language writing instruction. Because L2 writing classes typically bring together individuals from a number of cultural backgrounds, intercultural communication and the norms and values associated with the target language may be areas of significant topical interest to learners. Thus, while teaching about culture may not be an explicit goal of most ESL writing courses, the cultural patterns and values nevertheless form a significant part of the content through which second language writing skills are taught. ESL writing classrooms serve as arenas for cultural orientation and brokerage, and ESL teachers often serve not only as writing instructors, but also as explainers and mediators of American culture and cultural values.

Culture is an elusive construct that shifts constantly over time and according to who is perceiving and interpreting it. Yet, teachers are often called upon to explain or name the target language culture. In doing so, they must in a sense reify their own interpretation of culture, making static something that is in constant flux, and making unified something that is inherently multiple. The resulting "representations" of culture appear both implicitly and explicitly in the work of ESL writing classrooms. Representations of culture are embedded in a broader sociocultural context that is imbued with differential power relationships, a context that both shapes and is shaped by the interactions of students and teachers in the classroom (see Auerbach & McGrail, 1991; Benesch, 1993; Canagarajah, 1993; Raimes, 1991). Thus, instructional practices representing culture in the classroom continually tread a thin line between informing students of cultural norms that will further their L2 writing development and ability to function as L2 writers in academic contexts, and prescribing and enforcing dominant cultural norms in and through writing.

The role of ESL writing teachers as cultural brokers and mediators has been shaped in large part by a newcomer clientele in need of basic cultural information and orientation. Increasingly, however, college ESL writing classrooms serve another group of students who are not novices to American culture. Since 1965, immigration laws favoring the relocation of entire family groups have resulted in growing numbers of school-age immigrants. Many of these students arrive in the United States in late elementary or secondary school and enter college while they are still in the process of attaining the level of English proficiency they need in order to function in college academic contexts. Colleges and universities have several options when placing these students in writing courses. In some settings, linguistic minority students who are American high-school graduates are placed in mainstream college composition alongside native speakers of English. In other settings, long-term residents who are nonnative language writers are redirected into ESL classes, either in combination with international students or in classes designed specifically for them. With few exceptions (see Valdes, 1992), little consensus or even explicit discussion of these options has emerged in the literature. In this chapter, I discuss a study documenting what happens when long-term

U.S. resident language minority students are placed in ESL composition courses. I use these students' experiences as a means of illustrating the pitfalls we face in addressing cultural issues with language minority students, individuals who bring with them very different levels of familiarity with American culture and different cultural adjustment issues than their newcomer or international student peers. I will argue that their experiences have broad implications for the way teachers address culture in ESL writing classrooms.

Method

In 1994, I conducted a yearlong study to describe the transitions that ESL students make in the demands of reading and writing tasks as they move from high school to college. Four female subjects, three Vietnamese (Claudia, Penny, and Hanh) and one Turkish (Aeyfer), participated in the study.[1] All had attended the same western New York urban high school in spring 1994. The four were selected for the study with the assistance of the school's ESL teacher based on the likelihood that they would attend college after high school. Three of the subjects had come to the United States in sixth or seventh grade; one (Claudia) had arrived in second grade. The study employed ethnographic case study methodology. Students' experiences with and perceptions of high-school reading and writing demands across the curriculum were documented throughout the spring semester of their senior year in high school. The same students were then followed throughout fall semester as they made the transition to college-level tasks. Three of the students elected to study at nearby Lakeland Community College. Hanh enrolled at State University, just outside of the city. All four subjects enrolled full-time in fall 1994. All were placed in ESL writing courses that semester. Additionally, students at Lakeland were placed in ESL reading courses that also required composition assignments. In this chapter, I focus on writing instruction in these college ESL classes.

Data consisted of interviews, classroom observations, collections of students' work, field notes, and written artifacts collected from the study sites. Each student was interviewed between 10 and 13 times over the course of the study, and on five occasions each during fall semester, at 2–4-week intervals. Interviews typically lasted about 45 minutes, with some lasting up to 1½ hours. Each of the students' college instructors was interviewed as well. ESL faculty at Lakeland invited me to two meetings to discuss their concerns about the American high-school-educated students in their program. Each study participant's classes were observed twice.

---

1 A fifth subject who did not enroll in college was dropped from the study. All names are pseudonyms.

Lakeland was a 2-year college with an enrollment of approximately 13,700 students. The college had a sizable ESL program, with 231 students, five full-time instructors and several part-time instructors. More than 30 different countries were represented in the student population, with the majority of the students originating in Southeast Asia and East Asia, and an increasing number from former Eastern bloc countries. They varied considerably in the academic training and socioeconomic status in their countries of birth, and although many were newcomers who had been in the United States for three years or less, a rising proportion were long-term residents. State University, where Hanh enrolled, was a 4-year institution with an enrollment of 5,700. Minority students formed a small proportion of the student body. Although there was no compulsory ESL program, nonnative language writers such as Hanh who entered through the Educational Opportunity Program were often directed by advisers into an English department course titled "English Language and Culture."

Writing assignments in Lakeland Community College's ESL reading and vocabulary courses were based on articles in the newspaper, a college ESL textbook consisting of short readings with a multicultural focus, and a novel (*Flowers for Algernon* [Keyes, 1966]). Writing courses utilized various composition and grammar texts intended for a college ESL audience. Instruction covered the organization, content, mechanics, and a substantial amount of grammar and error analysis. Students were instructed in archetypal genres: argumentative/persuasive, compare/contrast, and classification. The State University ESL writing course curriculum was similar. It included a college ESL grammar text from which students were assigned exercises. Writing in various expository genres was emphasized. Instructors at both institutions were experienced, knowledgeable, and thoughtful. Instruction in both contexts included sound pedagogical techniques such as dialogue journals, multiple drafting of writing assignments, portfolio assessment, peer editing, and utilizing computers in order to promote fluency and editing skills.

Nevertheless, the case study subjects were far from satisfied with their ESL courses. They found it difficult to articulate exact reasons. They all believed that their instructors were good teachers, and liked them on a personal level. They said they found much in the classes that was useful, and had no specific complaints about the materials or assignments. Yet, over the course of the semester, increasing irritation, frustration, and resentment crept into their accounts of what was happening in their college ESL classes. Likewise, classroom observations showed them to be listless, fidgety, and occasionally sullen. Aeyfer and Claudia used excuses for not attending class regularly, and Aeyfer left her homework until the last minute. They began to complain that the classes were boring and of limited use to them. Claudia wrote in her writing course journal, "I don't like my advisor. I think that she gave me a wrong advise [sic] to take ESL 103 [reading] class. The class is too easy that it bored me."

In fact, students' behavior and attitudes were consonant with resistance – the sense of discomfort, perplexity, and frustration that occurs when students feel that "something deep and personal is threatened or offended" (Fox, 1994). Resistance can take many forms, and while some students may recognize what and why they are resisting, for many others resistance remains below the level of conscious recognition. Resistance in ESL writing classrooms has been linked with representations of culture. Many (e.g., Reid, 1993, pp. 139–140; Fox, 1994) have attributed it to students' reluctance to change their rhetorical patterns and logical style to better reflect American English cultural norms for expository prose. Some (Fox, 1994; Greene, 1993; Patthey-Chavez & Gergen, 1992; Rodby, 1992; Tucker, 1995) have further noted the affective difficulty that language minority writers may experience when asked to approximate the cultural norms of a discourse community that may nonetheless marginalize or exclude them. Accordingly, as I watched these students become increasingly discontented in class and spoke with teachers who were puzzled, concerned, or simply put off by students' behavior and attitudes, it seemed logical to examine how cultural representation was accomplished in the classroom. As I looked at manifestations of culture in writing assignments, class discussions, and student work, I came to see new significance in some of the very practices that our profession and I as a (nonimmigrant and nonminority) teacher have taken to be most mundane and self-evident. With the researcher's luxury of looking at these classroom practices through the eyes of students, I began to view some of these seemingly sensible, common practices as the very ones most likely to cause contention between culturally related perceptions, assumptions, and experiences of students and teachers, and thus the very ones most likely to precipitate student resistance. Despite these students' diverse instructors and different institutions, several strikingly consistent potential areas of contention ran throughout their experience in the classroom where: (1) Cultural orientation provided through reading and writing assignments was inappropriate for those already immersed in American culture; (2) assignments and class activities implied a polarization of cultures and cultural identity; (3) students' efforts to shape and articulate their own cultural identities conflicted with other classroom agendas; and (4) depictions of culture and cultural mixing were reductionist or one-dimensional. I will address each of these areas in turn.

Inappropriate cultural orientation

While teachers were aware that some of their students had already resided in the United States for a number of years, they nonetheless directed instruction toward the majority who had been in the United States for a relatively short time. As a result, through teacher talk and writing assignments, they frequently proffered cultural orientation and cultural brokerage to long-term residents who neither wanted nor needed them. For example, the goals of the program at Lakeland Community College, as stated by one of the ESL writing teachers for a College Day information program, included not only "Through language study, to open the door to a college degree program" and "Better communication," but also goals less related to academics than to cultural orientation: "Acculturation to life in America" and "Personal growth." When asked about these goals, all three of the study participants attending the community college (Claudia, Penny, and Aeyfer) believed the latter two to be inappropriate. Claudia commented, "I don't think ESL should be teaching those things. . . . What does this got to do with college, anyway?" Similarly, when asked if acculturation was an appropriate subject for ESL writing class, Aeyfer asserted, "you learn it the minute you come to the airport, really. So we learn it better than they teach at school, so they can't really teach that to us." The goal of acculturation and introducing the novice to American society was also evident in the name of the State University ESL writing course, "English Language and Culture." The teacher noted that there was some ambiguity in the intended population and goals for the course. The title of the course indicated its original intent, which was to serve newcomers to the United States who were presumably in need of both English-language instruction and American cultural orientation. Although most of the students had turned out to be U.S. residents coming from American high schools, the original intent of the course was still reflected in its title and its curriculum.

Teacher talk frequently reflected the assumption that students were new to the United States. Hanh's teacher often prefaced comments to the class with statements such as "As people new to American culture, . . ." Claudia and Penny's reading teacher, discussing branches of the U.S. government, noted, "This will be important if you want to become citizens eventually." In fact, Penny and Claudia were already U.S. citizens, and the comment only served to reinforce their impression that the class was not appropriate for them. Claudia's teacher wrote in her journal that her writing was continuing to improve and she should keep practicing. While meant as encouragement, the teacher's lack of acknowledgment of Claudia's previous decade of "practicing" written English in U.S. educational contexts rendered such encouragement hollow.

Writing assignments often had an American cultural orientation component, assuming cultural novices as their audience. For example, Aeyfer was given an assignment to find a stranger, interview him or her, and then write a composition based on the interview. While the intent of the assignment was to coerce cultural novices into interacting with native speakers of English, the effect for Aeyfer and students like her was quite different. It was not a particular linguistic challenge, because she already interacted with native speakers in appropriate communicative contexts, such as conversing with fellow Travel and Tourism majors in her content area classes. For her, then, the assignment entailed simply an awkward imposition on a stranger. Aeyfer, who had kept all the books for her father's small business in the United States, was also given several assignments intended to orient students to American credit cards and banking. Similarly, Claudia was asked in one of her writing assignments to write a letter responding to a job want ad in the newspaper, with the assumption that newcomers to the United States need help in learning how to find employment. Considered in light of her impressive range of previous work experience in the United States, the assignment was not appropriate for Claudia.

It must be emphasized that teachers at Lakeland Community College and State University were not unaware that these students had different needs than did the newcomers. In fact, in conversations and meetings with them, they frequently expressed concern that they were not meeting those needs. Nevertheless, with more training and experience in dealing with newcomers, and with greater numbers of newcomers in their classes, they tended to respond to the majority whom they perceived to be in need of this sort of orientation.

When such cultural orientation assignments are given to long-term residents, they arguably go beyond simple irrelevance: They risk making students feel as if their experience in American culture does not count, that their teachers still implicitly consider them newcomers, and that they will always be considered newcomers. In response to curricula and instructional practices that seemed to ignore students' hard-won experience in American culture and render them perpetual newcomers, it is no wonder that they might feel alienated or resistant. Resistance sometimes took a playful, if slightly sarcastic, form in students' writing. For example, in her letter to the want ads, Claudia asked for a fictitious job "flipping burgers," citing her 5 years of real-life experience working as a waitress, cashier, and hostess at restaurants.

Enforcing foreignness and polarization of cultural identity

Prominent among the composition topics in these ESL classes were "your country" topics. They included variations such as "My country – a great place to visit," "Holidays in my country," "Problems of students in my country," and "A food served on special occasions in my culture." They included compare/contrast variations as well, such as "The way children are raised in the United States and your country," "Shopping in the United States and your country," "Attitudes toward the elderly in the United

States and your culture," and "Attitudes toward wealth in the United States and your culture." These topics have long been a staple of ESL writing instruction, and I count myself in the legions of teachers who have used them. Why are they so ubiquitous? For one thing, they (presumably) build on personal experience, and it is a long-held tenet of writing instruction that it is best to begin with what students know (Britton, Burgess, Martin, McLeod, & Rosen, 1975; Elbow, 1973; Raimes, 1991; Spack, 1985). Students found this a sound notion. Penny observed, "Maybe it's easier to write if you see it happens, you know? Like you know more ideas, you find more things." These topics, then, are viewed as building a bridge between personal experience and academic, expository writing. They also accommodate students' desire to talk about their home cultures, and lend themselves quite naturally to comparing and contrasting.

In many cases, however, the "your country" topics did not build on the personal experience of long-term residents, who had left "their country" as children. Rather, it forced them to speak hypothetically about issues either that they had not experienced as children in their natal culture or that had changed greatly since their departure. Perhaps the best example occurred in Penny's ESL writing class, where, at their own request, students did reports on "their country." While Penny is Vietnamese, she is also ethnic Chinese and speaks Cantonese at home. The teacher encouraged students to collaborate on their projects, and Penny chose to work with someone who spoke her home language, who happened to be from Hong Kong. As a result, Penny's "your country" report was about China, a country she has never seen and can only remotely claim as her own. She thus completely circumvented the intent of the report topic, which was to elicit personal experience in service of writing instruction. In another instance, Penny's teacher asked students to write about the "Return Home." Because most of Penny's relatives preceded her to the United States and she has only distant cousins left in Vietnam, her report naturally took on a rather speculative tone, again completely missing the intent of making use of personal experience. So far removed were some of these nominally personal experience topics from Penny's experience, that she admitted "Sometime I make it up!"

Aeyfer told a poignant story of a woman in her class – Stephanie – who had immigrated to the United States very early in life and had only distant experience with her natal country or culture. When the teacher, Ms. Grayson, asked students to write about "their culture,"

Stephanie told her that she could not write about "her culture." Accordingly, Grayson directed her to write about some other culture that Stephanie knew better. When Stephanie turned in a report on Germany, Aeyfer relates what happened: "So she [Grayson] picks up the paper, and she . . . goes, 'This is not your work!' She's yelling like this. She [Stephanie] got red. . . . And then, she said, 'I did that, Ms. Grayson.' She [Grayson] said, 'No, I don't believe it. This is perfect. You could have not do it.' She goes, 'And why would you write about Germany unless, when you are Chinese?' She [Stephanie] goes like, 'Because you told me to write about other cultures maybe I know about.' And she [Grayson] goes like this, 'No! . . . It's *odd* for you to write about Germany!'"

Aeyfer reported that the issue was resolved only when Stephanie showed Grayson her notes and sources. In this case, then, a student was made to feel that there was something "odd" about her because she could not conjure up "her" country.

The issue of how "your culture" topics represent cultural difference and students' relationship to American culture has implications that go well beyond long-term residents' particular situation, however. In ESL classrooms, "*your* country" and "*your* culture" are frequently utilized as a shorthand, as a means to signify students' country of birth or origin and their home culture. That usage may seem sensible and innocuous enough when dealing with newly arrived students or those who will only be in the United States for a short time. Johnson (1994) has argued, however, that pronominal usage also serves as a powerful, if implicit, means of indexing inclusion and exclusion. Likewise, critical discourse analysts have argued that readers' and writers' social identities are implicitly conveyed and constructed through discourse (Ivanic, 1994). If we believe that learners forge "a sense of who they are and how they relate to the social world" through their interactions – spoken and written – with native speakers (Pierce, 1995), then we must recognize the latent potential of such prompts to signify a dichotomous, polarized view of the relationship between American culture and students' culture. This view can hold students at arm's length and foster a sense of alienation. Tucker (1995), discussing the work of Edward Said (1978), has cautioned that examining cultural and linguistic differences has the potential to set them in "contrived and misleading opposition." This potential is most evident in compare/contrast topics such as "Compare the way that children are raised *in the United States* and *your culture.*" When instructors dichotomize culture, they may implicitly suggest that they view American cultural perspectives and students' cultural perspectives as mutually exclusive. Furthermore, because of teachers' dominant role in the classroom, that implicit view is not likely to be challenged. Rather, it is likely to be reproduced in the writing of students, who come to believe that teachers expect them to emphasize the foreign, the different. Consider, for example, Claudia's introductory essay to her writing teacher. Claudia writes:

Hello! My name is Claudia. I come from Viet Nam. I was born in August 10, 1975. I came to the United States of America in 1983 of November.
 When I leave Viet Nam I was eight years old. I came to the United State with my mom, sister, grandma, and I.
 I have a sister and a brother, my brother is ten years old and my sister is

twenty-three years old. My sister name Trinh she also go to Lakeland Community College.

I like the United State is because here I can get good education. In Viet Nam you can't go to school if your family doesn't have money.

My goal is to complete my Education on Dental Hygiene, and find a good job in order to take care of my mom, and grand parents in Viet Nam.

Notice that perhaps half of this essay is devoted to issues relating to Claudia's "foreignness" – where she was born, when and how she came to the United States. This essay would not be unusual, perhaps, for someone who has only recently arrived in the United States. However, after spending more than half of her life in the United States, one expects Claudia's cultural identity as a Vietnamese-American to be important to her, but probably not the only way that she identifies herself. Missing from this account, for example, is any mention of the fact that she graduated from a local high school, that she works part-time at a nearby restaurant, that she is taking other classes at Lakeland Community College, and that she likes to read novels in her spare time. One also suspects that Claudia could give a much more sophisticated critique of life as an American than a simplistic statement comparing education in the United States and Vietnam. Nevertheless, from her essay it is apparent that Claudia believes that her teacher expects to see a one-dimensional cultural novice or perpetual foreigner stance. The classroom dynamics and representations of culture that give impetus to such a stance are reinforced in the broader sociocultural context, where Greene (1993) has remarked on the tendency to think of newcomers in terms of their foreignness rather than other, more individualistic traits. She points out "the invisibility that has been imposed upon those thought of as 'other,' those perceived as alien in the familiar world," and comments that, "we do not and somehow cannot do justice to them in their particularity and distinctiveness."

"Your country" topics also hold the potential to play into stereotypes of Asian-Americans in American society, becoming classroom manifestations of those types. Scholars (Lee, 1992; Takaki, 1989; Wong, 1987) have asserted that Asians in the United States have historically been portrayed as unassimilable to American ways of life. Lee argues that the portrayal of Asian-Americans as inscrutable, as "dangerously foreign with no alliance or identification with America," has given way to the equally sterile rendering of a "model minority" of "quiet, well-behaved, hard workers" who are nonetheless still seen as perpetual foreigners. Third- and fourth-generation Asian-Americans tell stories of being asked, "Where [i.e., what *other* country] are you from?" Similarly, Aeyfer encountered stereotypes depicting Muslims as unenlightened fanatics who oppress women and are prone to violence. In her reading class one day, for example, she encountered a newspaper editorial titled "PBS Program Maligned the Muslim Community." Mura (1992) notes that long after it has become unacceptable in American popular culture to use derogatory and simplistic stereotypes of African-Americans, stereotypes of Asian-Americans (and, one might add, Islamic people as well) disappear more slowly. He believes that this creates a "problematic relationship to America and the English language." In light of stereotypes held in the larger society, interpretations of composition topics about "your country" in the classroom can easily, if unintentionally, serve the polarizing function of telling students that they are different and that they must keep their distance from American culture.

The duality engendered by such topics produces a sort of cultural schizophrenia in long-term resident students' writing. For example, Penny, in responding to the prompt "Are blue jeans popular in your culture?" writes: "Blue jeans are very popular in *my own culture* and around the world. *They* wear it like *we* it in the United States" (emphasis added). In the first sentence, *my own culture* refers to Vietnamese culture, in which Penny includes herself. In the second sentence, though, *they* means the Vietnamese, not Penny, and in the same sentence she includes herself in *we,* meaning Americans. Despite the fact that she recently became a U.S. citizen, Penny is so accustomed to hearing references to Vietnam as "her country," that it does not particularly bother her. Note the following exchange I had with her:

L: When she [the teacher] says like, *your* country, do you feel like Vietnam is your country, or is the United States your country, or are they both your countries?
P: I feel Vietnam.
L: Really?
P: Yah, 'cause I get used to it, you know! (*laughs*)
L: You get used to what? (*laughs*)
P: Like, saying, "Our own country," you know? (*laughs*)

While Penny laughs about this, I find it troubling. Penny will build her future in the United States, and yet she has evidently been made to feel that "her own country" does not include the United States, but rather is limited to a distant place that she has not seen in years.

It must be acknowledged that the exact circumstances under which learners come into American society, as well as their future relationship with English and American culture, affect where students place themselves in terms of culture, and whether they see any implicit conflicts with such a duality. For example, international students who plan to study in the United States and then return to their country of origin may not be particularly troubled by the dichotomizing of home and U.S. cultures. No matter what students' background, however, many believe that one cannot truly learn how to write in a language without taking on the perceptions and viewpoints of cultural participants. Shen (1989), for example, has argued that learning how to write in English entails a redefinition of the values acquired from one's social and cultural background. In order to write well in English, Shen maintains that one must develop an "English identity," a sort of second "skin" for perceiving the world. Likewise, Fox (1994) argues that learning how to write in another language produces profound changes in those who live and work in other countries. She believes this is because "writing is so tied to thinking – the inner expression of a person's being – and to communicative style – its outer expression – thus touching the core of the writer's identity" (p. 71).

When students feel they are being pressed to conform to American linguistic and cultural norms and perhaps even to transform their ways of thinking through writing instruction, but at the same time feel that they are receiving a conflicting message to keep their distance, resistance is likely to ensue. For example, in an essay on the topic "Shopping in your country and the United States," Penny shows her resistance to the tendency of "your country" essay topics to emphasize difference and distance between cultures over the universal, what Geertz (1983, p. 14) has observed as the tendency for outsiders to focus on the exotic and to minimize the normality of the culture. After a dutiful cataloging of the differences between Vietnamese and American shopping as she vaguely recalled them, she adds a final parting shot, writing, "The way they do it [shop] is the same, because they need money to pay for it in both countries"; and, just in case her teacher takes her seriously, she adds, "This is just a joke."

Conflicting classroom agendas

For the informants in this study, as well as for many of their American-born peers, enrolling in college served as the catalyst for thinking about and grappling with identity. Students' struggles with these issues took outward signs – Aeyfer and Penny changed their hairstyle, and Penny and Hanh made significant changes in how they dressed, for example. Students' evolving views of their identities manifested themselves in other ways as well. Upon becoming citizens, Claudia (formerly Ngan) and Penny (formerly Tuyet) changed their names in a sort of metaphoric rebirth, literally looking through baby name books for new identities. Aeyfer reported frequent arguments with her parents about her major and her future, toying with the unlikely possibility of leaving her entire family to return alone to Turkey. Although the nature of the struggles might have been different, it is likely that newcomer students in these students' classes were working through cultural identity issues as well. Like long-term residents, they too face the continuing task of functioning in American culture, and placing themselves on various continua of cultural values and beliefs. Students' writing classes, with their emphasis on eliciting student opinions and beliefs through journals and class discussion, ostensibly provided ideal environments to explore culture and to tap those explorations in order to develop L2 writing skills. Nevertheless, students' attempts to engage these issues in L2 writing classes sometimes seemed at odds with other agendas in the classroom and were thus rebuffed, setting off resistance.

The most striking example of such a conflict in agendas took place in Hanh's writing class. Of the four students in this study, the exploration of cultural identity appeared most intense for Hanh, whose life had changed the most in college. She was separated from all of her high-school friends, living in a dormitory and immersed in campus life. She was associating with a number of Asian-American acquaintances dealing with similar identity issues. Her deliberations on culture and identity frequently found a place in her ESL writing class compositions and journal entries. In one essay, for example, she wrote that she thought that there should be a foreign language section in the school newspaper so that "Students who lost their nationality can learn more about their roots." In another composition, she wrote:

I have been in America for almost six years. I'm still not used to American's lifestyle. I still need to learn more and have more experience about it. I have live in my country for twelve years, but I still needed to learn a lot of things. I left my country when I was young therefore I don't know much about my culture and my language.

Clearly, Hanh's need to locate herself culturally was a powerful motivating force for her writing. Hanh's teacher seemed to be caught unawares by this need of his students. Intent on his charge from the English department to address expository writing, he considered Hanh's essays on this subject to be inappropriate. He complained that she was writing very "romantic" essays talking about cultural identity and feeling stranded between cultures, which he characterized as expressive writing that did not meet course goals. Over the course of the semester, Hanh and other students grew increasingly unresponsive in class, and the teacher noted that they did their work halfheartedly and did not seem invested in the course – if he was rejecting their agenda, they were rejecting his as well. In this case, then, the instructor's understandable impulse to hold to his objectives acted only to intensify student resistance, and at the same time rendered him unable to utilize students' consideration of cultural identities as a means of motivating writing development.

Aeyfer's religion was an important part of her identity. In interviews, she often prefaced statements with "In my religion, we. . . ." When she registered for courses, she told me that she looked for instructors' names that might indicate Islamic origins. It is not surprising that she felt somewhat of a personal investment in an assigned reading for her writing class titled "The Arab World." When the teacher opened up class discussion on the article, Aeyfer immediately asserted that she already knew a lot about the article because she came from a similar culture. Her comment set the class off on a discussion of religion. The teacher seemed uncomfortable with the direction the discussion was taking. She attempted to steer the discussion into a more relativistic discussion of religion, directing turns to Christians and the Buddhists in the room. Aeyfer, with rising frustration, persistently bid for turns. Moreover, despite the teacher's best efforts to redirect the discussion, other students in the class kept returning to Aeyfer with questions. The discussion culminated in a pointed exchange in which the teacher asked Aeyfer if religion is the same as culture, and Aeyfer responded, "I thought religion was part of culture." Watching this exchange, I understood the teacher's inclination to tread carefully in the potentially explosive topic of religion as well as her concern to distribute turns equally among her students. At the same time, however, Aeyfer's exasperation with the discussion was palpable. I could imagine her growing sense that an important part of her cultural background and identity was being disregarded in class. Later, Aeyfer and her teacher both told me that they had engaged in several similar exchanges over the course of the semester. Again, one can see the miscues between teacher and student intent and goals, and the missed opportunities to channel the intellectual and emotional energy that students have invested in cultural identity issues into English writing instruction. Rather, these encounters intensified resistance.

"Mainstream" and "travelogue" depictions of culture

Another way in which representation of culture in these classrooms potentially generated resistance was through the tendency to depict culture as "mainstream ways of thinking held by mainstream citizens of well-defined nation-states" (Kramsch, 1993a). Such a view tends toward reductionist and unidimensional images of culture, and fosters a "travelogue" depiction of cross-cultural experiences in which culture is portrayed as picturesque, a "sightseeing curiosity" (Kramsch, 1993a; Mar-Molinero, 1992). These views of culture and cross-cultural encounters were well represented in students' course work, in which they were asked to read several actual travelogues – for example, a sentence-combining exercise about an exotic beach vacation locale, and a reading passage about a Japanese tourist in New York. Not only did writing prompts such as "My country: A great place to visit" explicitly invite a travelogue portrayal of students' first culture, but students also construed other "your country" topics as asking for a travelogue as well. Hanh, for example, concluded her composition on the topic "Food served on a special occasion in your country" with the travelogue coda, "I hope you have enjoyed learning [about] the moon Festival." Resistance to the travelogue view of culture was demonstrated by several students in Claudia's writing class, who spent the class break creating a raucous parody of a "My country – a great place to visit" composition that highlighted tourist attractions such as prostitutes.

Hanh's textbook for writing class also evidenced a travelogue ethos. Her text, intended for a college ESL audience, was organized around recurring characters, a band of international and American-born college students safely ensconced in a university campus, who strike up earnest conversations about how hard they are all studying and whose worst problem seems to be the cafeteria food. The reductionism implicit in the unidimensional, "travelogue" depiction of culture in such texts and writing prompts did not invite students to probe the complexities or potential contentiousness of cross-cultural communication. Such depictions of culture, which are not uncommon in textbooks aimed at a college ESL audience, are perhaps most consonant with the experiences of "privileged" students (Vandrick, 1995). For some international students, for example, who bring with them the certainty that they will eventually return home to a secure place in the social hierarchy, the dilemmas of culture shock and intercultural communication may be uncomfortable, but they are nevertheless transient. These individuals may choose whether to address or to retreat from the questions raised by cross-cultural encounters about self-identification, power relationships among ethnic or linguistic groups, and potential cultural change. For students such as Hanh, however, who had confronted these questions daily in an ethnically and socioeconomically diverse high school, the text was rather incongruous. The construal of culture as "mainstream" fosters a static rather than dynamic view of multiculturalism – a live-and-let-live relativism in which cultural mixing is always a cordial exchange among equals, where cultural boundaries remain intact and immobile, and where contact among individuals from various cultures does not imply any influence, transformation, or re-creation of their respective cultures. These travelogues suggest that there is nothing more to crossing cultural boundaries than knowing what to pack, how to dress, what to see, and what to eat.

In opposition to the travelogue representation of culture, scholars influenced by sociocultural thought and postmodernism have stressed the multiplicity of culture and cultural identity, and the impossibility of fixing them or reducing them to stereotypes. Lum (1992), for example, notes that because a group such as Chinese-Americans is extremely heterogeneous in terms of class, education, sex, generation, and point of origin, answers to questions about "your culture" can only be answered from within each individual's own place in the constellation of variables that make up culture. Similarly, Penny, Claudia, and Hanh saw their orientations as very different. They noted differences among themselves and among other Vietnamese-American classmates in characteristics such as literacy and educational level in L1, socioeconomic status, attitudes toward schooling, and family networks in the United States and Vietnam. When a "your country" question in one class resulted in different answers from Vietnamese-American students in Penny's class, however, the teacher wrote on her paper, "Other people from Vietnam disagreed. You'll have to talk to one another!" Given the recurrent patterns of cultural essentializing in these students' classrooms, the comment holds at least an implication that people from "their culture" necessarily share uniform perceptions and attitudes, and that the Vietnamese students in Penny's class need to get their stories straight. The mainstream view of culture and the travelogue view of cross-cultural encounters potentially hinder L2 writers from drawing on the polyphonous voices of both the native and the target culture (Bakhtin, 1981; Kachru, 1995b; Rodby, 1992) to which they have access.

In sum, then, while explanation and discussion of culture were not an explicit instructional goal in these ESL writing classrooms, they were nonetheless a substantial, and perhaps inevitable, part of the curriculum. When representations of culture in these classrooms took predefined or assumed form, they potentially engendered resistance. In some instances, the version of culture forwarded by the instructor or the curriculum did not match students' needs and experience. In other cases, it did not allow for multiple or non-"mainstream" views of culture, or for a dynamic and contentious view of cultural mixing. At times representations, perhaps reflecting dominant sociocultural norms, implicitly dichotomized cultures and alienated students who were already a part of American culture. Finally, students' countering representations of culture sometimes were tacitly rejected.

One might conclude from this discussion that language minority students who have been schooled in American public schools simply do not belong in ESL classes at the college level. It might be argued that whatever academic and linguistic needs students bring with them from American high schools are best addressed in mainstream freshman composition and developmental writing courses, where they will be among students with the same previous academic training and experience. This has indeed been the route taken at a number of American universities. On the other hand, as conscientious advocates of language minority students at their respective institutions, instructors at Lakeland Community College and State University felt that they needed to protect students from mainstream courses that would not serve them as well as ESL. They pointed out that few of the mainstream instructors at their institutions possessed the training and expertise necessary to sort out students' academic writing ability from their language-specific instructional needs, or to respond appropriately to those needs. They believed that students' most intractable and fossilized nonstandard language features were the product of previous instruction in mainstream classrooms. They worried that students would be unfairly penalized by mainstream composition instructors confounding English-language proficiency with writing or general academic ability. In view of the paucity of research evidence about language minority students' experiences with reading and writing in mainstream college classrooms in the years after they leave ESL or freshman composition, these teachers' fears must be given serious consideration. In any case, long-term resident students at these two institutions, as at many other institutions in the United States, were likely to continue to be directed into ESL-specific writing instruction.

We are left, then, with the question of how ESL instructors might best simultaneously address the needs of both the newcomers and the long-term residents in their classes. A number of approaches for the instruction of linguistically and ethnically diverse students have been offered in which students' inevitable efforts to define their multiple cultural affiliations become a means of motivating writing development in the target language.

Cultural inquiry through L2 writing

In her writings on learner motivation, Pierce (1995) stresses the significance of incorporating "the lived experiences and social identities of language learners" into the curriculum. Advocating a Freirian "problem-posing" approach to language education, Pierce emphasizes that we cannot assume what those experiences and identities are. Rather, she promotes exploration of culture and social identity by students as the means through which language and writing skills are developed. Other writing instructors from diverse perspectives suggest similar approaches. Rodby (1992), for example, proposes countering what she sees as the enforced "outsiderness" of ESL literacy students with the formation of a classroom community or "communitas" (Turner, 1974) where students can collaborate as a group to explore their multiple cultural affiliations, and become aware of how these affiliations are mediated by written language. Similarly, Pratt (1991) and Lu (1994) advocate the creation of a classroom "contact zone," an arena in which "cultures meet, clash, and grapple with each other, often in contexts of highly asymmetrical relations of power" (Pratt, 1991). Lu (1994) asks students to give conscious consideration to "the context of their personal life, history, culture, and society" in the choices they make as a writer. Other formulations are described by Patthey-Chavez and Gergen (1992), who apply a "problem-posing" approach to college ESL writing instruction, and Tucker (1995), who describes the implementation of an American Studies course for ESL students.

These approaches share a deliberate avoidance of received representations of culture in the curriculum. Starting from the premise that culture is not self-evident, they ask students to take an active participatory role in defining culture in the classroom and, while acknowledging teachers' continuing leadership and power, describe a more facilitative and less directive role. These accounts suggest that the function of cultural content in ESL writing classrooms can be to problematize culture, and to facilitate students' explorations and evolving understandings of culture from their own varied individual backgrounds and experiences as a productive means of developing second language writing proficiency.

We have seen how some of the cultural assumptions and depictions of culture conveyed to students in the college ESL writing classrooms in this study potentially fostered alienation and resistance among students. This was by no means the only way that culture was dealt with in these classrooms, however. In fact, a good share of the ESL curriculum at both Lakeland Community College and State University held the potential to engage students in a process of cultural exploration and construction, utilizing instructional practices that built on student perspectives and thoughts about culture as a creative force for second language writing.

One topic area that was conducive to this approach addressed U.S. attitudes toward racial and ethnic diversity, immigration, and "multiculturalism." Aeyfer, for example, was asked to read and respond to two very different editorial views on immigration. One, by University of California chancellor Chang-Lin Tien, discussed immigrant bashing and scapegoating, while a contrasting editorial was titled "Lest We Become the Tired, Poor." Aeyfer was also asked to read and respond to a newspaper article discussing whether speaking a different language at home impedes the school performance of children. Students in Lakeland Community College reading classes were assigned an article that discussed the place of immigrants among U.S. small-business owners. Similarly, in Hanh's class at State University, students were asked to write an essay addressing the subject of racism. Assignments such as these facilitate an awareness in students that culture in the United States is diverse and multivocal. They counter what Wong (1992) has described as "the potency and persistence of existing hegemonic discourses on American ethnic groups, which pit each minority against a quasi-monolithic 'mainstream,' ignoring the realities of an already multi-ethnic America."

Another area of inquiry in the ESL writing classes in this study that seemed to lend itself naturally to problematizing culture pertained to American values and their manifestations in current events and students' own experiences. Topics in this area held the potential for students to link their own personal experience to larger sociocultural issues. For example, Aeyfer engaged in a dialogue journal by E-mail with her teacher regarding an encounter she had on the bus with a Christian who was extolling the virtues of his religion at the expense of others. Such an experience can serve as rich material for the further exploration of various manifestations of religious values in American society. Topics pertaining to American cultural values and perceptions were particularly conducive to engaging students in dialogue or debate. For example, students in ESL reading classes at Lakeland Community College discussed an article titled "America's Best-Kept Secret: Things Are Going Pretty Well," which addressed whether continuing pessimism in the American public was justified in light of many improving social conditions. Claudia and Penny read and responded to an article on the dangers of realistic-looking toy guns, and were invited to give their opinions on the broader issue of gun control legislation. These topics invited students to address issues that all participants in U.S. culture face, and to weigh in with their own opinions and ideas. Confirming the value of exploring these themes, all of the study informants concurred that discussing and writing personal opinions regarding elements of American culture were their most useful and interesting writing assignments.

Finally, although, as we have seen, received representations of culture in the ESL writing curriculum may result in reductionist or alienating renderings of students' native cultures, that is not to say that discussion of culture must be suspended, but only that such discussions must be motivated by and have their origin in students' perceptions and needs. There are compelling reasons to address students' natal cultures and issues of cross-cultural adjustment, anomie, and cultural identities. Wong (1992), for example, asserts that newcomers to American society try to reconstruct and recover their past life in their natal culture – "the lost center" of the past – as a means of equipping themselves to change culturally and develop a new reference point, or "center" in the United States. Thus, discussions of students' native cultures can serve as a powerful generative force, facilitating students' evolving understanding of their multiple cultural identities even while they are developing L2 writing skills. Nevertheless, just as a comparative stance holds an implicit risk of conveying a self-evident and static view of culture, discussions of cross-cultural adjustment may implicitly elicit, or even explicitly mandate, expressions of immigrant angst, nostalgia, and anomie. A good example of this genre was produced by Claudia, who had just spent her first summer in 10 years in Vietnam with her extended family. She wrote in her journal:

"My Dream"
I had a wonderful dream last night. my dream was that, I went back to my native country, an there I saw my grand parents, aunt, uncle, and cousin. they treated me very good. Then when I got into the dreaming loving them and hugging them suddenly I wake up. It seem like they to far from me wich make me can't hug them.

The very real and powerful emotions that generate such expressions of nostalgia, sadness, and confusion must be acknowledged. Students may need to capture and explore these feelings in writing, and ESL writing class is a logical place for them to do so. In fact, the need for expression is sometimes so great that students will produce such sentiments even if they conflict with the instructional agenda. Hanh's teacher complained that students were producing these sorts of reflections in spite of his lack of enthusiasm for them: "She's one of the students who keeps expressing . . . the nostalgia for Vietnam, being without a country, and not fitting into the United States." On other occasions, however, assignments and essay prompts may explicitly demand such displays of anomie. For example, Claudia was assigned essay topics such as "I miss my hometown," "Leaving my country," and "Coming to the United States." Such topics hold the potential for "recentering" or coming to terms with the past as a means to shape a future cultural identity, but they also hold the real possibility that students will produce a display of immigrant angst merely for the benefit of the teacher. In fact, at the same time that Hanh was writing some reflections that her teacher felt were too personal in nature, she was also expressing some resentment of assignments that she felt asked her to make a public display of private thoughts. Hanh commented, "Sometime it's like, it's too personal, and you don't want to write about it." Aeyfer complained that her teacher was pressuring students to publish essays containing information that Aeyfer considered private in the department's semiannual magazine of student writing. There is a potential danger in such essays becoming coercive (i.e., students find that they need to make such displays of private thoughts and angst in order to secure the teacher's sympathy and goodwill) or becoming a means for students to resist and to mitigate the power relations between the teacher and themselves (i.e., students produce them because they realize that it makes it difficult for teachers to address other aspects of their writing for fear of appearing insensitive). In either case, writing produced is not genuinely motivated by students.

Despite this risk, most ESL writing teachers would agree that, treated with sensitivity and caution, explorations of students' natal cultures, cross-cultural adjustment, anomie, and identity can serve as powerful generative issues in the classroom. Classroom tasks must somehow ensure, then, that students are not coerced into making displays of emotion or private thoughts, while at the same time ensuring that the validity of such displays is acknowledged as legitimate when proffered. The assignments in this study that seemed to do this best involved experiences of others who have crossed cultural boundaries. In one assignment, for example, Penny read and responded to vignettes ostensibly written by two second language learners, each posing a dilemma faced in crossing linguistic and cultural boundaries. In another assignment, Penny read and responded to a short story about a Native American man returning home to the reservation for the first time in years. Both assignments allowed Penny the option of directing her analysis outward and commenting on the protagonists' experiences and feelings about cultural adjustment in the third person, as well as the option of responding in the first person and relating their experiences and feelings explicitly to her own cross-cultural adjustment process.

Conclusion

In this chapter, I have utilized the perceptions of ESL students who are long-term residents as a unique vantage point from which to critique how culture is dealt with in ESL writing classrooms. The presence of these students in ESL college composition raises many larger questions, to be sure. There is the fundamental question, for example, of when enough is enough. When should students be regarded as second language learners whose written language features indicate a developing command of the English language. When should they be considered proficient and functional bilinguals whose writing may nevertheless exhibit fossilized or contact variety features – features that arguably should be expected and tolerated in a diverse, multilingual society? Valdes (1992) has argued that the current compartmentalization of ESL and mainstream composition stems from the false belief that ESL composition instruction will transform students into writers who are virtually indistinguishable from mainstream monolingual writers. She argues that this belief penalizes bilingual language minority students whose language skills may be fully functional in college communicative contexts, and yet whose English production may never precisely match a mainstream monolingual's language use. In terms of this study, we might ask if Claudia is still best served by ESL. After a decade of U.S. education, it is likely that further ESL instruction will have diminishing returns, and yet it is also quite possible that mainstream instructors would penalize Claudia for the nonnative-like features still evident in her academic writing. Valdes argues that the presence of bilingual language minority students in college writing courses calls for a fundamental rethinking of the relationship between ESL and mainstream composition instruction, and more responsibility on the part of mainstream instructors for bilingual student writing development. While such issues are beyond the scope of this chapter, findings from this study indicate that they deserve wider attention.

This chapter illustrates how teachers' views of ourselves, our students, and the relationship among cultures are represented not only through explicit instruction regarding cultural differences in rhetorical and aesthetic values for texts, but also implicitly in the course content, assignments, and class discussions in which we engage with students. In order to counter implicit assumptions about culture and resulting student resistance, areas of cultural inquiry were identified in these same classrooms that facilitated a multifaceted representation of culture and that potentially invited students to define culture for themselves. By proposing such an approach to instruction, I do not mean to imply that ESL writers in our classes will or should come away with any conclusive determinations about culture or cultural identity. On the contrary, because constructions of culture are multiple and shifting, such determinations will remain elusive. The point, then, is not to find a final resolution to inquiries regarding culture, but rather to engage in the process itself of questioning representations of culture. Grappling with cultural issues maybe a useful and potentially transformative experience not only for long-term resident language minority students, anyone who crosses cultural boundaries, including the teachers who utilize these approaches.

Instructional practices that problematize culture and engage students in its definition do not preclude explicit training and modeling of American academic cultural norms for written prose, nor do they preclude the representation of mainstream types of culture and cultural values in the classroom. These norms and types are part of the sociocultural and political context in which instructional practices are embedded, and their pervasive influence must be acknowledged and dealt with. After all, to explore these issues without an explicit instrumental goal of developing students' ability to function in L2 academic contexts is to invite further student resistance. We must be very clear, however, with our students and with ourselves, about the nature of what we are presenting in the classroom, and its sociocultural and political origin. As Tucker (1995) notes, it is "an unavoidably political enterprise to engage, to read, to 'write' other cultures. For that matter, ESL teachers soon discover, it is equally an ideologically charged endeavor to teach one's culture to others." In dealing with culture in ESL writing instruction, we have the potential to take students' individual explorations with cultural adaptation and to transform it into collective work of meaning and identity. Even while acknowledging that the broader societal context shapes how and what of we represent culture in the classroom, we must also believe that classrooms can be a space from which we creatively construct, contest, and redefine culture.

PART III:
CULTURE AND SECOND LANGUAGE TEACHING MATERIALS

Edward Sapir's theory of language use as socialized behavior gave rise to analyses of interactional practices in cultural communities and the ethnography of speaking inaugurated by Dell Hymes and John Gumperz in the 1960s and 1970s. Additionally, the work of philosophers John Austin and John Searle in the 1950s and 1960s formed the basis for speech-act theory, which today serves as a foundation for the study of pragmatics in interaction and speech act behaviors. Hymes and Gumperz first made explicit the connection between culture and language and treated interaction and speaking as culturally defined practices. They emphasized the need for studying the social contexts of speech acts, cultural influences in interaction, and the interactional competence of language users.

In his influential work, Hymes in the 1960s and 1970s proposed that language competence necessarily includes speakers' ability to use language appropriately in various sociocultural contexts. He argued that the social function of specific linguistic structures and discourse has to be examined together with syntax because the sociocultural parameters of interaction often determine the syntactic construction. Although Hymes and his followers largely focused on ethnographic, componential, and taxonomic descriptions of speech, they approached language as a social, rather than exclusively linguistic, phenomenon. The ethnographic analysis of interaction addressed such important components of sociocultural interactional contexts as participants and their social status, setting, purposes, speech-act sequencing, and norms of appropriateness, all of which play a role in speakers' communicative competence. Hymes's description of what represents communicative competence also included pragmatic dimensions of sociocultural contexts and cultural frameworks of discourse.

The pragmatic features and uses of speech acts, such as contextual and speaker meaning, presupposition, and explicitness, have been examined extensively following John Austin's highly influential theory, further elaborated by John Searle. Austin and Searle were primarily concerned with the meaning of linguistic structures as they are used by speakers in various interactional contexts. The study of pragmatics examines assumptions, communicative goals, and types of speech actions that are used to achieve these goals. Thus, pragmatic analysis explores how people understand particular forms of speech acts and their implications, and how assumptions and presuppositions that affect the speaker's intended meaning are understood. Speech act theory relies on the regularity of language use by members of social and cultural groups who are expected to behave politely and appropriately. However, when using a second language, nonnative speakers may not always be familiar with the parameters of social contexts and cultural norms to achieve their interactional and/or intended meanings. In addition, their nonlinguistic knowledge of the world, as well as pragmatic presuppositions in interaction and speech acts, may be distinct from that of native speakers.

While the earlier chapters focused on the role of culture in second language learning and the place of culture in second language writing, the next five chapters more narrowly address issues associated with applied linguistics research to examine the implications of culture in teaching materials and methods. In keeping with the framework for the analysis of interactional practices and speech acts, the chapters in Part III employ applied linguistics findings to heighten the interactional and pragmatic competence of second language learners. Building on the notion of communicative competence (Hymes) and speech act theory (Austin and Searle), the authors approach the development of teaching materials from a variety of perspectives, all of which serve to raise teacher and learner awareness of the influences of culture on second language teaching and learning. The five chapters in Part III take the position that the teaching of the second or foreign language cannot be separated from teaching the culture of its speakers. However, because culture and its many facets are often difficult to define and describe, little applied linguistics research has been carried out to deal with the manifestations of culture in language use. As an outcome, few ESL and EFL texts and pedagogical approaches address second or target culture, and the task of developing the necessary teaching materials is often left to the classroom instructors. The chapters in Part III examine what is known about the influence of culture and pragmatics on second and foreign language pedagogy, and the implicit cultural influences on second and target language teaching.

In Chapter 7, Joan Kelly Hall presents an overview of parameters implicit in second and foreign language interactions. Her pedagogical method focuses on developing learners' pragmatic and interactional competence as an aspect of linguistic competence, first introduced by Dell Hymes in 1962. She points out that interactional competence extends beyond linguistic competence and requires learners' context-specific knowledge of interactive practices in a second culture. Learning to interact in a second language necessitates a systematic study of interactive practices on the part of the learners, as well as teachers' guidance and facilitation. To become competent interactants in a second culture, learners need to be taught to become astute observers of behaviors, pragmatically appropriate language use, and interactional moves employed in another culture. Learning to "notice" interactional practices can allow learners to make informed choices of behaviors and linguistic structures when communicating with members of a second culture. However, Hall notes that learners can rarely accomplish these learning goals without formal instruction. While in second language classrooms emphasis is often placed on teaching grammar and lexis, ubiquitous and prosaic aspects of interaction require consciousness-raising on the part of both teachers and learners. She concludes with a discussion of the specific parameters of interaction for which materials can be developed and used in second and foreign language instruction and provides guidelines for preparing instructional tasks designed to develop the learner's interactional and pragmatic competence.

In Chapter 8, Elliot L. Judd continues with some issues that more narrowly focus on the considerable complications in the teaching of second language pragmatics. Like Hall, he stresses that although few available pedagogical approaches have been developed for teaching second and foreign language pragmalinguistic norms, such instruction seems to be essential in many cases. He begins with a description of incidents in which linguistic proficiency was not sufficient to assure successful communication. Using the work of Austin and Searle devoted to speech act theory, Judd proposes a framework for the teaching of speech acts to overcome the considerable pitfalls and possible negative consequences that can result if nonnative speakers employ inappropriate pragmalinguistic forms. Although some techniques for teaching second language pragmatics have been developed, few have found their way into the available teaching materials. Additional complications with the existing approaches are that they may not be appropriate for all learners and that it is not known whether they are effective. One of Judd's concerns also lies with the divergent needs of ESL and EFL students, who may see their priorities differently. He cautions that teaching and learning of speech-act forms may be particularly constrained in EFL environments, where many teachers have a limited access to naturally occurring language events, and thus may be simply unable to teach L2 pragmalinguistic rules.

In Chapter 9, Kenneth Rose proposes an approach to teaching L2 pragmatics of speech acts in an EFL setting. He addresses the development of pragmatic competence and creates a framework for learner consciousness-raising, taking a cue from Hall and Judd. Rose emphasizes the applicability of linguistics research to second and foreign language pedagogy and makes a particular use of rudimentary ethnographic data gathering, carried out by students in their L1 with the goal of making them aware that, for example, requests can be linguistically and pragmatically complex. The employment of similar learning strategies in L2 seems more difficult to accomplish when teaching EFL, and Rose suggests employing excerpts from movies (or other authentic media) to bring learners' attention to the forms and sociolinguistic variables in which a similar speech act occurs in L2.

In Chapter 10, Ronald Scollon presents a research-based view of cultural values and constructs. Significant cultural differences in the expectations of conversation participants in Asian–English intercultural communication center on Errin Goffman's "focused interaction," first noted in 1963. The divergent social situational paradigms in Ronald Scollon's perspective are fundamental to all conversational activity, including initiations and dissolutions of interactions. He comments that the cultural identity of the participants represents a crucial aspect of ritual practices on which many human activities are based. As noted by Judd and Rose in Chapters 8 and 9, investigating and teaching cultural and pragmatic paradigms of face-to-face interactions may be difficult without direct contact with members of the community in which a particular language is spoken. Scollon analyzes conversation-opening rituals among Hong Kong Chinese, Koreans, and Japanese and white middle-class Americans, based on the data obtained from television shows. His study demonstrates that cultural codes (and their violations) can find various manifestations in the media and go unnoticed by the members of the community for which they are produced. Codes for entry, conversation initiations, and calls are rarely recognized as culturally determined rituals simply because they remain within the frameworks established for these activities. Nonetheless, the differences between them are readily noted by an observer who expects the ritual scripts to follow a different path – that is, someone whose membership is in a different culture. Scollon explains that by watching how characters in television shows proceed along the cultural scripts, it may be easy to understand why, for example, members of Asian and American cultures often see one another as rude and how interactions can go wrong. Television shows are frequently accessible to many language teachers and learners. In Scollon's view, they may provide valuable materials that can be used in teaching contrastive and comparative analyses of cultural codes and even a second culture.

In Chapter 11, Martin Cortazzi and Lixian Jin take a broad look at the overt and implicit representations of culture in EFL/ESL teaching media and methodologies. In their view, culture is portrayed not only in the instructional materials, but also in the dynamics of the teaching and learning processes that reflect the core values of teachers' and students' socialization into classroom interaction. Building on the notion of communicative competence originally defined by Hymes in the early 1960s, Cortazzi and Jin argue that merely integrating second language teaching and the culture of its speakers is insufficient for learners to develop intercultural competence and social effectiveness. Although research has long recognized a need for materials to facilitate the development of learners' intercultural competence, textbooks and methodologies reflect the source and target cultures in ways that lead to mismatches and create obstacles to learning. What constitutes good teaching and learning is often based on the socialization processes and the internalization of roles and expectations that teachers and students take for granted. These are closely intertwined with attitudes, values, and beliefs that underlie the teaching of culture. To be effective and to help students achieve intercultural competence, the teaching and the learning of culture need to become a dialogue between the source and the target culture. An ethnographic stance of both teachers and learners can only promote an awareness of their own and others' identities that can lead to creating better teaching materials and methods.

7 A prosaics of interaction

The development of interactional competence in another language

Joan Kelly Hall

Introduction

Interacting with others in another language involves more than knowing the appropriate syntax and lexicon. It is also, minimally, a matter of interactional competence. This competence involves such context-specific knowledge as (1) the goals of the interactive practice, the roles of the participants, and the topics and themes considered pertinent; (2) the optional linguistic action patterns along which the practice may unfold, their conventional meanings, and the expected participation structures; (3) the amount of flexibility one has in rearranging or changing the expected uses of the practice's linguistic resources when exercising these options and the likely consequences engendered by the various uses; and (4) the skill to mindfully and efficiently recognize situations where the patterns apply and to use them when participating in new experiences to help make sense of the unknown (Celce-Murcia, Dornyei, & Thurrell, 1995; Goody, 1995; Sanders, 1987, 1995).

Elsewhere (Hall, 1993b, 1995), I have argued that the development of such competence involves minimally two related activities: (1) guided practice in those interactive practices considered significant by and to the learners, and (2) the systematic study of L2 interactive practices, including their conventional resources and typical meanings, their varied uses by the participants of the practices and the consequences engendered by these uses. It is the second activity that is of interest here.

In what follows, I first define and explain the notion of "interactive practices." Next, I summarize research related to consciousness and language learning that provides a sound rationale for the kind of pedagogical approach to the study of language that I propose here. I then move to the primary focus of the chapter, the explication of a specific approach to developing L2 interactional competence, which I call a prosaics of interaction. I argue that engaging learners of another language in such an

A version of this chapter was presented at the 1995 TESOL Colloquium "Cultural Competencies in the ESL/EFL Classroom," Long Beach, California. Thanks are extended to Jim Jones, Denise Overfield, and Lucinda York for their careful readings of and comments on earlier drafts.

137

activity not only helps them to develop both L2 practice-specific and practice-general interactional knowledge and skills, but can also involve them in learning about L2 practices in ways that are less likely to lead to negative social or other consequences for them as they are learning, and that would not otherwise be possible outside of a classroom.

Interactive practices and their resources

It is through our everyday engagement in face-to-face interactions that we develop, articulate, and manage our memberships in our communities as well as our interpersonal relationships with one another (Gumperz, 1982, 1992; Hymes, 1972a; Vygotsky, 1978). Much of this talk consists of interactive practices, that is, goal-oriented, recurring moments of face-to-face interaction, through which we manage our family relationships, engage in a variety of community- and work-related tasks, and nurture our social networks. The linguistic and paralinguistic resources of these practices provide structuring frameworks for the creation, articulation, and management of our collective social histories (Hall, 1993a, 1993b; Wertsch, 1987, 1991). The resources are sets of prototypical elements particular to the enactment of an interactive practice, and include lexical and syntactic choices, participation structures, act sequences, and prosodic and other formulas to signal opening, transitional, and closing moves.[1] Such discourse markers as *okay* and *now* are examples of formulaic devices characteristic of teacher talk associated with particular sociocultural groups, for example, and are often used by classroom teachers to signal to students that what follows is likely to be the summation of the salient aspects of what had just occurred and/or the beginning of the occurrence of something new (Dorr-Bremme, 1990; Schriffrin, 1987). Similarly, the linguistic utterance "What can I get for you?" is a formulaic opening associated with a type of interactive practice, typically signaling the beginning of certain kinds of service encounters among certain sociocultural groups.

The conventionalized nature of these resources provides us with fairly predictable ways of using and interpreting their uses in a practice, and thus aids in the reduction of the cognitive complexity of participating in the interaction, in the acquisition of the resources needed to competently interact, in the perpetuation of the goals, values, and customs associated with the practices, and in the maintenance and/or modification of the status of our group membership(s); that is, when we interact with others, we use the resources as cues that signal who we are and what we are do-

---

1 These resources have also been referred to as "mediational means" (Wertsch, 1991) and "contextualization cues" (Gumperz, 1982).

ing at that interactional moment. This conventionality helps us to set up expectations about what is "going on" and to place us in a context in which our actions are mutually intelligible. To use the example given above, the utterance "What can I get for you?" has a typical pragmatic function, and is associated with a set of typical contexts and participant roles within those contexts. When those who are familiar with the utterance hear it, certain trajectories of interaction and contextual conditions are called to mind and are then used to make inferences about what the subsequent talk is most likely to be (i.e., the typical sequence of speech acts, possible sources of misunderstanding, and the likely consequences of the various moves). In short, the predictable uses of the resources provide us with the tools necessary for structuring and interacting with others in ways that are both socially and cognitively meaningful to us and to those around us (Ervin-Tripp, Strage, Lampert, & Bell, 1987; Snow, 1989; Wertsch, 1991).

There is one final point to make about interactive practices. All of our practices are sociocultural constructions, developed, maintained, and modified by the members of the groups to which we belong as we together engage in these practices. It is this common knowledge of our practices, their resources, their likely unfoldings, and the consequences of our varied participation that make interaction with our group members possible. Our shared sociocultural knowledge not only constrains to some degree how our practices are defined and structured, but also partially defines the frequency with which the practices are realized, and the criteria by which our and others' moves are judged as appropriate, relevant, and likely. How it is that we develop this knowledge and what happens when we participate in practices that are unfamiliar or in which we have little prior experience is discussed in the next section.

Learning to become interactionally competent and the role of consciousness

There are two general spheres of practices, primary and secondary, in which we become experienced participants (Gee, 1990). The first set of practices is acquired during childhood, and consists of those practices important to our families and those social groups of significance to us in our early years. As we are schooled, begin to work, and become involved in our communities during adolescence and into adulthood, we acquire secondary spheres of interactive practices, practices whose resources, goals, optional paths of talk, and likely outcomes can be quite different from those of our primary practices.

We begin developing our interactional competence in our primary practices from our earliest years. Studies of child language development (e.g., Butterworth, 1993; Gibbs, 1984; Miller & Hoogstra, 1992; Reeder & Wakefield, 1987; Shatz & McCloskey, 1984) have shown that we learn to participate in our practices by first perceiving what is most salient and then making connections between these cues and their contexts, that is, formulating figure-ground relationships, and then generalizing these patterns to similar contexts. We develop categories of linguistic action patterns that are organized around prototypical instances of their uses, including where it is they occur in the unfolding interaction and what usually precedes and succeeds them, their most prominent linguistic and extralinguistic cues, and the social meanings engendered by their uses.

Generally, as we gain more experience in the various practices important to the accomplishment of our daily lives, we become more interactively competent; that is to say, we build up habits of uses and responses to the uses of their linguistic resources within those practices, and develop social histories of participation with the other participants (Snow, Shonkoff, Leer, & Bruner, 1986).[2] The more competent we become, the more we (1) use our knowledge to better interpret and respond to the ensuing talk, (2) become creative in the ways we choose to participate, and (3) become adept at realizing our individual goals within the larger practice-related goals, and, in some cases, at changing the practice in light of our changing goals.

There is evidence in research on language and cognitive development (e.g., Perkins & Salomon, 1989; Tulviste, 1991; Wertsch, 1991; Vygotsky, 1978) that these pragmatic patterns of interaction are developed via two specific processes: through guided participation with more experienced participants, and through the conscious, systematic study of them in which learners mindfully abstract, reflect upon, and speculate upon the patterns of use. In a study by Snow, Perlman, Gleason, & Hooshyar (1990), for example, it was shown how important the role that caregivers play in guiding children's participation is to the successful development of the children's interactive competence. Not only do they provide a substantial amount of input, but, more important, it was found that they also provide verbal instructions that direct the children to notice important connections between forms and their contexts. Similarly, Rogoff and her colleagues (Rogoff, 1990; Rogoff & Lave, 1984) claim that engaging in social interaction with people who are more expert is an important "cul-

---

2 I do not mean to suggest here that the development of competence in a group's practices is always and only an individual concern, depending solely on the individual's ability to learn. It is more often the case that the competence to perform appropriately in the significant practices of a group is dependent on the degree of access to the knowledge, access that is in turn dependent on sociohistorical conditions that constrain in various ways the opportunities that an individual has to participate, and thus become proficient in participating in the significant practices of the group(s) to which she belongs. See Boster (1991) and Hall (1995) for a more extended treatment of this point.

tural amplifier" necessary to the development of children's cognitive processes. There has been ample research into schooling practices (e.g., Tharp & Gallimore, 1988; Lave & Wenger, 1991), much of it springing from Vygotsky's (1978) theory of development, in which it is demonstrated how such "assisted performance" facilitates the linguistic, cognitive, and social development of the novice participants. Reciprocal teaching (Palincsar & Brown, 1984) is an example of one such instructional activity in which students are actively guided in the use of cognitive strategies needed for successful reading comprehension (for a review of this procedure, see Rosenshine & Meister, 1994).

There is also research (e.g., Light & Butterworth, 1993; Stone & Forman, 1988) that suggests that the process of developing an awareness of these patterns via their systematic investigation, including activities such as reflecting on and theorizing about the patterns, facilitates both cognitive and linguistic growth. Of specific interest here is the research on second language acquisition. Recently, there has been renewed interest in the investigation of the relationship between consciousness and the learning of another language. The findings here are provocative and make clear that an input-rich environment alone is not a sufficient condition for learning.[3] Schmidt (1994), in a summary of this research, notes that the learning resulting from unattended processing is insignificant compared to the results of attended processing. He concludes that simple exposure to the language being learned will not suffice. What is also needed is explicit use of such top-down processes as focusing attention and expectations. Much research concerned with the role of consciousness in L2 development has addressed only the acquisition of linguistic forms. However, one study (Lyster, 1994), provides evidence that conscious attention enhances the learning of pragmatic knowledge as well. Schmidt (1993) and, more recently, Kasper and Schmidt (1996), propose that what is needed for such pragmatic development, which includes the learning of patterns of language organization such as that involved in interaction, is a pedagogy that focuses the learners' attention in ways that help them take notice of co-occurring features of context and the relevant linguistic resources. Bardovi-Harlig and Hartford (1993), in their study on the development of nonnative speakers' pragmatic competence in university advising sessions, also note the need for such a pedagogy. Based on their findings, they conclude that nonnative speakers need to be provided with models of and opportunities to learn and practice the specific linguistic realizations of those schooling practices that are essential to their development of the competence needed to be successful university students.

---

3 Readers are directed to *AILA Review* (1994, vol. 11) for a series of articles summarizing much of this research.

Given this need, the question then becomes: What are some reasonable pedagogical activities that would help to promote the development of the learners' consciousness of these patterns, and lead to the development of pragmatic and interactional competence? Recently, there has been interest in the field of second language development in designing and investigating the potential of collaborative learning tasks for such purposes, that is, for helping students to raise their awareness of linguistic forms (e.g., Donato, 1994; Kowal & Swain, 1994). The findings from these and other similar studies demonstrate that the successful learning of language forms does indeed result from such activities.

There is a greater reservoir of studies outside the mainstream of SLA whose findings are also relevant here. Their concern is with the development of pedagogical approaches whose aim is the cultivation of learners' awareness of key concepts, and their subsequent cognitive and linguistic development. Moll (1990), for example, presents a range of studies that, drawing on Vygotsky's (1978) theory of development, propose classroom practices whose primary focus is on the creation of specific conditions that foster the creation of communities of learners who are mindful of and actively engaged in their own learning. An approach that has been shown to be particularly successful is what Brown and Campione (1994) refer to as "guided discovery." The goal here is to provide opportunities for students to create shared bases of knowledge about different areas of interest. In doing so, the students participate in a variety of semistructured and recurring research activities about particular concerns or issues, which include noting repeated themes and patterns, making claims and providing warrants for them, resolving inconsistencies, and providing possible interpretations.

The classroom activity I propose here has its foundations in this and similar work. Specifically, I argue that guiding students to detect patterns used in interaction through the systematic study of interactive practices – that is, the development of a prosaics of interaction – will facilitate the development of interactional competence in the second language. Included as part of this competence are the skills needed to (1) "notice" a particular linguistic resource and its function, (2) reflect on its interactional meaning (i.e., its use by a particular interactant, its particular placement in a sequence of speech acts in an interaction, the consequences emerging from its varied use, etc.), (3) formulate and test hypotheses about its conventional uses, interpretations, and consequences of use, (4) develop knowledge that is both domains (i.e., practice-specific and domain-general), and (5) develop alternative uses of the resources that may lead to the realization of the learners' individual goals within the larger practice. In the next section, I first provide a brief overview of the Bakhtinian roots of this approach, and then describe in detail how the approach might be carried out in both second and foreign language classrooms.

Developing a prosaics of interaction

Much of Mikhail Bakhtin's (1981, 1986, 1990) work is a philosophical treatment of language and language use.[4] Among the many useful concepts he proposes three are directly related to the discussion here: dialogue, transgredience, and the prosaics of the novel. I briefly summarize each of these.

According to Bakhtin, our lives as we live them develop into sets of speech genres, that is, interactive practices, with discernible patterns of language whose uses are typically associated with sets of socioculturally important goals, and defined by constellations of values. The goals of the practices act as structuring webs to which unfolding talk orients. Our everyday involvement in the creation, maintenance, and modification of these practices is not rooted solely in individual motivations. Neither is it only and always the imperfect instantiation of some larger system. More appropriately, our involvement in our interactive practices is a movement between the two, a dialogue; that is, our individual participation is constrained by the degree of sociocultural authority embedded in the conventionality of the practices' linguistic resource. In some practices, we find that there is more room for our individual voices, whereas in others our participation is more constrained by social and other factors. For some sociocultural groups, for example, the talk that ensues among close social friends when engaged in a practice whose general goal is to have fun is likely to be far less constrained than the talk of many classroom practices. The interactants are likely more able to say what they want and in ways they choose, making it fairly difficult to predict the trajectories of utterances that may take place at any given moment. In the classroom, on the other hand, many of the practices are more conventionally structured. One common structure is the three-part act-sequence frame of a teacher-initiated question, a student response, and a subsequent teacher-produced evaluation of the response (I-R-E). What counts as an appropriate range of possible uses of the linguistic resources and sequences of moves by students in classroom practices is constrained by the degree of sociocultural authority attached to the frame, by the varying consequences of moving within or away from it, and by a variety of extralinguistic, socioculturally defined factors, such as the kind of class it is (e.g., the grade level and/or area of study), the topic being discussed, the ages of the students, and the role that the teacher plays in directing the talk.

For Bakhtin, the development of consciousness about our lives, our

---

4 This is not the appropriate place to review Bakhtin's philosophy of language. Readers are directed to the numerous works written by and about him, including those given in the References, and Holquist (1990) and Morson and Emerson (1990). Readers are also directed to Hall (1995) for a discussion of how his ideas can be related to SLA.

practices, our roles within them, and the consequences of our participation is necessary to the development of our ability to change the ways in which we live our lives. To develop this understanding, we need to step outside these practices, and engage in the analysis and reflection of our own and others' actions. He calls such a process transgredience, that is, the ability to see an interaction as a dialogic event between the resources and the utterances from a vantage point outside of that event and not as a member within it.

Bakhtin proposed the study of the novel, what he calls the prosaics of the novel, as a powerful tool in this process for enriching our understanding of ourselves and our surroundings, because he saw the novel as a chronicler of the everyday dialogues by which we live our lives. In proposing the study of interactive practices here, the prosaics of interaction, I am making the same case as Bakhtin, namely, that by standing outside of interactive practices that are of significance to the group(s) whose language is being learned, and analyzing the conventional ways that linguistic resources get used, the movement that occurs between their conventional meanings and their individual uses, and the consequences that are engendered by the various uses, we can develop a far greater understanding both of ourselves and of those in whose practices we aspire to become participants.

A model for classroom practice

In this section, I first define and explain the "texts" of interest, and outline a framework of interaction as a possible unit of study. I then discuss some implications for designing classroom activities that involve the students in the study of these texts. Parenthetically, much of what is proposed here is a synthesis of considerations and methodologies that are common to the fields of linguistic anthropology, discourse analysis, and, to a lesser degree, conversation analysis.

Texts

The "texts" pertinent to engaging in a prosaics of interaction are those that are of recurring interactions, that is, goal-directed talk among members of a group that takes place on a regular basis, in regular ways with the same participants, or different participants acting in the same or similar roles, and able to be captured on audiotapes and/or videotapes. These can include family practices such as mealtime talk or other recurring gatherings; classroom or other schooling practices that occur regularly, such as faculty meetings and advising sessions; and community practices, including those enacted as situated face-to-face gatherings, such as service encounters, and those that are broadcast via either television or radio and include talk shows and other regular features to which we have easy access.[5]

The study of such practices in a second or foreign language classroom is useful for a variety of reasons. First, because they are an essential part of the fabric of our everyday lives – that is, we define and live our daily lives through them – these practices are repositories of important sociocultural knowledge. The recurring themes and topics of these practices contain important information about the practices and their goals, the participants and their larger social communities, and the issues they consider important.[6] Thus, they function as "cultural maps" of the social environment, and, as such, can serve as exploration sites of significant sociocultural information for the cultural newcomer. Second, because the practices are important to those who engage in them, they must be considered of significance to the learners of the language as well, if the learners are indeed interested in coming to know about those who are native speakers of the second or foreign language on the native speakers' terms. Finally, the fairly predictable patterns of language use in the everyday practices of a community function as important linguistic and cognitive scaffolds for language learners. They provide learners with some cognitive security in that they help develop structures of expectations for the use and interpretation of a practice's linguistic resources. These expectations become the tools learners use to think about what they and the other interactants are doing in a practice. At the same time, they function as building blocks in the development of more complex and creative linguistic and interactional behaviors.

Less ritualized language use, like more locally situated, and/or less goal-directed talk, although equally important to the realization of people's everyday lives, may be too unwieldy, linguistically and cognitively, for any other than the most advanced second or foreign language learner to collect and analyze. Perhaps, as the learners gain experience in interactional analysis and develop their interactional competence, they will be

5 It will make a difference as to the practices chosen whether the language is being taught as a foreign or second language. When studying a foreign language in a first language setting, we will most likely be constrained to choose those practices most readily accessible, which are, for the most part, those practices that are broadcast interregionally or internationally. Those studying a language within a community that speaks that language have more opportunity to study the practices of everyday lives of the members of that community. It is worth noting here that not all face-to-face encounters are considered interactive practices, and therefore that not all videotapings and audiotapings can be used in the way I propose. A feature-length movie, for example, is not considered in and of itself to be an interactive practice, although it is possible for practices – structured, goal-directed recurring talk like family mealtimes – to constitute part of the film.
6 See Hall (1993a) for an example of the significant sociocultural information contained in the seemingly unimportant practice of gossiping.

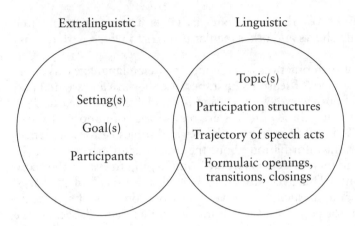

Extralinguistic   Linguistic

Setting(s)

Goal(s)

Participants

Topic(s)

Participation structures

Trajectory of speech acts

Formulaic openings,
transitions, closings

Figure 1   Frame of analysis: features of an interactive practice.

better able to deal with and make sense of talk that is less conventionalized.

A FRAMEWORK FOR ANALYSIS

The framework proposed here consists of a set of structuring elements
the realizations of which have been shown to define and foreground the
kind of practice it is (see Figure 1). It consists of two interrelated spheres,
the extralinguistic elements and the linguistic resources. In the first sphere
are three extralinguistic components: the setting(s), the participants, and
the expected goals. Each is described below.

The setting(s).   This includes both the physical space conditions and
temporal considerations, such as usual time(s) and duration of the practice, as well as larger geographical considerations. Classroom practices,
for example, generally occur in specific kinds of buildings, located in particular parts of a community, which in turn are located in specific geographic regions, and so on. In addition, they typically occur in rooms that
are likely to have, among other items, desks and chairs arranged in a particular pattern or patterns, and an array of audiovisual items. Finally,
these practices are likely to occur at the same time on a regular basis.

The participants.   This involves descriptions of the actors' social identities, which include such ascribed features as age, ethnicity, gender, and
geographic origin, as well as those social and professional identities and
relationships typical of the practice. To continue with the preceding example, in some classroom practices the participants typically include one
person who plays the part of a "teacher" and others who are "students,"

the number and social identities of whom can vary depending on other factors.

The expected goals or outcomes of the activity.   These are defined as the typical expectations that the participants have of the practice (e.g., "to maintain and/or solidify social bonds," "to make a purchase," "to learn about something," "to tell a story," "to participate in an advising session"). Practices can have one or several expected outcomes. The social actors of these practices use these expectations to help them know what the others are doing, decide the appropriateness of a particular move, and determine whether their participation has been successful.

These three considerations can generally be discerned through observations of the practices, interviews with the interactants whose practices they are, and, if available and accessible, readings about them.

The second sphere consists of four linguistic resources: the topic(s), the speech acts and their rhetorical connections to each other, the participation structures, and the formulas used to open, move through, and close the practice. Each is explained below.

The topic(s).   This resource is concerned with what gets talked about in the practice, that is, the recurring stories or themes with which the social actors concern themselves. In some family mealtime practices, for example, talk about the members' activities of that day, or plans for the next, might be those usually broached, while others, such as stories about displays of social impropriety by known community members, more likely might be considered verboten. In classrooms, the topics are likely to center on a particular area of study, and talk about these topics is likely to include certain kinds of information that is valued by those members as "germane" to the development of that topic.

The constitutive speech acts and their sequential development.   This resource includes the pragmatic meaning that each utterance plays (e.g., as a request, an invitation, a solicitation), which is a function of, minimally, (1) what is considered to be a conventional linguistic display of a particular act, (2) its placement in the sequence of utterances, and (3) the intent of the interactants. It also includes the typical patterned arrangement of utterances. A common arrangement of acts of many classroom practices is the I-R-E: the initiation of a question by the teacher (T: Who wrote the story?), followed by a student response (S: Wasn't it Maya Angelou?), which in turn is followed up by the teacher with some kind of an evaluative act (T: Yes, that's right *or* Are you sure?). The more conventionalized the practice, the less flexible the arrangement is likely to be. Catholic masses, for example, are quite rigidly structured, while other religious services may be less so, allowing for more optional pathways of talk.

The participation structures.   Of concern here are the turn-taking patterns among the participants, including how speakers' turns are determined, and the number of speakers who can speak at a time. Turn-taking procedures can range from self-selection (e.g., whoever wants to talk, does) to other-selection. Other-selection can be decided on the basis of first come, first served, or some other criterion. Getting one's turn can involve speaking loudly until the floor is relinquished to the loudest, or the use of a particular utterance such as "excuse me," which signals to the other(s) that a turn is being requested. In addition, the number of speakers can range from one to several at a time. "Teacher-selected one-speaker-at-a-time" is a participation structure common to many mainstream American classroom practices.

The formulaic openings, transitions, and closings.   This element consists of the formulaic utterances that are used to open, move through, and close a practice. An opening formula helps set up the expectations of the other participants by signaling to them what practice is to come. In certain classroom practices, for example, the linguistic token "OK, let's see" quite often is used by the teacher to signal movement from one activity to the next. Similarly, the utterance "Once upon a time" is a conventional opening to a particular kind of storytelling practice for certain sociocultural groups whose use sets up certain expectations about the talk that follows. Finally, "Y'all come back" is a typical way to close certain kinds of service encounters among some sociocultural groups.

In sum, these features highlight the socioculturally patterned webs of linguistic behaviors with which interactive practices are structured. Their use as a frame in the analysis of these practices by SL/FL learners will help them to make sense of, and subsequently develop, some of the interactional competence needed to participate in the interactive practices of those whose language is being learned. It will also aid in the comparative analysis across practices in the target language or between L1 and L2 practices. As a final note, this is not meant to be an exhaustive list of all possible elements relevant to the description and analysis of interactive practices. Rather, it is meant as a heuristic to help novices in their descriptions and analyses. Clearly, other resources such as grammatical structures, prosodic cues, and even interactional rhythm can be, and have been shown to be, recurring features of practices, and thus can be added to the frame as they are deemed relevant by the learner-researchers.

Pedagogical considerations for the study of practices

There are several points to keep in mind when designing curricular activities involving the study of practices. The first concerns the practice itself. In choosing one as an object of study, one must be concerned with student interests and needs as well as the accessibility of the practice and the feasibility of collecting data. A focus on family practices, for example, requires that these be easily accessible to the learners, and that the family or families in question be open to having their practices become part of a classroom project. This might be possible for learners living with families in the target culture. In other cases, it might be feasible for SL learners to collect data from target culture classrooms. This would be an appropriate choice for those learners who aspire to be participants of such classrooms, such as, for example, students of intensive language programs who plan on attending a regular university in the United States. For FL learners living outside of the target culture, practices that are regularly broadcast and thus most accessible (e.g., televised talk and entertainment shows, or serial dramas) may be those practices most easily collected and studied. It is recommended that the less L2 interactionally competent the learners are, the more ritualized the practice to be studied should be.

Also to be considered are the methods of data collection. Although videotaping would best capture the relevant goings-on in the practice, audiotaping is also possible. Because the examination of recurring patterns of talk is the concern of the activity, repeated tapings over a period of time are necessary. Interviews with the participants of the practice are also a crucial source of data. Having the learners ask the participants to articulate what it is they are "doing" with their talk (e.g., the pragmatic intent of their utterances, and the functions the practice plays in their lives) will provide them with essential sociocultural information and thus help to focus the learners' attention on the relevant aspects of the interaction. Where it is not possible to have access to the actual interactants, people from the culture whose practice is being studied, and who speak the target language, can be asked to help. Their intuitions about and knowledge of the practice can help guide the learners' analyses. As a final assessment of learners' development of interactional competence, teachers should consider asking their students to construct some kind of summary report on their findings and/or perhaps a constructed and taped simulation of the practice.

Some final pedagogical considerations of relevance to this approach should be noted. First, engagement in the study of a prosaics of interaction is itself its own practice. It is a "guided inquiry," a particular academic activity with which L2 students may not be familiar. It would be useful, then, for the teacher to provide a variety of linguistic resources to guide the learners' participation in the various activities. Helping them to construct a set of possible interview questions, for example, by providing them with the words, phrases, and other linguistic cues in the target language that they will most likely need would be beneficial. In addition, allowing students the freedom to move between their first and second languages, especially in the early stages of their participation in the various activities, would provide them with the cognitive security they will often need, because engagement in these academic pursuits can be quite cognitively demanding.

Second, it is not at all the case that the language teacher needs to be an expert conversation or discourse analyst, or ethnographer. It is required, however, that she be interested in and knowledgeable of what constitutes active learning – for example, that she be willing to help guide the students to the appropriate resources, and to help them ask relevant questions of the data, and adequately justify the claims they make about the data they collect. It is important to remember that the primary pedagogical focus of a prosaics of interaction is not on the production of some report that "correctly" describes a practice. It is instead on the development of L2 interactional competence, the facilitation of which includes providing the students with opportunities to "take notice of" significant interactional features and their situated meanings, to search for and develop patterns of talk, to learn to make predictions about possible future moves, and to become aware of the various linguistic and social consequences of these optional moves within particular practices that are significant to the groups whose language is being learned. Such an approach in no way suggests that learners are expected to assume the roles of native-speaking interactants in the interactive practices under study. Quite the contrary: In learning about the various ways of meaning making within L2 groups, the students develop a critical awareness of language use, and thus, to a certain degree, are empowered to make choices about whether to participate in practices and, when doing so, how to use the resources in ways that will enhance the realization of their own individual goals. The classroom provides a safe environment for such learning in that it allows the students to explore the various uses and consequences of talk in the L2 in ways that are likely to have fewer negative social and other consequences for the learners.

A final consideration has to do with the sociocultural and practice-specific nature of talk that is assumed in the kind of study proposed here, and the kinds of decisions that need to be made about which practices to study. The thought exists in some circles that, because it is difficult to know the kinds of L2 interactive situations that learners will find themselves in, what language teachers do, indeed what they can only do, is to provide their students with generic language skills that can be used in any situation, and with any group who speaks the language being learned. What we know, however, is that the skills needed to competently participate in face-to-face interactive practices are both practice-generic and practice-specific; that is, how we learn to become a competent participant in a practice very much depends on the opportunities we have to participate in and develop a familiarity with the practice. Our own experiences in the practices of our everyday lives make this clear. We feel more confident, and thus perform more competently, in those practices with which we have experience. Research on first and second language (e.g., Berman & Slobin, 1994; Snow, Cancino, de Temple, & Schley, 1991; Snow et al., 1986; Wu, De Temple, Herman, & Snow, 1994) corroborates our intuitions by providing data that shows rather compellingly the sociocultural and practice-specific nature of the acquisition processes of both first and additional languages, and the significant role that the conventionalized language of practices plays. This being the case, the concern for both language teachers and language learners becomes having to make a choice about which culture groups to deal with, and, more specifically, which practices within those groups to study. In making such choices, we are engaging in the same activity and must confront issues similar to those who teach literature, namely, Whose texts from which cultures do we choose to bring into our classrooms? The concern is a valid one, and one with which language pedagogues must deal in creating instructional space for a prosaics of interaction.

Conclusions

I have argued that learning to interact with others in another language involves the development of pragmatic competence, principally, interactional competence, and that this development is aided in part by the systematic study of L2 interactive practices by the learners themselves. Specifically, such study helps the learners "notice," and subsequently facilitates the learning of the various practice-specific, pragmatic uses of language, the likely optional sequences of moves in the practice, and their typical interpretations and consequences. This mindfulness of language use in turn provides opportunities for the learners to reflect on and make informed choices about their own individual participation as users of the L2.

One final point: Engaging in a prosaics of interaction cannot be considered an activity that is peripheral to, and thus less important than, the traditional grammar and vocabulary lessons of language classrooms. If we expect learners to develop interactional competence in another language, consciousness-raising approaches such as the one presented here, and other similar ones, must become essential practices of SL/FL classroom experiences.

8 Some issues in the teaching of pragmatic competence

Elliot L. Judd

Introduction

It is considered almost axiomatic that those who are acquiring a second language need to gain mastery over the sociolinguistic and pragmatic rules of the target language (Paulston, 1975; Canale & Swain, 1980). Linguistic accuracy in a second language is one important feature to be learned, but a person needs to achieve functional abilities in the second language as well. It is necessary to learn how to understand and create language that is appropriate to the situations in which one is functioning, employing the proper illocutionary patterns in accordance with the sociocultural parameters of the specific situation, because failure to do so may cause users to miss key points that are being communicated in either the written or the oral language and/or have their messages be misunderstood. Worse yet is the possibility of a total communication breakdown and the stereotypical labeling of the second language users as people who are insensitive, rude, or inept (Thomas, 1983, 1984; Bardovi-Harlig, Hartford, Mahan-Taylor, Moorage, Reynolds, 1991).

In this chapter, I discuss current approaches used for the teaching of sociolinguistic and pragmatic skills and offer some practical suggestions on how teachers can create activities to develop those skills in second language learners. In particular, I focus on the problems involved in developing such skills in both English as a second language (ESL) environments and in English as a foreign language (EFL) situations, where native English speaker models may be difficult to find and where the English spoken by native English speakers may not be the only norm to follow. The goal is not to present a new approach to teaching pragmatic forms, but to provide concrete teaching ideas to those who are unsure of how to incorporate these forms into their regular instructional programs. Some of the issues to be explored are whether or not it is possible to teach pragmatic and sociolinguistic rules to second language learners, whether there is a difference between the needs of students in ESL and EFL environments, and whether it is necessary for EFL learners to master these rules.

Defining the issue

To illustrate how communication can be impeded when pragmatic and sociolinguistic rules are not shared by an interaction between participants, I will relate a series of incidents in which I was involved. In 1988, I was fortunate to be awarded a Fulbright lectureship to do teacher training and staff development at two Venezuelan universities. At one, I taught a course in curriculum development and materials design that was open to both the local faculty and other EFL teachers in Caracas.

After several of the lectures in the course, a coordinator of English courses at a military academy came to me and said in clear, understandable English: "I really like what you are saying in the class. You will come to my school to give the information to my teachers." Mindful of my duties as a Fulbright lecturer, but unsure of the exact parameters, I checked with the Fulbright adviser on how I should arrange this visit. Her response was that I should go when I wanted to and if I wanted to. A little puzzled, I asked her whether I was obligated to go, and she said no, that the decision was up to me. It seemed that I had misunderstood the "will" in the teacher's comment. I was being asked to give a lecture, not being ordered to. There was no obligation implied. As Thomas (1983, 1984) defines a similar situation, pragmalinguistic failure occurred when words were transferred from one language to another, but communicative functions of the speech act were distinct in the two languages.

As the class continued, I received several other invitations, some of which sounded quite interesting and exciting. Some of these invitations were even given two or three times. I responded favorably to the invitations, encouraging people to call me to set up a specific time for the visit. Yet, no calls came and I never got to make the visits. At first, I doubted the sincerity of those who had offered the invitations. Then I began to realize that I had not been invited at all; I was being complimented on my course. This is another type of speech act breakdown, one that Thomas (1983, 1984) has labeled as "sociopragmatic failure," where a compliment was misinterpreted as an invitation.

The final incident occurred at the annual Venezuela TESOL conference. I was introduced to an American teacher who had been living and teaching in the country for a number of years. Over coffee, she suggested that I come to speak at her university and give a number of lectures to the staff. Having learned my lessons, I thanked her for the offer and assumed that I had received another compliment. Three weeks later, it turned out that the invitation was genuine. Embarrassed, I mumbled some sort of apology and told her that the reason I had not replied was that I thought she was just being nice, but was not seriously inviting me. She laughed and commented, "Elliot, I was speaking to you in American English, not Venezuelan English."

It is easy to find other examples of pragmatic misinterpretations. One of my graduate students, a fluent, nonnative speaker of English from Russia, commented to me that "Americans are so insincere; they are always giving compliments, but don't mean it," echoing findings found by Wolfson and Manes in their studies (Wolfson, 1983, 1989; Manes & Wolfson, 1981). A university colleague claims that some of his international students behave inappropriately when they come to his office to haggle over grades. It may be that he does not realize that they are asking for clarification rather than challenging his authority. It would be easy to furnish additional examples – perhaps humorous, perhaps unpleasant – of other such failures in sociolinguistic/pragmatic skills. Likewise, many of us can recall our own frustrations in second language use when our lack of pragmatic ability caused conversations to go awry.

It seems fairly clear that knowledge of speech acts and their function is a basic component of communicating in a second language. Unlike those who feel that second languages can be learned naturally without formal training in the second language classroom, I believe that instruction in pragmatic skills and speech acts needs to be carried out formally, as part of the regular content in second language curricula. The issue is how these features of language should be taught and how to integrate them into the teaching of discoursal, syntactic, and lexical features of a second language, both oral and written. Further, we must devise practical strategies for instruction based on an understanding of what conditions facilitate or hinder the learning of these essential features of language.

Teaching speech acts

Several writers have discussed techniques for developing pragmatic/sociolinguistic awareness in second language learners. For the sake of simplification, these activities can be largely divided into three broad categories: (1) cognitive awareness, (2) receptive skill development, and (3) productive use. Each is presented and then analyzed in terms of its benefits and shortcomings for both ESL and EFL language learners.

Cognitive awareness

Cognitive awareness activities are designed to make learners consciously aware of differences between the native and target language speech acts. The rationale for this approach is that such differences are often ignored by learners and go unnoticed unless they are directly addressed (Schmidt, 1993). The emphasis is usually placed on both the linguistic manifestations of the speech acts (i.e., the grammar) and the sociolinguistic features (i.e., the situations, the participants, the status of those involved, etc.).

Two major techniques are commonly employed: presentation and discussion of research findings on speech acts, and a student-discovery procedure based on students' obtaining information through observations, questionnaires, and/or interviews.

Using presentation/discussion techniques, information from research on speech acts is presented to students so that they can study how speech acts manifest themselves in the second language (Bardovi-Harlig et al., 1991; Bardovi-Harlig, 1992). Generally, the works on speech acts are distilled, and the information is presented to students in manageable, understandable forms (Olshtain & Cohen, 1991). When employed by teachers, it is best done in a way that provides detailed information on the participants, their status, the situations, and the speech events that are occurring, because merely presenting linguistic formulas without such background information can lead to overgeneralizations on how speech acts function in real-life situations. For example, simply to state that one way of apologizing is by saying "I'm sorry" or "Excuse me" does not capture the intricacy of when to apologize, to whom, and to what extent (Borkin & Reinhart, 1978; Olshtain & Cohen, 1991). Research has identified the complexity of these parameters and the cultural assumptions inherent in apologies (Wolfson & Judd, 1983; Wolfson, 1989).

While the information provided to students in cognitive, consciousness-raising activities can indeed be of value and may help them develop some awareness of pragmatic features in another language, several shortcomings need to be pointed out. As many researchers have noted, few studies are available to confirm the pedagogical usefulness of these kinds of activities, in part because of the limitations of the available research methodologies (Kasper & Dahl, 1991; Rose, 1994a and b; and Aston, 1995), as well as their generalizability across varieties of English and interactional situations (Holmes & Brown, 1987); that is, can we be sure that the information is accurate enough for students to use in real-life interactions?

A second issue deals with very practical and real constraints. Does the typical classroom instructor have the access to these studies and the time needed to become familiar with their findings so that the instructor can be up to date? Generally, the answer is no, especially in EFL situations, where resources are scarce and costly. Finally, there is the question of whether familiarity with current research findings is actually implemented in second language use. Certainly, instructors have all encountered students who can recite grammatical rules but are unable to contextualize that knowledge into daily language performance. The same phenomenon can occur in studying speech acts. Even if the students have been exposed to research findings, there is no guarantee that they will be able to incorporate such knowledge into their own speech acts, especially in uncontrolled, naturally occurring language situations.

Another cognitive technique, suggested by Bardovi-Harlig (1992) and Bardovi-Harlig et al. (1991), is to have learners act as amateur ethnographers and collect their own examples of speech acts. This helps to overcome the lack of published, available research findings in certain areas or the lack of accurate depictions of speech acts in available student texts. It can also provide realistic information on how speech acts function in the particular environment where the students find themselves. Students can either be sent out to observe and record naturally occurring speech acts in actual speech situations or they can devise and administer questionnaires or conduct interviews to solicit more focused data.

While both of these approaches expose students to natural language (natural input, unrehearsed speech, and meaningful negotiations of language), each suffers from pedagogical weaknesses. Observations of naturally occurring situations can be quite time-consuming and, considering the time limitations in most structured second language programs of study, may take away the time necessary for students to learn other crucial elements of language. These approaches also assume that the learners possess the linguistic skills to process natural language in natural language environments and have sufficient ethnographic skills to recognize speech acts when they occur. The problem with the alternative, more focused means of elicitation is that native speakers often do not report accurately what they really do in natural language situations because they may not want to reveal that information to strangers (especially, to nonnative speakers of the language). In addition, native speakers may want to help the solicitors of information to obtain easy answers, at the expense of the truth.

Research has indicated that what people say they do with language and what they actually do are not always the same, because language use often is beyond the level of conscious analysis (see Wolfson, 1989; Kasper & Dahl, 1991; and Aston, 1995 on research methods). Further, a certain amount of linguistic skill is necessary to both design and administer interviews and questionnaires, and second language students may not yet have reached this level of proficiency. Still another challenge is that both natural and structured methods require a representative English-speaking population, something that may be lacking, especially in an EFL environment. Finally, as has been noted, it is not known whether the cognitive knowledge can be transferred to actual speech understanding and production.

Receptive skill development

In this category of pragmatic skill development are techniques that seek to have students recognize and understand one or more speech acts. These activities go beyond cognitive awareness techniques to show students formally the functions of speech acts and to provide them practice in understanding these features of language as they naturally occur. Again, two types of materials are common: teacher-generated material and natural data. In the former, a textbook or the instructor first presents a discourse excerpt. Then the speech act is pointed out to the students (a deductive approach) or students are asked to identify the speech act that is occurring (an inductive approach) (Holmes & Brown, 1987). Attention is drawn to both the linguistic forms that are employed and the sociolinguistic variables of the speech event (i.e., the physical environment; age, gender, and status of the participants; and the levels of formality). Once this is done, similar examples of the speech act are presented until students are able to recognize the structural and sociolinguistic dimensions of the speech act(s) being studied.

Several shortcomings can diminish the usefulness of such activities in the classroom. First, many texts do not include examples of speech acts that are representative of naturally occurring discourse, or the examples are often inaccurate or limited in regard to the sociolinguistic variables. As an outcome, students either lack exposure to speech acts or are provided with inaccurate information about them. To counter this, teachers are advised to check published materials to establish their pragmatic validity (Bardovi-Harlig, 1992). Alternatively, instructors can try to create their own materials to compensate for the deficiencies in published media. However, this solution has to be implemented with care. Materials created by teachers – native and nonnative speakers alike – to re-create natural language often suffer from the same shortcomings as published texts and may not be representative of real, authentic language use. The lack of authenticity in teacher-generated materials often stems from the teachers' not being aware of how language is used in various sociolinguistic settings: Speakers generally use language on an unconscious level and do not specifically focus features of speech acts and/or discourse. When we try to re-create on paper what language users do, we often superimpose our assumptions and cannot always separate them from real language use. If the instructional purpose of supplementation is to expose students to a more natural language than published media provide, teachers who create their own materials should exercise caution and seek a second opinion on its accuracy and naturalness.

Second, teacher-generated or commercially available material frequently lack accurate and situationally specific sociolinguistic information, essential in real-life interactions. As an outcome, second language learners may overgeneralize and apply inappropriate forms of speech acts. Without information on the specifics of the metalinguistic situation, the participants involved, their status, and other sociolinguistic variables, students may not truly grasp the variability entailed in most speech acts. For example, information on apologies (see Cohen & Olshtain, 1981; Olshtain,

1983; Cohen, Olshtain, & Rosenstein, 1986; Olshtain & Cohen, 1991; and Bergman & Kasper, 1993) must include the crucial details of who is apologizing to whom, for what offense, the degree of the offense, and even the nature of the relationship between the situation participants. When such information is lacking, students may fail to apologize when they should or apologize when they should not. To provide language learners only one apology formula to apply on the many occasions when apologies are necessary in English is a misrepresentation of the complexity of this speech act. Such an approach can mislead students when they encounter real English language use in natural discourse. To remedy this shortcoming, it may be prudent to expose students to contrasting samples of natural discourse in which different pragmatic and sociolinguistic variables are involved. For example, students can be given one utterance in which a person apologizes and one in which no apology is given, one in which a full apology formula is employed and one in which only a partial apology is given. With the teacher's guidance, students can discuss why the differences occurred. By being exposed to these multiple contrasting language examples, students can become attuned to the various factors that affect pragmatic usage.

Because of the pitfalls involved in either using published textbooks or designing materials, a teacher can obtain more natural and reliable data by employing audiocassettes and videocassettes or television (with a satellite hookup in EFL situations), with or without closed captioning. Sections from such media can be recorded and analyzed for their speech-act content (Lovejoy, 1981; Holmes & Brown, 1987). In addition, various snippets can be compared to see whether or not certain forms emerge and why the similarities or differences occur. These uses of media provide natural language samples because they were not originally designed for teaching purposes but for genuine communication. Because videotape is becoming more accessible in most classrooms, it offers great possibilities, especially where there may not be a lot of native speakers of English available. However, collecting appropriate speech act examples from media can be beyond the time resources available to many instructors. Additionally, it requires pragmatic knowledge and awareness that teachers, especially nonnative speakers with little training, may lack.

Productive use

While the two previous categories of activities provide learners with an exposure to pragmatic usage, neither ensures that second language users will actually incorporate the patterns into their own speech production. Therefore, many methodologists advocate teaching strategies that encourage students to use specific speech acts. While this approach makes intuitive sense, it is not without its problems. For the sake of examination, let us consider two common techniques: cloze-type exercises and simulation/role plays.

Cloze-type activities are conversations with the speech acts deleted (Bardovi-Harlig et al., 1991). Students are instructed to fill in the blanks, either orally or in writing, with the correct pragmatic forms. This is done only after students have been exposed to the receptive and/or cognitive techniques discussed earlier. While cloze-type exercises are helpful to some extent, they are certainly not natural (Aston, 1995). In real conversation, people do not encounter partial discourse and then "fill in the blanks." Furthermore, there is no guarantee that students will be able to successfully transfer their speech act knowledge to situations where no language is provided. Will they be able not only to create the proper pragmatic form, but also to produce the language that surrounds these forms? More important, a user must determine if it is culturally appropriate to employ the speech act at all. Pragmatic knowledge is more than just utilizing a series of formulaic utterances; it entails a vast knowledge of culturally appropriate behavior functioning in a variety of novel situations.

Another type of activity recommended for speech-act mastery is simulation/role play (Paulston, 1975; Holmes & Brown, 1987; Bardovi-Harlig et al., 1991; Olshtain & Cohen, 1991). Here students are asked to assume certain roles that would produce pragmatic features. Generally, such role plays/simulations are guided in the sense that background information on the situation and the participants is provided. For example, to practice clarifying information, arguing, and apologizing, students are given the following:

Student A: You have ordered food in a restaurant and the server brought you
a different dish.
Student B: You know that you brought the correct meal and that the customer
has forgotten what was originally ordered.

The advantage of this activity is that students are not provided with any specific language. One disadvantage is that often students who are engaged in role plays create language that is unnatural, that is, language that sounds like a role play, not human language (Aston, 1995). Another disadvantage is that it is very hard to create situations that are realistic and meaningful for both parties in the role play. For example, if students are asked to participate in a role play in which a student is apologizing to a teacher, the role of the student is relevant, but the role of the teacher is not, because students are not teachers. The same can be said of typical role plays in which students are asked to assume the roles of a ticket agent, store owner, and so on. How many students will have these occupations?

An additional problem with both of these productive activities is one that we have encountered before: Do teachers themselves have the pragmatic knowledge to create valid activities and to provide meaningful feedback to the students? This may especially be a problem in EFL situations where teachers may not have pragmatic knowledge of natural situations, and is even true in ESL situations where the teacher has not received formal training and may possess incorrect assumptions about the forms that natural language takes. One of my nonnative graduate students, in fact, voiced this exact concern to me when she said, "How should I teach the pragmatic rules? I'm still unsure of these myself."

Is native-speaker pragmatic knowledge necessary?

Any discussion on native-speaker pragmatic knowledge poses many complications. First, there is the issue of variation within English. We know that certain pragmatic rules differ among varieties of English (American Northern or American Southern, Jewish-American or African-American, British or American, etc.). Further, newer varieties of English are appearing worldwide (see Kachru, 1982; Lowenberg, 1986; Wolfson, 1989). Because each of these forms of English has differing norms and pragmatic forms, it is virtually impossible for any native, let alone a nonnative, speaker of one variety to be familiar with all the rules of all the others. Thus, mastery of all varieties is a pedagogical impossibility and often just one is selected in ESL/EFL classes as the target model. Even after one model is chosen, one basic question remains: Should ESL or EFL students be expected to master native pragmatic norms?

The answer to this question revolves around two key variables: (1) Who are the students in the class? and (2) Who are the classroom teachers? In terms of the students, we need to assess what their needs for English are, both current and future. If our students are now in an ESL environment, they will certainly need to be exposed to and gain mastery of the pragmatic knowledge of the English that they will encounter on a daily basis. Failure to do so can only expose these students to frustration, and perhaps ridicule, when dealing with native speakers. Yet, we cannot, and should not, require ESL students to adopt native speech acts any more that we should require our students to assimilate culturally. After exposure in class, some students may elect not to use native forms as a matter of individual choice, perhaps signaling a desire to maintain their own identity or their unwillingness to join the ESL cultural environment. On the other hand, others may need and want to adapt to native-speaker norms. Thus, it is incumbent on those of us teaching in an ESL situation to present pragmatic information to our students so that they have the tools to use such knowledge, should they desire. If we do not, we have failed in our responsibilities as teachers, and this type of philosophy will hurt our students and damage our credibility as teachers (Holmes & Brown, 1987).

In an EFL situation, the students' needs are different and the answer differs accordingly. Here, pragmatic accuracy may be less important, and in some cases may even be unnecessary. Some students are only interested in acquiring English to obtain information written in English (i.e., to read articles written in English in their areas of specialization). They do not interact on a regular basis with native speakers of English, and pragmatic knowledge may not be especially useful. In other EFL situations, where students are interacting with other nonnative speakers in English, there is less likelihood of their encountering sanctions for violating native-speaker norms because local sociolinguistic and pragmatic rules of the native language override the use of English in this environment (Olshtain, 1983; Beebe, Takahashi, & Uliss-Weltz, 1990; Bergman & Kasper, 1993; Eisenstein & Bodman, 1993; Olshtain & Weinbach, 1993; Takahashi & Beebe, 1993; Weitzman, 1993). Therefore, there is no urgency for productive pragmatic ability in English (Bentahila & Davies, 1989). For EFL students who are planning to go to an ESL environment in the future, such as those who are applying to universities or planning to immigrate, there is a need to acquire pragmatic knowledge of English, but it is not an immediate, pressing one. They need to obtain fundamental knowledge of basic English skills, and once they obtain such knowledge, they can begin to acquire cognitive and receptive knowledge of pragmatics. When they arrive in the ESL situation, they can either enroll in classes where they will fine-tune their pragmatic skills or learn through experience to apply their receptive knowledge. Finally, there are cases of those who live in an EFL environment, but who need to communicate with native speakers of English on a regular basis, either in face-to-face interactions or by phone, E-mail, or other media. This group, a minority among EFL learners, needs to acquire both receptive and productive use of pragmatics. However, they still may be granted some tolerance when errors are committed, since they are functioning as recognizable nonnative speakers engaged in cross-cultural communication activities.

The teacher's ability is the other factor in determining whether or not to teach the pragmatic features of a second or foreign language. Simply stated, you cannot teach what you do not know. If teachers are unfamiliar with the pragmatic rules of English, they cannot teach them to their students. Yet, for teachers who lack this knowledge, and who are in situations where students need to acquire pragmatic ability, four possible alternatives are available. First, teachers can find second language teaching material that has the information. Second, if possible, a teacher can seek out other teachers who possess pragmatic knowledge and consult with them about speech-act features and/or have them work on materials for classroom use. Third, a teacher can read studies on pragmatic usage and, with care, adapt these findings for classroom activities. Finally, as mentioned earlier, media that show naturally occurring speech acts can be used in classrooms. These suggestions will not provide a complete remedy in situations where teachers are unfamiliar with pragmatic features, yet using them will partially solve the problem and provide students with some exposure.

Teaching pragmatic competence in the classroom

Even given all the problems previously discussed, it is imperative for some students to master this type of linguistic knowledge. Ironically, although while much research on pragmatics has appeared in the literature in the past few decades, little of it is addressed to classroom instructors who need to devise and implement practical teaching strategies for their classrooms beyond a general caveat to somehow include this information in a teaching curriculum (however, see Scarcella, 1990; Bardovi-Harlig et al., 1991; and Olshtain & Cohen, 1991 for exceptions to this statement). Therefore, what I am proposing is a model for teaching second language learners pragmatic competence. In employing this model, I advise instructors to be mindful of the pitfalls discussed earlier and to adapt this framework to the specific conditions (teacher, student, and material) in each classroom. The model is divided into five components: (1) teacher analysis of speech acts, (2) cognitive awareness skills, (3) receptive/integrative skills, (4) controlled productive skills, and (5) free, integrated practice.

Teacher analysis of the speech act

In order to teach a speech act, the classroom instructor must first determine exactly what is to be taught and under what circumstances. This means that the teacher must first identify the speech act and its specific manifestations. For example, if the lesson is to focus on compliments in English, the instructor must first identify what linguistic forms are used for compliments. This information can be obtained from some scholarly articles or in some published textbooks. Teachers can also engage in their own investigations (see Bardovi-Harlig, 1992).

Then the teacher must relate this material to the specific class in which the lesson will be taught. Basic questions should be asked:

1. In what situations, if any, will my students employ or encounter the pattern (at work, at home, at play, etc.)?
2. With whom will the pattern be used (native or nonnative speakers of English, friends, associates, acquaintances, teachers, bosses, etc.)?
3. What is the social status of each speaker (equal, superior, inferior)?
4. Are there other factors involved when the speech act will be used (age, gender, etc.)?
5. What topics will be discussed when the speech act is used (clothing, work habits, personal behavior, etc.)?

Because speech-act usage varies based on all of these factors, teachers need to focus on the specifics to see if the material is accurate and meets the students' needs. Without such questioning, what is taught to students may be of dubious value if it does not represent real language use.

One additional question should be asked, if possible: How does the speech pattern manifest itself in the students' native language (in both its linguistic forms and occasions for use)? As has been pointed out (Thomas, 1983, 1984; Kasper & Blum-Kulka, 1993), pragmatic usage differs across languages, and it is important to see if there are differences between the first and second languages. In ESL situations, this may be difficult to accomplish owing to the multiplicity of native languages among the students and/or the teacher's unfamiliarity with the students' native languages. However, in an EFL situation, where classes are more linguistically homogeneous and the teacher may be a native speaker or quite familiar with the students' first language, the information may be useful in understanding how the speech act may or may not cause difficulties for students. Further, it can help an instructor determine if it is important for students to learn the speech act at all, because they may only be talking to similar nonnative speakers.

Cognitive awareness skills

Now that the instructor has defined what needs to be taught, the information should be presented to the class. This stage involves presenting the materials to the students so that they develop an understanding of the pragmatic feature. The teacher should present naturally occurring examples of the speech act. These models should be representative of the situational, participant, status, and topical factors discussed earlier. The actual approach can be inductive (from data to rules) or deductive (rules to data); the explanation offered can be in English or in the students' native language. The important thing is that students understand the linguistic components of the pattern and how they function in English so that they can use this knowledge in meaningful ways in the activities that follow.

One activity that can be used is to have students obtain their own data on the speech act. Native speakers can be observed or questioned about their speech-act usage, if they are available. Alternatively, and more readily available in EFL situations, natural media (films, videotapes, radio broadcasts, or printed sources) can be presented for examples of the pragmatic feature being taught. The information obtained can be linked to the materials made in the teacher's presentation of the speech act.

Receptive/integrative skills

The third stage is to integrate the students' cognitive knowledge with actual language use. This begins by having the instructor ascertain if students can recognize the speech acts when they are presented within natural discourse, not in isolation. Learners should be asked both to identify the speech act within the discourse in terms of its linguistic features and to comment on the sociolinguistic environment that causes the speech act to occur. For example, the student may hear the following, as part of studying how to disagree:

Professor A: I think we should continue our study to see if additional factors can be identified.
Professor B: You may be right, but I think we'd better recheck the statistics first.

Students can be asked to identify who disagrees with whom, what features indicate that there is a disagreement, where the conversation is occurring, and what the participants' social relationship is.

Similarly, students can also be exposed to contrasting pieces of discourse and be asked to identify the factors that account for the differences in language behavior. By way of example, students can listen to another conversation and hear the following:

Susan: I really think the concert was awesome.
Barbara: Well, I don't. I think we got ripped off.

Here, students are asked to compare the two pieces of disagreement discourse not only in terms of linguistic differences, but also of the factors that may account for the differences in style, directness, and other features.

These types of exposure are necessary for two reasons. First, students often study speech patterns in isolation, but fail to recognize them when they occur within natural language because they are surrounded by other linguistic features. Natural discourse often masks speech features, and second language students are not adept at identifying features as they occur naturally. Second, students often believe – and this may be partially the fault of teachers and textbooks – that there is only one way for a speech act to appear and that this form works in all situations. Multiple exposures to many forms of the speech act are necessary to disabuse students of this assumption.

Controlled productive skills

To this point, students have been taught to recognize and understand pragmatic features in the language of others. It is now time to activate that knowledge and refine production of the speech acts by those students who will be in situations where active, productive use is necessary. To ensure success, instructors should provide some guided practice to aid students in this task. One activity is based on a cloze exercise. The teacher provides a language situation and natural linguistic data and the students are asked to fill in the appropriate speech act. For instance:

Situation: Your friend invites you to her house for the first time.
Friend: Why don't you come in?
    You: Thanks/ (*After looking around*) _____ house you have.
(Possible answers: *What a great/wonderful/beautiful*)

Or:

Situation: A colleague at a business meeting makes a point and you disagree.
Colleague: I think we should immediately contact all the parties involved and
           proceed to market the product directly.
    You: Well, _____, but I think we should wait until more tests are in
       before going on.
(Possible answers: *I see your point/That's a good point/Maybe we could*)

The advantage of a controlled exercise such as this one, in which the students are asked to complete sentences, is that students can concentrate on the speech act itself without having to come up with the entire piece of discourse. Such exercises can concentrate on one or more speech acts and can be more or less teacher-guided.

Another familiar language-teaching activity that can help students produce pragmatic features is a role play. Teachers write out the situation and include the appropriate sociolinguistic information, and then ask students to act out the situation. The degree of advanced linguistic and pragmatic guidance that the instructor provides for the scenario would again depend on the students' proficiency level – with lower-level students, who have limited linguistic abilities, there is a need to provide more specific lexicon and syntax than with more proficient students. For example, when studying apologies, the teacher can tell the students that they have just spilled coffee on a friend and ask them to act out the situation.

A variation of the role play is contrastive role plays. Here, a series of role plays is presented, with differing sociolinguistic features, and acted out to show how these factors can affect the forms that speech acts take. For example, with apologies, first the students are asked to apologize to a stranger whom they have accidentally bumped into on the street, then to a friend after coming 20 minutes late for an appointment, and finally to a professor with whom the students had an appointment to discuss a term-paper topic. These contrasting situations, and others like them, would illustrate how differing situations affect both the linguistic forms that an apology can take and the amount of explanation that needs to be offered when making an apology.

These three activities are merely examples of the types of controlled, teacher-guided practice that can be used to help students form speech acts. Many others could be used. The important thing to remember is that students need to be taught how to create speech acts and what situations impact on the various speech acts. The more proficient the students become, the less the act should be scripted by the teacher.

Free, integrated practice

The last stage is to have students integrate pragmatic usage into natural language patterns, without teacher guidance. It is this last stage that is absent from many textbooks, with the result that teachers need to devise their own teaching materials. Here, the teacher should set up an activity that produces not only the speech act pattern under study, but other forms of language as well. This is the true test of learning: Can students appropriately employ the speech acts when they are embedded within natural conversations? Activities that may generate speech acts are general scenarios that approximate real language use, such as students' pretending to be at a business meeting, at a social get-together, or in a classroom. Within these contexts, students can greet, agree, disagree, compliment, and so on. Teachers can give general guidance or perhaps provide students with character information. Similarly, naturally occurring speech acts arise in the course of discussions, debates, and other problem-solving activities that are widely used in communicative language classrooms. Teachers should set up the activity, step aside while students perform it, and then offer feedback after the activity is completed. The key point at this stage is to have students engage in meaningful language activities so that occasions for pragmatic performance will naturally arise.

A cautious conclusion

As stated earlier, for some ESOL students, pragmatic ability is not the highest priority in second language learning. For those who need to gain mastery of this feature of language, we should be mindful of several things: Is it possible for second language learners to obtain complete pragmatic competence through classroom activities? Probably not, nor is it possible to obtain total mastery of any other aspect of the English language. Will students master all of the information presented in class? Of course not; would that it were so for anything we teach. Will pragmatic miscues continue to occur? Yes, they are just like any other type of error that persists after we have taught it to our classes. The point is that some of the pragmatic knowledge we teach can be retained. Equally important is the general development of awareness that we instill within our students so that they can figure out pragmatic meaning when they encounter it outside of our classrooms. If we can succeed in giving our students some pragmatic awareness and knowledge, in spite of all the limitations that have been discussed in this chapter, we have much to feel proud of.

9 Teachers and students learning about requests in Hong Kong

Kenneth R. Rose

Introduction

Although most of the chapters in this volume address the development of cultural competencies in English as a second language (ESL), this chapter deals with the development of pragmatic competence in English as a foreign language (EFL). The title is based on a paper by Holmes and Brown (1987) on the teaching of compliments, and it is offered with a similar intent, that is, of making the most of pragmatics research in language teaching. The differences between this chapter and the earlier work are the speech act chosen for exemplification (in this case, requests), the consideration of teaching in an EFL context, and the focus on a consciousness-raising approach. This chapter does discuss the small-scale data collection of requests in Cantonese, but it is not a report of research results per se, so the emphasis is not on pragmatics research but rather on the application of pragmatics research to EFL teaching. Since this chapter deals with EFL contexts, it begins with a discussion of the advantages and disadvantages of teaching in foreign language contexts. Next is a consideration of the nature of pragmatic competence and pragmatic consciousness-raising (PCR). Finally, some techniques for PCR are discussed. Examples are taken mainly from PCR activities that focus on requests and were carried out with students in Hong Kong.

ESL and EFL contexts

There is a widely accepted distinction between ESL and EFL contexts based on the language spoken by the host community in which English is being learned or taught. When the host community is (primarily) English-speaking, there is an ESL context (e.g., Australia, Canada, England, New Zealand, the United States); when the host community is not English-speaking, there an EFL context (e.g., China, France, Japan, Peru, Saudi Arabia, Thailand). Of course, as is the case with any dichotomy, the ESL/ EFL dichotomy is a convenient overgeneralization that fails to reveal the inherent complexity in many contexts, such as those in which an indigenized variety of English has emerged (Kachru, 1986) or in which English has had, largely for reasons associated with colonization, a more prominent role than is usually accorded a foreign language. Hong Kong is a prime example of the latter. As Pennington (1994) notes, although as much as 98% of the population of Hong Kong is Chinese, most of whom are native speakers (NSs) of Cantonese, approximately 6% of the local Chinese population is made up of fluent Chinese-English bilinguals, with another 30% or more possessing some capacity to function in English. This situation is more complex than implied by the commonly accepted distinction between ESL and EFL. However, many of the characteristics found in "pure" EFL settings are also present in Hong Kong, so the ESL/EFL distinction will suffice for the purposes of this chapter. Given these distinctions, we can move to a discussion of the advantages and disadvantages of teaching in EFL contexts.

First the disadvantages. At the level of logistics, EFL settings often involve large classes and limited contact hours. Although there is considerable variation in class size, it is certainly not uncommon to have at least thirty students in a language class and, in some cases, as many as a hundred or more. Since EFL is generally treated as a compulsory subject, the allocation of contact hours is similar to that for other subjects – often two to three hours per week, sometimes less. Such conditions, that is, large classes and limited contact hours, are generally not thought to be conducive to successful language learning. Virtually any teacher, if given the choice, would opt for smaller classes and more contact hours.

Two additional disadvantages in an EFL context are related to motivation. In most cases, EFL is a compulsory subject; this, too, has certain negative implications for learning. It is not without reason that in EFL contexts an acronym applying to English language teaching has been invented: TENOR, or Teaching English for No Obvious Reason. ESL students, who know from real-life experience that they need what is being taught in order to survive in an English-speaking environment, are generally more integratively and instrumentally motivated learners than EFL students are. Of course, there is a source of instrumental motivation in many EFL contexts, particularly in Asia, and that is for passing entrance examinations. Although an exam focus can lead to short-term gains in, say, grammatical competence, more often than not it has little long-term effect. For example, it is something of an embarrassment to teachers of English in some Japanese universities that their students' English scores are higher *before* they enter university than when they graduate with an additional two years or more of English under their belts. The gains from cramming for exams seem to fade rather quickly.

Another obvious difficulty in EFL contexts has to do with the availability of NSs of English, which is generally very low. Learners thus have little or no contact with NSs and little or no opportunity to experience the enlightening dimensions of cross-cultural (mis)communication. Even in a place like Hong Kong, where one might expect frequent interaction between nonnative speakers (NNSs) and NSs, research on code choice has generally shown that Chinese-English bilinguals' use of English with NSs is restricted to a very small set of contexts (see, e.g., Gibbons, 1987), and most Cantonese speakers seldom (if ever) interact in English, with NSs or NNSs. Further, in EFL settings there are generally more NNS teachers than NS teachers. Although this has obvious ramifications for English language teaching in general, it poses special difficulties for the teaching of pragmatic competence because current approaches to the teaching of pragmatic competence present certain obstacles for NNS teachers. That is, given the lack of comprehensive, detailed accounts of the pragmatic system of English, materials development and teaching aimed at addressing pragmatic competence rely primarily on NS intuitions. Such intuitions are, by definition, not available to NNSs. This is not to say that NNSs of English have no knowledge of the pragmatic system of English; many NNSs have extensive knowledge of English pragmatics, just as they have knowledge of English syntax or phonology. Such knowledge, however, does not constitute NS intuition. Research has shown, for example, that NNSs do not share the same intuitions as NSs concerning grammaticality judgments (see, e.g., Johnson & Newport, 1989). Why should the case be any different for pragmatics? When it comes to pragmatics, there are no available published sources akin to those for English syntax found in descriptive and pedagogical grammars. The lack of such materials puts NNS teachers at a disadvantage in dealing with pragmatics in the classroom (see Rose, 1994a and b, 1995 for further discussion).

Concerning the advantages of EFL settings, one of the obvious possible pluses is the inherent homogeneity. Although this can at times be a problem (because they have in common a language other than English, students are not forced to use English with one another), it can also be an advantage, for it can allow specific focus and detailed comparison with regard to pragmatics. The diversity inherent in many ESL classrooms can result in a dizzying variety of pragmatic preferences, which can obscure a given point. In an EFL setting, though, there is the possibility of in-depth comparison between learners' L1 and English, which can be helpful in clarifying difficult points. There is an advantage, too, in the teacher's position as learner, which is of particular relevance in the area of pragmatics, and especially in PCR. Most EFL teachers spend a good deal of time and effort learning and/or attempting to cope with their students' language and culture, and comparative discussions of pragmatics in the classroom are often as enlightening for the teacher as they are for the students. The teacher's efforts do not escape the students' attention, and these efforts contribute to the development of rapport. Of course, there are also advantages to having NNS teachers (see, e.g., Medgyes, 1992). Having had similar learning experiences, NNS teachers can better empathize with learners; this often leads to interesting solutions to persistent problems. Also, having a language and culture in common can be a tremendous asset in the classroom because NNS teachers can either make pertinent comparisons themselves or more efficiently help students do so. Only a NS teacher who has achieved a high level of proficiency in his or her students' language can make such comparisons.

So there are disadvantages and advantages in EFL contexts. This is, of course, true of virtually all teaching environments. Knowing what sort of difficulties one may encounter and what inherent contextual strengths one may employ is important nonetheless. EFL settings do, however, present certain challenges in addressing pragmatic development. Such challenges require the use of techniques aimed at developing pragmatic competence in situations in which learners have little or no opportunity to interact with NSs, which is the perhaps the greatest hurdle in teaching EFL.

Pragmatic competence and PCR

A fundamental question in dealing with pragmatics in EFL teaching is this: Just what is meant by *pragmatic competence?* Although it is beyond the scope of this chapter to provide a detailed discussion of the nature of pragmatic competence or to attempt to arrive at a satisfactory definition of it (but see Kasper, 1997; Rose, 1997), it should be noted that the lack of a definition of pragmatic competence – though perhaps not an impediment to research – is rather problematic for language teaching. Just how problematic is an open question, but the fact that we currently lack a widely accepted definition of pragmatic competence or a comprehensive taxonomy of its various components presents numerous obstacles to language teaching, for example in the selection of elements for inclusion in a syllabus and the writing of materials for classroom use. Nevertheless, the tyranny of the moment leaves language teachers with no choice but to teach. The classroom cannot wait for researchers to provide complete taxonomies and comprehensive definitions – lesson plans must be made today for classes to be taught tomorrow. Still, it would be helpful to arrive at a working definition or conceptualization of pragmatic competence.

One alternative is to follow Leech (1983, pp. 10–11), who points out that there are two elements of pragmatics to consider: pragmalinguistics and sociopragmatics. Pragmalinguistics is related to grammar and is concerned with "the particular resources which a given language provides for conveying particular illocutions." Sociopragmatics, on the other hand, is related more to sociology, and is what Leech has called the "sociological interface of pragmatics." Sociopragmatics, then, deals what qualifies as appropriate linguistic behavior, which, of course, depends on a given context or culture. Bachman (1990) takes a similar approach to pragmatic competence, which for him consists of illocutionary competence, that is, knowledge of speech acts and speech functions, and sociolinguistic competence, knowledge of (among other things) dialect, register, and various cultural factors in language use. Concerning Leech's sociopragmatics, it is important to note that what is considered appropriate in one context or culture may not be appropriate in another.

As Thomas (1983) rightly points out, questions concerning what is appropriate behavior (linguistic or otherwise) must be treated carefully in the classroom. Ethnocentrism is to be avoided, and comparative discussions should steer clear of making value judgments and should always note the viability of different norms for different settings. It is essential that learners be informed of the various options offered by the pragmatic system of English without being coerced into making particular choices regarding those options. For example, an important part of pragmatic competence no doubt involves the knowledge of what constitutes rude behavior and when one might wish to exercise the options provided for achieving this end. So, then, a basic orientation for pragmatic competence might be the ability to use available linguistic resources (pragmalinguistics) in a contextually appropriate fashion (sociopragmatics), that is, how to do things – appropriately – with words.

Having arrived at a working conceptualization (however tentative) of what is meant by pragmatic competence, it remains to explain what is meant by *pragmatic consciousness-raising (PCR)*. Like earlier work on grammatical consciousness-raising (see, e.g., Sharwood-Smith, 1981), PCR is basically an inductive approach to developing awareness of how language forms are used appropriately in context. The aim is not to teach explicitly the various means of, say, performing a given speech act (request, apology, compliment, etc.) but, rather, to expose learners to the pragmatic aspects of language (L1 and L2) and provide them with the analytical tools they need to arrive at their own generalizations concerning contextually appropriate language use. Although this may seem relatively straightforward, it should be noted that consciousness-raising is not without its problems. As Schmidt (1994) points out, in second language acquisition (SLA) research, the term *consciousness* has been used by various researchers to refer to intentionality, attention, awareness, and control, all of which represent quite distinct phenomena. In addition, very little is known as yet concerning the effects of consciousness-raising activities, that is, whether or why such activities achieve the desired result. These problems are similar to the ones mentioned earlier concerning the definition of *pragmatic competence* and will ultimately need to be dealt with to contribute to more informed language teaching. For now, however, the rather loose definition of PCR offered here will have to suffice for the following discussion of PCR techniques.

Some techniques for PCR

Since PCR is aimed at developing learners' awareness of pragmatic properties in language use, any technique that accomplishes this task would, of course, be fair game. The following discussion of PCR techniques is not intended to be exhaustive, then, but rather it is illustrative of some techniques that have proved to be useful in teaching EFL. PCR generally involves the following four steps: an introductory phase in which learners' interest (it is hoped) piqued for the activities to follow, familiarizing learners with a particular aspect of pragmatics to be studied in some detail, analyzing data from the learners' L1 as a means of making the new concepts more accessible, and conducting analyses of similar phenomena in English. Each of these steps is discussed in turn, with examples taken mainly from PCR activities that focused on requests and were carried out with university students in Hong Kong.

First the introductory phase – the time when learners' interest should be gained. In preparing to engage in PCR activities with students, it is often useful to start by collecting examples of interesting and potentially problematic interactions that evidence some sort of pragmatic peculiarity and then present these examples to students for discussion. Having a notebook handy for taking "field notes" is essential in collecting such samples. Relying on memory to record relevant details of an interaction is generally not productive, especially if one is involved in the interaction, and a reliable account of the event is beneficial for later discussion with students. I will discuss two examples to provide an idea of the types of incidents that have proved to be fruitful in introducing pragmatics to students.

The first example occurred in the United States and involved an encounter with an elderly Korean couple who lived next door to me. As I was returning from the hospital after my daughter was born, I met the couple in the parking lot. Upon hearing of my daughter's birth, the woman said (rather solemnly) that I "looked much older." Needless to say, I was initially taken aback. Having had little sleep, I knew I may have looked a bit tired – but older? I was about to question the remark, but fortunately I remembered that for my Korean neighbor, being "older" was a good thing: Now I was a father, and so had taken on a new role, one with much responsibility. Her utterance was intended to be a compliment, and once I realized this, I thanked her. Of course, in American English, this statement would not be appropriate as a compliment, and it thus illustrates well the type of sociopragmatic issues teachers and learners of English must confront.

The second example comes from Hong Kong. I was struck, after arriving in Hong Kong, by the frequent use of direct requests in the English spoken by local Chinese-English bilinguals, especially in contexts in which they would be inappropriate in the United States. For example, I have been told by bank tellers to "sit down over there and wait," by university library staff to "just put those books down over there," and by various other salespeople to "Give me your ID." Once again, my pragmatic sensibilities were ruffled on these and other such occasions, but I kept them in check by remembering my Korean neighbor and assuming that none of these people intended to offend me. These encounters raise an obvious question: Why was there an apparent preference for direct requests in the English of many Hong Kong Chinese-English bilinguals for situations in which directness would be inappropriate in American English?

Although there are a number of possible explanations, I will offer two obvious ones. The directness could be the result of low proficiency in English, or at least of limited pragmatic development due to limited opportunity to interact with NSs of English. Recall that, as Pennington (1994) points out, Hong Kong is really not a bilingual society, as many people seem to believe, but rather is primarily a monolingual, Cantonese-speaking one. Another possible explanation is that direct requests may be more appropriate in Cantonese than in English. That is, in sociopragmatic terms, speakers of Cantonese may not place the same negative value judgment on directness in these contexts that speakers of American English would. If that were the case, the various people I encountered may simply have been transferring their sociopragmatic norms from Cantonese to English. This is an empirical question which can be answered only by conducting a contrastive pragmatic analysis of requests in Cantonese, American English, and the English of Chinese-English bilinguals in Hong Kong. Nevertheless, the obvious pragmatic differences between American English and the English of Hong Kong Chinese, and the possibility of sociopragmatic transfer, are fruitful ways of introducing pragmatics to learners.

What these two examples have in common, then, is that in each case the utterances produced seemed not to match the speakers' intention. If so, both could be considered pragmatic failure (Thomas, 1983). In the first case, a compliment was intended, but the utterance produced would likely be taken as an insult, at least in American English. In the second case, the directness used would more than likely offend American English speakers, which is generally not the intention of individuals involved in service encounters. The point here is that material can be derived from such encounters and shared with students during the introductory phase of classroom PCR. The various examples can be presented to learners with an aim to determine whether the interaction seems acceptable to them. Following that, learners can offer tentative explanations for the pragmatic peculiarities in these exchanges. After doing so, students will have developed at least some notion of the kind of stuff pragmatics is made of, and ideally some interest to know more. This, of course, is only the beginning. Some techniques that can be used effectively for PCR in EFL contexts are discussed in the next section.

After pragmatics is introduced in the classroom, it is often useful to choose one specific area of pragmatics and provide students with a brief overview of it. In the case discussed here, students were introduced to a basic understanding of what constitutes a request (i.e., attempting to get someone to perform an act), the various strategies for performing requests (i.e., directness, conventional indirectness, hinting), and some of the mitigating devices used with requests (e.g., downgraders, supportive moves). Although the manner in which this material is presented will vary from one group to another, presenting the material necessarily involves the introduction of some pragmatic metalanguage, but doing this generally presents little difficulty. Even at an intermediate level, students have already mastered quite a bit of grammatical metalanguage, so it is not likely that pragmatic metalanguage will be a problem for them. After ensuring that the basic elements of the item in focus are understood, one can move to the next phase.

It is often expedient in getting started with the details of PCR to have students collect data on the area of focus from their L1. Doing this means that the emphasis is first on pragmatics, rather than on English, and there is the added benefit of validating the learners' L1 as a useful resource and not merely as a source of "negative" crosslinguistic influence. Once learners have a good sense of what to look for in conducting a pragmatic analysis, English can be the focus. Again, for the purposes of this chapter I will discuss one case in which I asked a group of students to collect data on requests in Cantonese. Following the initial discussion of the components of requests, I provided the students with a data-collection worksheet designed to permit collecting naturally occurring requests (see Figure 1). I asked them to complete the worksheet by noting on it the next ten Cantonese requests they heard or made.

This round of data collection produced some interesting results. Since the sample was small (students collected a total of 154 requests), and the method of data collection rather limited, no attempt will be made here to conduct a thorough analysis of the data, nor do I intend to imply that the results of this classroom PCR exercise are representative of all Cantonese requests. A controlled study that yielded considerably more data would be required to achieve such ends. The focus here will instead be on the various insights that students drew from the collection and analysis of requests in their L1.

Of the 154 requests students collected, 37% (57) were direct requests. This is considerably more than has been found in previous request re-

---

Participants

Speaker	M/F	AGE:	
Hearer	M/F	AGE:	
Dominance	S > H	S = H	S < H
Distance	1	2	3

Situation

Request

Figure 1   Data collection worksheet (requests).

search (see, e.g., Blum-Kulka, 1989). This may indicate that in Cantonese directness is, in fact, appropriate in more contexts than in other languages studied. This suggests that pragmatic transfer may be the cause of the directness in the English of Hong Kong Chinese-English bilinguals. The following are some examples of direct requests in Cantonese. (Note: Transcription conventions follow Matthews & Yip, 1994.)

(1) Béi go yìuh-hung lèih
     Give CL remote-control come
     "Give me the remote-control."

(2) Gâ-máhn àh daai-fâan deui hàaih béi ngóh a
     [name] PRT bring-back CL shoe give I PRT
     "Carmen, bring me back the shoes."

(3) Hôi mùhn a móuh daai só-sìh
     Open door PRT not – have bring key
     "Open the door – I forgot the key."

(4) Yáuh faahn sihk la jâp tói
     Have rice eat PRT tidy table
     "Time to eat – clean up the table."

One important observation made by students in analyzing the direct requests they had collected is that, although directness is often the appropriate strategy in making a request, direct requests usually occur along with other elements, such as supporting moves. That is, bare direct requests seem to be rather infrequent. Students thus realized the importance of mitigating strategies, especially with direct requests.

Conventional indirectness, which is generally the most frequent request strategy in most studies (see, e.g., Blum-Kulka, 1989), was the least frequent in this small sample, with a mere 19.5% (30) of the requests falling into this category. The following are some conventionally indirect requests in Cantonese:

(5) Sîn-sâan, mh-gôi néih hó-mh-hó-yíh hôi síu-síu chêung a
Mister, not-should you can-not-can open little-little window PRT
"Sir, can you open the window a little bit, please?"

(6) Néih gaai-mh-gaai-yi bông ngóh-deih léuhng go yíng jêung séung a
You mind-not-mind help I-PL two CL take CL photo PRT
"Would you mind helping us to take a picture?"

(7) Mh-gôi hó-mh-hó-yíh béi go gâau dói ngóh a
Not-should can-not-can give CL plastic bag I PRT
"Excuse me, can you give me a plastic bag?"

(8) Hó-mh-hó-yíh je bá jê béi ngóh a
Can-not-can lend CL umbrella give I PRT
"Can you lend me an umbrella?"

In analyzing the conventionally indirect requests they had collected, students discovered the essence of conventional indirectness, that is, pragmatic duality. Direct requests have one interpretation – making the speaker's intent obvious – and hints have multiple interpretations, making it possible for both speaker and hearer to deny or ignore requestive intent, but conventionally indirect requests have two possible interpretations – one that refers to the hearer's willingness or ability and one that is interpreted as a request for action. Conducting this analysis of L1 data, then, made a seemingly complex concept – pragmatic duality – more clear.

Much to everyone's surprise (including my own), the most frequent request strategy used in this data set was hinting. Of the 154 requests, 43.5% (67) were hints. This is markedly higher than in English or other languages (see, e.g., Blum-Kulka, 1989). The following are some Cantonese hints:

(9) Lohk yúh la yauh móuh jê tîm
Down rain PRT and not have umbrella PRT
"It's raining, and I don't have an umbrella!"

(10) Yùh Mâ yáuh-móuh hiuh-mêng nûk-sí hái sân a
[name] have-not-have Humanities notes at body PRT
"Shirley, do you have your Humanities notes with you?"

(11) Ngóh tîng-yaht yiu fâan gûng ga
I tomorrow have-to go work PRT
"I have to work tomorrow!"

(12) Néih tau-mìhng gàh
      You transparent PRT
      "Are you transparent?"

Given the opaque nature of hints, some explanation is needed for these examples. Utterance (9) is a relatively straightforward request to borrow an umbrella, as (10) is clearly a request for the lending of class notes. Examples (11) and (12), however, are not as clear. In the case of (11), a sister was asking her younger brother to turn down the volume of the television so that she could get to sleep. In (12), another sister is requesting that her younger sister not obstruct her view of the television. In analyzing these hints, students were able to understand that often the most effective and appropriate means of asking someone to do something is not to ask directly but to produce an utterance that allows the hearer to intuit speaker intent based on contextual factors. They also saw, as demonstrated above, that not all hints are the same – some are more or less opaque than others. They understood intuitively, then, what Weizman (1989) refers to as the opacity scales of propositional content and illocutionary force. This knowledge can be put to strategic use in interacting in English, and it is no doubt an important aspect of pragmatic competence.

One of the most important discoveries students made in carrying out their analysis is that there is no one-to-one correspondence between linguistic forms and interactive functions; that is, students saw firsthand the multifunctionality of utterances. Any given utterance can have many functions, and context is essential for interpreting speaker intent. This is, perhaps, the core of speech act theory, and undoubtedly a vital component of pragmatic competence. Analyzing requests made this clear, especially when an utterance that appeared to function as one speech act was actually intended to perform another, as in the following example:

(13) Dáng ngóh bóng néih béi-màaih â
      Wait I help you pay-V-PRT PRT
      "Let me pay for you."

In this case, an individual was waiting to get on a bus, when the person next in line (a stranger) produced utterance (13). Although the linguistic form of (13) would normally be interpreted as a direct request for a particular action (i.e., that the speaker pay for the hearer), the contextual details (i.e., the speaker held out his hand to show that he did not have the required exact change for the bus fare) informed the hearer that the speaker was asking for change. By definition, then, the request in (13) is a hint because the desired act is not mentioned by the speaker.

Once students have collected data in their L1, it is helpful to have them compare their data with whatever research is available, both for their L1 and for English. There are a number of studies on requests in English that are useful in this regard, most notably Ervin-Tripp (1976) and Blum-Kulka (1989). Although I am not aware of any published research on requests in Cantonese, studies by Lee-Wong (1994) and Zhang (1995) on requests in Mandarin provide some points of comparison. Such comparisons get students thinking about a number of issues, such as how they make requests in their L1, how they make requests in their interlanguage (IL), how NSs of English make requests, how their L1 differs from the L2, and how their IL requests compare to NS requests. That's a lot to think about, and this range of issues helps make students aware of some of the complexities of learning to *use* another language, which, of course, is what pragmatics is all about. Again, discussion of pragmatics research will vary from one group to another, but learners at an intermediate level and above are surely capable, at the least, of digesting carefully prepared summaries of research.

So far, techniques that rely heavily on the use of students' L1 in the classroom have been discussed. One point to make here is that the use of the L1 provides for a substantial amount of role reversal in the classroom. That is, at many points during the instruction (depending on the extent of the teacher's knowledge of the students' L1) the teacher assumes the role of learner by appealing to the students' L1. This is often appreciated by students, and it does a great deal in helping teachers come to grips with the host language. Although there was a time when use of the L1 in the language classroom was considered unthinkable, many teachers would now agree that this is an extreme position. I, for one, have no problem with judicious use of the L1 in the classroom. The use of students' L1 in PCR generally enhances rapport and motivates students (and teachers).

The last technique to be discussed has to do with the pragmatic analysis of data from English. In employing this technique in an EFL setting, we run into some difficulty. In an ESL environment, it would be simple to tell students to go out and collect data on the target language, but it is a lot harder to do this in Asia than, say, in the United States or Australia. One source that can be used to great advantage in an effort to remedy this problem is film or video. To convey some idea of the utility of film for PCR, a short transcript from Woody Allen's film *Annie Hall*, which I have used fruitfully in the classroom, is given below. Although only a minute and a half in length, this segment provides substantial material for discussion. In this scene, Alvy Singer (AS) has been standing in front of a movie theater waiting for his girlfriend, Annie Hall (AH), who is late. As he waits, Alvy (a well-known comedian) is recognized by a few thugs, who approach him asking for autographs and begin to call attention to his presence. Annie finally arrives in a taxi, and after they make their way into the theater to buy tickets, Alvy refuses to go in because the film has already started. (Note: Transcription conventions follow Schiffrin, 1987.)

```
 1  AS: Jesus, what did you [do, come by way of the Panama Canal?
 2  AH:              [Sorry.        All right.        I'm in a bad mood,
 3      OK?
 4  AS: Bad mood, I'm standing with the cast of The Godfather.
 5  AH: You're going to have to learn to deal with it.
 6  AS: Deal- I'm dealing with two guys named Cheech.
 7  AH: OK: Plea:se. I have a headache. All right?
 8  AS: You are in a bad mood. You you must be getting your period.
 9  AH: I'm not getting my period. Jesus! Every time anything out of the ordinary
10      happens you think that I'm getting my period.
11  AS: A little- a little louder, I think one of them may have missed it. Has the
12      picture started yet?
13  WO: It started two minutes ago.
14  AS: That's it. Forget it. I can't go in.
15  AH: Two minutes, [Alvy.
16  AS:            [No, I'm sorry, I can't do it. It's- we've blown it already.
17      I, you know, ah, I can't go in in the middle.
18  AH: In the middle? We'll only miss the titles. They're in Swedish.
19  AS: You want to get coffee for two hours or something?
20  AH: Two hours! No uh uh. I'm going [in. I'm going in.
21  AS:                             [Go ahead. Good-bye.
22  AH: Look- while we're talking we could be inside, you know that?
23  AS: Hey, can we not stand here and argue in front of everybody, [cause I get=
24  AH:                                                          [All right.
25  AS: =embarrassed.
26  AH: All right all right. So what do you want to do?
27  AS: I don't know now, you want to- you want to go to another movie? Let's
28      go see The Sorrow and the Pity.
29  AH: Oh, come on, we've seen it. I'm not in the mood to see a four-hour
30      documentary on Nazis.
31  AS: Well, I'm sorry. I I can't. I'm I'm- I've got to see a picture exactly from
32      the start to the finish cause cause I'm anal.
33  AH: /Laughs/ That's a polite word for what you are.
```

By the time they view a segment like this, students have become quite familiar with the components of requests, having been exposed to some request research and even done some analyses on requests they collected from their L1. They can now apply what they have learned thus far in the analysis of film data. In this scene, several occurrences of speech acts are worth analyzing. Apologies occur in lines 2, 16, and 31, and requests occur in lines 11, 12, 22, and 23. Since the focus so far has been on requests, analysis could begin with a discussion of their formal properties. For example, the request beginning in line 23 starts with an alerter ("Hey"), would be coded as conventionally indirect ("Can we not stand here and argue in front of everybody"), is made from the perspective of both speaker and hearer ("we"), and contains a supportive move ("cause I get embarrassed"), but no downgraders. These concepts are all familiar from previous activities, but now students are exposed to the linguistic resources available in English for realizing them. Discussions can also focus on why particular linguistic choices are considered to be appropriate in this and other requests. Although activities of this kind will not lead to taxonomies of the rules of requesting (that isn't the intention), they will help develop students' sensitivity to both the pragmalinguistic and the sociopragmatic aspects of English, as well as equip them with analytic abilities that they can apply in future language learning.

Conclusion

In closing, I would like to make it clear that PCR is by no means the only way of addressing pragmatic competence in the classroom. As discussed, it is perhaps more suitable for EFL contexts. No doubt there are students in ESL contexts who will need more explicit instruction in language use. When students have an immediate need to use the target language in daily interaction, PCR will probably not be sufficient, and available resources (i.e., whatever research is available plus NS intuitions) will have to be brought to bear to meet that need. PCR is not a comprehensive means of developing pragmatic competence in ESL or EFL contexts. However, it is a useful way of confronting students with the pragmatic aspects of language, and it provides them with some analytic tools to further their pragmatic development as the need arises.

10 Cultural codes for calls

The use of commercial television in teaching culture in the classroom

Ron Scollon

Getting culture into the classroom

There is a growing recognition among educators that teaching and learning in the classroom inevitably take place within a matrix of more general sociocultural practices. Flowerdew and Miller (1995) have argued, for example, that at least four notions of culture must be recognized: ethnic culture, local culture, academic culture, and disciplinary culture; that is, teaching and learning practices in the classroom will be significantly influenced by teachers' and students' ethnicity, by the degree of familiarity with local versus distant examples, by the practices of academic life governing lectures and discussions, and by the specific practices of the disciplines within which they are studying. From this point of view, what is of primary concern are the patterns of social interaction among students and between teachers and students, expectations on how teaching and learning should take place, and cultural-social-historical placement of teaching and learning within the society itself.

The problem of understanding the role of culture in the classroom is made more acute when culture itself is the subject of study, especially where the study of culture is being conducted across cultural lines, as in second or foreign language classrooms. Thus, in such classrooms, not only are students and teachers normally members of distinct cultural (ethnic, local, academic, and disciplinary) groups, but teachers have the responsibility for teaching social interaction patterns, cultural values, and other aspects of the subject culture while at the same time having to take into consideration the negotiation of a tension between students' cultural patterns and their own.

The case on which I will focus is where the classroom is located at some distance from the cultural matrix being taught; I am concerned with the problem of how to teach students outside of, say, the United States or Canada the social practices and communicative interaction patterns adopted in these countries. Teachers working in Asia, Africa, or Europe, for example, find that their students have very little access to native speakers of American English. When it is the teacher's concern to teach them common patterns of social interaction, his or her example as a

181

model in the classroom is confounded by being conducted in a negotiated tension between the teacher's cultures and the students' cultures.

With this problem in mind, I have studied a set of a commerical television sitcoms to test the idea that they might be useful as teaching materials to contrastively elucidate differences in cultural patterns for common social interactions. Specifically, I have analyzed materials on the initiation of social interactions from four cultural groups – Hong Kong, Korea, Japan, and North America – to see to what extent such ordinary television materials can be used to analyze and to illustrate cultural differences in patterns of conversational openings.

Intercultural communication

Intercultural communication takes place across a broad range of situations, from high-level governmental negotiations to hailing taxis while on vacation in another country. The paradigmatic social situation which has been most studied by researchers, however, is the face-to-face social situation, what Goffman (1963) has called the "focused interaction" in one place or, in another place, the "with" (Goffman, 1971). As he defines it, a with[1] is a party of more than one whose members are perceived to be "together" (p. 19).

When we see people walking along next to each other, reciprocally exchanging talking turns, gazing at each other from time to time, laughing in synchrony, and the like, we judge them to be together. These indicators of their "togetherness" such as synchrony, mutual gaze, and alternating turns Goffman calls "tie-signs," and participants in the social situations as well as analysts use them as evidence of with status.

Among the characteristics Goffman defines for the with are ecological proximity, civil inattention, territory marking, rights to initiate talk and other communications approximately equally distributed, and ritual practices for joining and withdrawing. Members of a with orient their bodies and gazes to each other while at the same time disattending to others in the vicinity. They jointly use the territory they have marked out among themselves and neither allow the intrusion of others without apology nor expand themselves outside of that territory themselves. Most crucial for my purposes here, there are socially recognized means for initiating and dissolving a with.

The openings of conversations have been most completely studied within the literature (Schegloff, 1972; Houtkoop-Steenstra, 1991) as a particularly fruitful site in which to analyze the social processes by which we open up withs. Unfortunately, with few exceptions such as the Houtkoop-

---

1 I follow Goffman's usage in using the term *with* and cite it without highlighting it in quotation marks or italics in the text. While this may need careful reading in a few contexts, in most situations there is no actual ambiguity.

Steenstra paper just cited, there are very few studies of how withs are opened up outside of the research domain of English-speaking analysts. Outside of language-teaching textbooks, one finds very little either in non-Western cultural groups or in intercultural situations.

In our own research in this area (Scollon & Scollon, 1981), we found, however, that there are significant cultural differences in expectations on how conversations should be opened and that there were consequences throughout the conversation of the opening pattern. Athabaskans, an indigenous North American group, expect that the person who opens the conversation will yield the topical floor to the other participant(s). This is directly opposite to the pan-North American expectation that opening the conversation grants the right to first topic to the initiator (Schegloff, 1972).

We found that in Asian-English intercultural communication there are also different expectations on who should have the right to introduce the main topic and when (Scollon & Scollon, 1991). In that case, however, the crucial consideration was that many Asians prefer to defer the introduction of the main topic until after a period of "facework" in which good interpersonal relations are established. While this difference might appear to be an Asian-Western cultural difference, further research demonstrates (Scollon, 1998) that this difference in inductive (topic-delayed) and deductive (topic-first) patterns should be considered to be rhetorical strategies equally accessible to members of any cultural group and the choice of strategy to depend on other aspects of the situation. Thus, a native English-speaking businessman used the deductive rhetorical strategy in speaking to clients but the inductive rhetorical in speaking to colleagues.

Thus, research indicates that the identity of the participants in a discourse constitutes one crucial aspect of the ritual practices of opening-up with status. We are still left with the question of discovering the cultural codes used to signal these opening up practices and it is that problem that this chapter addresses. I will argue that there are significant differences in the signals used by Hong Kong Chinese, Koreans, Japanese, and white middle-class Americans for ritually opening up the states of social interaction that Goffman calls the with and that these differences can be analyzed with data from ordinary commercial television sitcoms.

The use of television sitcoms in teaching culture in the classroom

Method in cross-cultural or intercultural[2] studies is often problematical as members of cultural groups may be blinded to significant aspects of

2 These two terms are often used interchangeably, but I prefer to make a distinction. Cross-cultural studies are those studies of different groups in isolation that are then compared or contrasted on the basis of structural differences, behavioral displays, habits, customs, and the like. Intercultural studies, as I use the term, are those that

their own cultural displays as seen by others, while at the same time non-members struggle to achieve the emic perspective of members and often only arrive at characterizations that are rejected by members as stereotypical. A dodge of this problem is to directly examine stereotypical behaviors for cultural differences and then to bring those to members for critical discussion. This is the strategy I adopt here by using television sitcoms as the raw data of my research.

Of course, cultural analysts often are highly critical of popular cultural analyses. Drotner (1992), for example, shows how "high culture" reactions to television programming recapitulate once again the media-panic frame of mind. From this point of view, popular culture is the degeneration of culture, and while it might demonstrate *that*, it is of little use in understanding more basic cultural issues.

For quite different reasons, most media research, while very interesting in itself, is of little use to my project as it focuses on the contents of television programming, not on the unconscious or out-of-awareness aspects of cultural behavior taken for granted in the production of television shows. An important exception to this is research such as that of Skovmand (1992), which does focus on the cultural codes used in the construction of television programming. By comparing American, German, Swedish/Norwegian, and Danish versions of the internationally popular program *Wheel of Fortune,* he demonstrated significant differences in studio audience participation, host and hostess roles, and decor in what is often taken to be "the same" television program. Carbaugh's (1989, 1990) studies of the American-produced but internationally broadcast *Donahue* show also indicate that close attention of the underlying structure of the discourse yields rich insights into the cultural codes of the presumed implied audience.[3]

My strategy in this research is to compare how ritual openings of withs, what Schegloff (1972) has termed "summonses" and we have preferred to call "calls" (Scollon & Scollon, 1991, 1995) are constructed in television sitcoms from four different countries and broadcast in Hong Kong. This comparison yields insights into how the producers of these television sitcoms call on cultural codes to signal these rather common day-to-day situations and contrastively displays them for the student of culture. But before entering upon the description of the study itself, I still need to account for why I consider these calls, these ritualized openings,

focus on situations in which members of different groups have direct contact with each other. Furthermore, as cultural groups are often large, nonhomogeneous, complexes, I prefer to focus more closely on interdiscourse communication, that is, on communication between members of different discourse systems – gender discourse, generational discourse, or professional discourse (Scollon & Scollon, 1995). Nevertheless, in this study I take a cross-cultural perspective.

3 It is still, of course, another inferential leap to assume that the implied audience of any mediated communication resembles in any way the real audience (Scollon, 1995).

to be cultural codes as opposed to codes of the medium itself, and it is to this question I now turn.

How "cultural" are television codes?

I consider the calls for ritual opening of social interactions that I will describe to be cultural for four reasons: they are regular, they are out-of-awareness, they are patterned, and they are distinctive.

The regularity of these calls can be seen across several instances within a single program, across many instances in sequel programs, and in other programs originating within the same country. This regularity does not mean that there are never departures – it is not rigidity of practice but stability of expectation. What most clearly demonstrates the regularity is that when there are departures from the code, these departures are considered marked by the participants and receive comment or other significant response. ⸺ *Unconscious*

These ritual opening calls are out-of-awareness, or at least they are presented as being so however carefully they might actually be scripted into the program; that is to say, they occur as part of the unmarked flow of the interaction and are not highlighted in any way except when violated. As I will show, in some cases they are so far from awareness that it is very difficult to get members of the cultural group to focus on them and to get nonmembers to perceive them at all.

Calls codes are patterned in that they correspond to behavior in other contexts than the ones first observed; that is to say, they are not specific to the single situation depicted. They are also patterned in the sense that they match independent ethnographic observations elsewhere in the culture – they are not *just* television codes.

Finally, I argue that these are cultural codes because they are distinctive. By that I mean that they differ from the codes used by members of other cultures. I do not mean to suggest that these codes are used *only* by members of a single group – they are often found more broadly used across other groups, as I will show. Nevertheless, across the four groups I analyze, I will argue that there is a particular distinctive code, a knock, a formula utterance, and so forth that is recognized by members to be "the right thing to do or say."

The data

The research I report here is based on a larger sample of television programs recorded across a 2-year period of time in Hong Kong that includes not only sitcoms but also television news, entertainment, documentary, and other feature programs.[4] Parallel to this television data is a body of data of printed public discourse in newspapers and magazines that is often keyed to the television programming. For example, the newspapers present television listings in one place and short summaries and commentaries in another. Newspapers and magazines also have critical articles discussing television programs, including sitcoms. Finally, my data includes interviews with viewers of these programs, both Hong Kong Chinese and Hong Kong expatriates.

The data I report on in this chapter is of three types:

1. video-recorded and closely charted and analyzed sitcom/soap operas;
2. other video-recorded and closely analyzed television programming such as feature-length films, news and entertainment features, and main news broadcasts;
3. nonrecorded viewings of other episodes or programs in the same series as those analyzed here.

These programs have been in Cantonese, Putonghua, English, Korean, and Japanese. All of these programs, except for the Cantonese, are broadcast with Chinese subtitles. The four public television channels in Hong Kong are TVB Pearl, TVB Jade, ATV World, and ATV Home. Pearl and World broadcast mainly in English, but also include other non-Cantonese-language programs or NICAM broadcasts. Jade and Home broadcast mainly in Cantonese.

Charting for analysis consists of marking the sequence of episodes and the time of occurrence and coding episodes for the contextual features I have studied, such as participant structure, location, and setting. Transcriptions have been made only of segments in which the dialogue itself was of direct relevance to my analysis.

I have chosen sitcoms with a family group or family setting as the organizing social setting to get at least some degree of comparability across the cultural groups I am studying. Specific details on the 10 programs I have closely analyzed and chosen from to illustrate are as follows:

LP: *Fate of the Clairvoyant,* Cantonese, Hong Kong. Tuesday, October 18, 1994, TVB Jade, 7:30–8:00 P.M.

HH: *Happy Harmony,* Cantonese, Hong Kong. Tuesday, October 18, 1994, TVB Jade, 8:00–9:00 P.M.

GR: *Gentle Reflections,* Cantonese, Hong Kong. Tuesday, October 18, 1994, TVB Jade, 9:00–10:00 P.M.

OH: *Korean Hour* [Dr. Oh's family], Korean, Korea. Sunday, October 2, 1994, ATV World, 6:00–7:00 P.M.

4 Research for this article was supported by a City University of Hong Kong small-scale research grant. I wish also to thank my research assistants, Janice Ho Wing Yan and Ivy Wong Kwok Ngan, for many useful ideas and observations.

OK: *Okakura Family II,* Japanese, Japan. Sunday, October 9, 1994, ATV World, 11:00 A.M.–12:00 noon.

DW: *Dave's World,* English, United States. [Exact date unknown: October 1994], TVB Pearl, 6:50–7:15 P.M.

RO: *Roseanne,* English, United States. Monday, December 5, 1994, TVB Pearl, 6:50–7:15 P.M.

HI: *Home Improvement,* English, United States. Monday, October 3, 1994, 6:50–7:15 P.M.

LC: *Love Cycle,* Cantonese, Hong Kong. Monday, October 3, 1994, TVB Jade, 8:00–9:00 P.M.

CH: *Chameleon,* Cantonese, Hong Kong. Monday, October 3, 1994, TVB Jade, 6:00–7:00 A.M.

In the text to follow, segments from these programs are indicated with a two-letter code followed by a number. Thus, LP 20 is the twentieth episode from *Fate of the Clairvoyant* ("LP" is based on the Cantonese name of the program). All translations from Cantonese, Korean, and Japanese are mine, in the latter case aided by Chinese subtitles.

Dad's home: Hong Kong Chinese calls

The first call I will discuss is seen contrastively by its absence. It has to do with the arrival in the family flat of first the father (as head of the household) and then, moments later, his wife.

LP3: The door to the flat opens. The male head of the household comes in drenched with rain. He is looking downward, somewhat bemused, holding an umbrella, and does not glance at his mother and daughter who, however, have turned to watch him enter. His mother, looking irritated with him, asks if his wife is not with him. In surprise he looks up and asks, "Isn't she home yet?"
    Just then his wife opens the door saying, "Waa! There's too much rain!" He goes to her and they begin talking, somewhat acrimoniously, about what they've been doing to have become so wet. At the same time, the daughter has come from her chair to take her mother's shopping bags from her hands and take them away.

The ongoing interaction within the household has geared itself to the arrival of these two. It is as though everything is constantly in readiness for this head of household to make his call and take the floor. When he does not, his mother shows her irritation and prompts by asking where his wife is, thus giving the floor over to him. The wife's entry seems more true to form as she exclaims loudly about the rain. The daughter comes quickly to her mother's assistance.
    But what is the basis for the mother's irritation with him for the *absence*

of an initiating call? This may be compared to another very similar entry later in the same episode.

LP20: The situation is nearly the same. We see a young girl and boy across the table from each other eating. The door opens and the father, smiling, says, "I've come back." The young boy cries out, "Daddy!" and runs to him, as does the young girl. At the same time, his wife comes onto the screen from our left, takes his hand, and leads him into the next room, where some family and friends are playing mahjong.

In this more normative scene we see two crucial aspects of the home arrival call: the head of the household says quite explicitly, "I've come back," and the waiting family gathers around him. As in the first case, the children actually leave their places and go to him.

Now we can see the reason for the mother's irritation in LP3. She has expected him to call out "I've come back" as his call, thus giving the others the opening they have anticipated. As it was missing in the first case, we see the mother become irritated.

Given two scenes, one in which a call is made and one in which it is not, do we have sufficient evidence that a call ("I've come back") is, in fact, the expected means of initiating the interaction? I believe that a case can be made that we do. For one thing, there is the mother's patent irritation with her son. While that might have other causes, of course, the fact that she requires some explanation from him as well as the fact that in LP20 he does make such a call indicates some expectation that he should have done so in LP3.

Why, then, does he not make the call "I've come back" in LP3? In the logic of this particular episode, there is an underlying reason for the absence of the call. In the preceding scene, this man has just met by accident the woman who will become the femme fatale of this series of programs. We have just seen him standing in the rain leaving her, and his downcast eyes as he enters his home clearly foreshadow what we later see is his quite extended separation from his happy home life.

These entrances have been from the outside into the residence. There are also entrances within the house into rooms. The following two episodes are examples.

LP5: The father passes the open door of his young daughter's bedroom and sees her reading in bed. As he enters, he knocks lightly with his knuckles, the back of the hand toward the door, and says, "What are you doing?" He tells her she should stop reading and go to sleep.

LP22: The father and mother are in their bedroom, dressed in pyjamas, preparing to go to bed. The bedroom door is open and they are talking. Their teenage daughter rushes through the open door saying, "Waa! I've had a telephone call . . ."

First, we can note that the inner doors of the flat's bedrooms are standing open. Second, the father enters without hesitation and begins speaking, but *as he does so* he performs the ritual knock. There is no alternation sequence in which he knocks and then waits for a signal from his daughter to enter. In the same way, in LP22 there is no hesitation from the daughter as she rushes into the bedroom. Her call "Waa!" is issued simultaneously with her entry and her comment about the telephone call. In cases from other programs in which the doors stand closed, there is a pattern of alternation. Thus, we can see that the open door signals readiness to resume social interaction, even though a ritual call is given. In the case of the father, it is a knock; in the case of the daughter, it is the cry "Waa!"

Such simultaneous calls and entrances are characteristic of other settings such as university offices. I have observed, for example, that Chinese and British colleagues normally keep their office doors closed, while American ones leave their doors open. Hall has noted (Hall, 1969; Hall & Hall, 1987) that there is significant cultural variation on this aspect of the use of space. Confronted with this difference in patterns, I observe that Hong Kong Chinese colleagues, upon entering an open office door, will knock with the back of their hands or knuckles, even if they have been seen coming and asked to come in before they have performed this ritual call.

The doctor is in: Korean calls

In the series of programs concerning the dentist, Dr. Oh, and the affairs of his family, the setting is a dental clinic that adjoins the Oh family's living quarters. OH2 shows Dr. Oh entering his clinic.

OH2: Two nurses or dental assistants are working at cleaning and arranging dental utensils in Dr. Oh's clinic. The camera is on one of them when we hear a distinct, sharp clearing of the throat. She turns in the direction of the door and the camera pans to show that Dr. Oh has entered and he begins to address his assistant.

The call in this case is Dr. Oh clearing his throat. What evidence is there that this is not simply accidental? In the first place, it is clearly audible on the sound track, although we do not yet see Dr. Oh. Second, the assistant turns her head in immediate response to the call; that is to say, there is nothing else presented to account for her quick turn of the head. Third, careful listening shows no other instances in which off-camera throat clearings are heard, and perhaps we can suppose that if this were accidental it would be discarded as an outtake and the scene done again without the noise.

Of course, there is much other evidence that this is a call as well. In OH17, we see a situation somewhat similar to LP5.

OH17: Mrs. Oh is in their bedroom with the door closed kneeling on the *ondol* floor [Korean-style heated floor] working. The door opens and, as Dr. Oh enters, he clears his throat. Mrs. Oh turns to look at him and he begins speaking.

In OH17 we see the full sequence of call-answer-topic introduction to support the argument that in OH2 it is simply a matter of the camera not displaying the moment of the throat clearing to view. In further support of the throat clearing as a call is the more general cultural pattern to clear the throat in such places as public toilets to determine if a cubicle is occupied. If it is, the person inside will answer with a clearing of the throat.

The throat clearing is not the only call that Koreans use, however, as OH9 indicates.

OH9: Mrs. Oh is in her bedroom working with the door standing open. Her sister approaches, and shuffles her feet quite noticeably as she removes her slippers and enters the room. [Note that shoes are not worn on the Korean *ondol* floor, but, at least in the Oh home, the living room is outfitted in Western style where shoes or some footwear are worn.] Mrs. Oh looks up in answer to this call and her sister begins speaking.

These throat clearings and foot shufflings are as clearly symbolic to Koreans are they are normally imperceptible to others. Non-Koreans to whom I have shown these clips can see that an interaction has begun, but take simple presence of the person to be the call. Only repeated viewing of the tape brings these noises up to conscious awareness.

Entrances from outside are few, but in each case there is an explicit call that is very much like the one used in the Hong Kong example. In OH14 we have an example.

OH14: Mrs. Oh is seen sitting in the living room. Her teenage daughter comes in from what we can presume is the area of the doorway, saying, "I've come back," as Mrs. Oh rises to greet her.

The principal Korean calls, then, are of two classes, those for entering from outside and those for entering inside rooms. From outside there is the explicit and formulaic statement that one has come back, and in entering inside rooms there is a clearing of the throat or a shuffling of the feet. Note that knocking is *not* used in any example, nor have I ever observed knocking in Korea.

"Tadaima!" – I'm home! When a cultural code is broken in Japanese calls

The Japanese call *tadaima* or *tadaima kaerimashita*, meaning "now" or "now I've come back," is formulaic to the extent that it is almost stereotypical. Many non-Japanese who know little else about the Japanese language or interaction formulas will know this entrance greeting from textbooks, from films, or from being directly told by Japanese to say this. Thus, it can hardly be argued to be out of awareness in its normal usage. In the Okakura family, there are many examples. OK5 is quite characteristic.

OK5: Mrs. Okakura's neighbor returns home, where her invalid mother-in-law is in bed. As she enters she calls out, "I've come back," and her mother-in-law returns the equally formulaic "Welcome back" from her bedroom. As the door is standing open, her daughter-in-law simply comes in, accomplishing the entire sequence from entering the front door to arriving at the bedside in one formulaic sweep.

One might ask just how characteristic this traditional formula is in contemporary Japan. Surely one aspect of the Okakura family is that, in many ways, they are shown as being quite traditional in outlook. In one segment, OK9, we see that the formula may in fact be missing, but not without consequences.

OK9: We see Mrs. Okakura watching television. The program is a police thriller and there is a woman being chased down by someone in a car. As the headlights get closer and closer and the woman begins to walk faster and faster in panic, the camera cuts to a man's stockinged feet stealthily entering Mrs. Okakura's room. He steps up, comes closer, and then we see that it's Mr. Okakura, who puts his hand on her shoulder. She has not yet seen him and screams out in fright. He picks up the remote control and turns off the television set. She grabs the remote control and turns it back on, saying that the program is almost over. He turns it off again and says that when people come home they expect to be welcomed. He is back from work.

We do not know if we should presume that Mr. Okakura has said "Tadaima" upon entering the house and that she has not heard because of the television set. What we do know is that we have been shown a man coming home from work without any call–answer sequence having been made. We also know that the scriptwriters have chosen this situation to illustrate how members may develop negative attitudes toward others when such ritual greetings are not offered.

"Enter and die!": American calls

Like Hong Kong Chinese, Koreans, and Japanese, Americans issue an explicit call when entering the house, as we can see in HI3.

HI3: We see three boys of about 10 to 14 sitting together on a sofa watching television with fixed stares. Behind them the front door of the house opens, their mother walks in, and says, "Hi, guys." They make no movement. She repeats, "I said, 'Hi, Guys'!" After a long moment while she walks toward them, one of the boys turns and asks, "How'd the auction go?" She sits down near them and they begin to talk about their father.

A few minutes later, their father comes in from the side door (from the garage) and goes directly to the refrigerator. As he goes there, he says, "Hi, guys." They all turn to stare at him. He stares back and then says, "Why are you looking at me like that?"

Although I doubt that "Hi, guys" would be found in a textbook treatment of American greetings upon arriving home the way "Tadaima" might be found in a Japanese text, nevertheless here it is shown to have formulaic status as both the father and the mother use it. Furthermore, the mother repeats it when she gets no response on the first utterance, thus indicating her expectation that her sons should respond to her when she says it.

What is different about the American call lies not in the utterance itself, though I believe it would be much more variable in form than the very fixed Japanese "tadaima." What is different is that the call is issued at a great distance from the others present and there is no movement on their part to close the gap. In the case of the mother, she moves closer to where they are seated – they do not budge from their places in front of the television – but in the case of the father, he does not go to them but to the refrigerator and continues speaking to them from there. They do not leave their place on the sofa either. Thus, the American pattern indicates something not so much about the call as the ecological proximity, which for Americans can be over a considerably larger distance than for any of the others observed. Furthermore, no assumption is made in the American example that the arriving person should receive much notice beyond his or her arrival. In all of the other three examples, whether the arriving person was a parent or a child, at least some of those present moved to close the physical gap as part of the answering response.

In another sitcom, the very popular *Roseanne,* a teenage daughter has taken to her room and refused to participate in preparations for Thanksgiving dinner. There are two scenes, RO2 and RO4, in which she does enter into the conversation, both of which are illustrative.

RO4: We see the daughter lying on her bed reading. There is a knock on the door and a pause. The girl says, "Enter and die" without looking up from her book. The door opens and her mother's sister enters. She says, "I need a breather." The girl, still without turning away from her book says, "Gramma, eh?"

First we note that the door to the bedroom is closed. The girl's aunt knocks as a call, but does not enter until she receives a response from inside. When she comes in she fills the topic slot in the call-answer-topic sequence described by Schegloff (1972). The second thing we notice is that, like the calls in HI3, the answerer makes no move from her position, and generally takes considerable distance from entering into social interaction.

In the other scene, the daughter makes the entry.

RO2: Roseanne and her other daughter are preparing dinner in the kitchen. The girl comes in and goes to the refrigerator without saying anything. Her mother says to her other daughter, "Becky, look! It came out of its hole to forage for food." And then, holding out a piece of bread in the girl's direction, she says, "I hear sometimes you can actually get them to eat right out of your hand. Get the camera." The girl looks blankly at her mother and says, "That was so funny I'm going back to bed."

In addition to the perhaps typical American parent–child acrimony that this scene displays, as well as the apparent American predilection for going directly to the refrigerator upon entering, we can see that the "Hi, guys" of HI3 is pointedly missing here. The withdrawal of the girl is displayed in her refusal not only to participate in Thanksgiving dinner preparations, but also in her refusal to issue the normal call as she enters the space where her mother and sister are cooking. Roseanne treats this refusal to enter into normal social-interactive relations as if it were animal behavior and launches into a parodic play as if it were an issue of dealing with a wild beast rather than her daughter.

Hong Kong Chinese, Korean, Japanese, and American code differences

The examples I have given illustrate that there are some significantly different calls, such as the Korean throat clearing, but they also show that there are many commonalities, such as some form of saying "I've come back" when entering the family's living quarters from outside. If we look first at the entrances from outside, we have the following:

OUTSIDE DOORS	*I'm back/Hi, guys*	*Ecological proximity*	*Arriver as center*
Hong Kong	+	+	+
Korea	+	+	+
Japan	+	+	+
United States	+	−	−

The American example is the clear departure from the general notion that one greets others as one enters and that someone among those already present will go to the arriving person to produce close ecological proximity.

If we look then at entrances through inside doors, we have the following:

INSIDE DOORS	*Closed*	*Knock*	*Speaking*	*Throat/noise*	*Sequence*
Hong Kong	−	+	+	−	−
Korea	±	−	−	+	+
Japan	−	−	+	−	+
United States	+	+	−	−	+

Taken together, I can now establish why it is necessary to refer to these as cultural codes rather than simply as calls or symbols. No single item in this list is sufficient to discriminate any one group from another. In each case, except perhaps the throat clearing or the Hong Kong simultaneity of call and answer, the feature indicated is shared by some other group. What sets the groups apart are the combinations of features. This, of course, is part of what lies at the basis of perennial discussions of whether cultural differences are really valid. One notes a particular feature such as throat clearing, which is quite distinctive as a call for Koreans. This leads one to believe that calls are indicated with unique symbols. Unfortunately, one does not find such unique symbols in other places and is inclined to treat the Korean case as simply idiosyncratic. If we treat code complexes, however, as the basis for comparison, it should be clear that the patterns are different from group to group and that cultural learning means learning both what is familiar to one and where the pattern differs.

Cross-cultural interpretability

Before concluding, I need to make a comment on cross-cultural interpretability. All of the programs that I have included in this study are regularly broadcast in Hong Kong, a bilingual Chinese-English speech community (Luke & Richards, 1982; Pierson, 1987, 1993). These programs in Korean, Japanese, and American English are very popular. Nevertheless, Dr. Oh's coughs and Mrs. Oh's sister's foot shuffling are not perceived by Hong Kong informants, even when their attention is first called to them. What this means for cross-cultural communication studies seems evident. In the first place, one can learn to interpret and thoroughly enjoy communication that is presented in codes other than those of one's own "home" culture. Furthermore, because the great majority of the viewers of the Korean, Japanese, and American English programs make no claim to understanding the languages used – the programs are all presented with Chinese subtitles – it is clear that their failure to interpret the subtle differences I have described here is no barrier to such entertainment uses.

What do we learn, then, if we can demonstrate differences in cultural codes, on the one hand, but then also say that in practice they make no difference to the normal viewer who pays little attention to such things? The answer lies, I believe, in the problem that viewers may well come to believe that, by understanding and enjoying programs such as *The Okakura Family* or *Roseanne*, they have come to understand Korean and American cultures. Further, they may well come to believe that there are no differences of major significance between them.

The falsity of this latter position is shown up every time a non-Korean, while visiting in Korea, finds that a Korean has entered his or her toilet cubicle *without knocking.* It is seen every time a Hong Konger, a Korean, or a Japanese visiting an American home finds that, on arriving, people *rudely* simply stay seated and yell out their greetings and other comments. It is shown every time an American and a Hong Konger greet each other and the Hong Konger is singing out the answer at the same moment the American is first making his or her greeting call. These are the moments when intercultural discourse goes wrong because a casual cross-cultural analysis has led one to believe that the differences one might have noticed are really not so important. One watches a Chinese film that has won an award in an international film festival and comes to believe that Chinese are not much different from one's own compatriots.

This brief sortie into the commercial television of four cultural groups has demonstrated that the cultural codes used to open up social interactions differ significantly from group to group. I also believe that this research demonstrates that, when used with care, the study of popular culture products may shed useful analytic light on differences across cultures.

Conclusion

Teaching culture in the classroom is a much more complex matter than just analyzing codes for opening up social interactions. I would argue, however, that it is a very useful bit of knowledge for students to have, as their ability to enter into social interactions may well depend on their ability to open social interactions. It could be said that a Korean student learning English might not need to do more than just watch a few North American, Australian, or British television shows, but I would argue that the key to the approach I have advocated here is the contrastive and comparative analysis of codes, not isolated behaviors. There are two steps to the process, both of which are crucial to a contextualized understanding of such cultural codes. The first step is seeing the cultural codes, and the second step is placing them into the context of daily usage. My argument in this chapter is that commercial television can provide a rich source for bringing unconscious cultural codes to the level of conscious perception. I believe that this first step is a useful one on the road to the effective classroom teaching of culture.

11 Cultural mirrors

Materials and methods in the EFL classroom

Martin Cortazzi and Lixian Jin

Introduction

In this chapter, we examine some ways in which culture is reflected in text-books used for teaching English as a foreign language (EFL) and English as a second language (ESL). We distinguish *cultural content* from *cultural medium*, or, as we will call it, *culture of learning*. We analyze a variety of English-language teaching materials from around the world to show a range of ways in which culture figures in textbooks. We show that there are several paradoxes arising from the cultural mirrors found in materials and methods used in language classrooms. To resolve problems associated with these paradoxes, we suggest a broader definition of the cultural content of texts. Further, we propose that teachers and learners take a more reflective and ethnographic stance when tackling the cultural content and cultural processes involved in learning a foreign language.

It is generally expected that second or foreign language textbooks should include elements of the target culture. The extent and quality of inclusion are sometimes assessed using textbook evaluation checklists. However, we will examine a range of textbooks from different parts of the world to show that this is by no means always the case: a target culture is not always represented; some books include, appropriately, a range of English-speaking cultures; others include non-English-speaking cultures, stressing more international uses of the language. The representation of culture is more complex than the kind of portrayal implied by many evaluation checklists.

Culture, we shall argue, is not only content, but also a series of dynamic processes, including those involved in learning. The medium for learning about target cultures in the classroom is therefore itself part of a culture of learning. From an early age, students (and teachers) are socialized into expectations about what kinds of interaction are appropriate in class, about how texts should be used, about how they should engage in teaching and learning processes. The expectations arising from a culture of learning can be powerful determinants of what happens in classroom interaction. This can lead to possible mismatches between those cultures portrayed in textbooks and the cultures of learning used by teachers or students to acquire appropriate knowledge, skills, or attitudes about the target cultures. When there are such mismatches, it will not be a solution to include more representative elements of target cultures in texts. It is necessary to go beyond this, to reflect on ways of using the human resources of the classroom more effectively for intercultural education.

Language teaching and intercultural competence

It is now broadly accepted in most parts of the world that learning a foreign language is not simply mastering an object of academic study but is more appropriately focused on learning a means of communication. Communication in real situations is never out of context, and because culture is part of most contexts, communication is rarely culture-free. Thus, it is now increasingly recognized that language learning and learning about target cultures cannot realistically be separated (Valdes, 1986; Robinson, 1988; Byram, 1989; Harrison, 1990; Kramsch, 1993a). In Britain, for example, many documents about foreign language teaching show three broad aims, as analyzed by Byram (1993b, p. 15):

- the development of communicative competence for use in situations the learner might expect to encounter
- the development of an awareness of the nature of language and language learning
- the development of insight into the foreign culture and positive attitudes toward foreign people

But, as Byram shows, these three aims must be integrated.

The term *culture* can, of course, have different meanings. Some language teachers use the term to refer to cultural products (e.g., literary works or works of art). Others use it to refer to background information (e.g., facts about the history or geography of countries where the target language is spoken). Here, the term *culture* includes such aspects, but it also includes behavior and attitudes, and the social knowledge that people use to interpret experience. Moerman's definition (1988, p. 4) is useful: "Culture is a set – perhaps a system – of principles of interpretation, together with the products of that system." In this way, culture can be seen as the framework of assumptions, ideas, and beliefs that are used to interpret other people's actions, words, and patterns of thinking. This framework is necessarily subjective and is commonly taken for granted. However, it is crucial that foreign language learners should become aware of differing cultural frameworks, both their own and those of others; otherwise they will use their own cultural system to interpret target-language messages whose intended meaning may well be predicated on quite different cultural assumptions.

Following this line of thinking, it can be argued that even to integrate communicative competence and learning about target cultures is insufficient. Indeed, *communicative competence* can be too general a term. In one well-known analysis, communicative competence is divided into the four aspects of grammatical, sociolinguistic, discourse, and strategic competences (Canale & Swain, 1980; Canale, 1983), but this list can be extended by adding *intercultural competence*. This concept has been widely used in social psychology and studies of communication (Dinges, 1983; Hammer, 1989; Martin, 1989; Kim, 1991; Wiseman & Koester, 1993). In these fields, intercultural competence is seen in social effectiveness (i.e., the ability to achieve instrumental and social goals) and appropriateness (i.e., suitable communication in a given situation in a particular culture) (Martin, 1993). It has been defined in foreign language learning as "the ability of a person to behave adequately in a flexible manner when confronted with actions, attitudes and expectations of representatives of foreign cultures" (Meyer, 1991, p. 137).

It is not difficult to see strong arguments for developing students' intercultural competence, given the increasingly international nature of the work of many professions. In the contemporary world, a person does not need to travel to encounter representatives of other cultures: popular music, the media, large population movements, tourism, and the multicultural nature of many societies combine to ensure that sooner or later students will encounter members of other cultural groups. Developing students' skills in intercultural communication is therefore appropriate as a part of language teaching. It is, moreover, a worthy aim of education in general. Damen (1987, p. xvi) summarizes this point forcefully: "The current dedication to the development of the communicative competence of language learners mandates the development of intercultural communicative skills and an understanding of the processes of culture learning on the part of students and teachers alike."

With these points in mind, one would expect EFL or ESL textbooks to reflect a range of cultural contexts and to include intercultural elements. One would expect materials that raise learners' awareness of intercultural issues and enable them to communicate effectively and appropriately in a variety of communicative contexts. One would expect English-language teaching (ELT) curriculum design and evaluation, including textbook evaluation, to include consideration of culture and intercultural communication. Surprisingly, none of these are necessarily what happens. In the case of curriculum evaluation, for instance, "culture" is not even indexed in some of the most widely used – and otherwise excellent – current texts on second language curriculum development and evaluation (White, 1988; Johnson, 1989; Alderson & Beretta, 1992; Rea-Dickens & Germaine, 1992; Brown, 1995; Lynch, 1996).

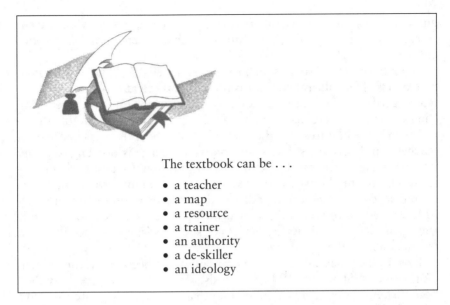

The textbook can be . . .

- a teacher
- a map
- a resource
- a trainer
- an authority
- a de-skiller
- an ideology

Figure 1   Roles of the textbook.

Evaluating textbooks for cultural elements

EFL textbooks can be analyzed as having important functions on several levels. The levels shown in Figure 1 seem a minimal framework for analysis. A textbook can be a *teacher,* in the sense that it contains material that is intended to instruct students directly about English-speaking cultures. A textbook is also a *map* that gives an overview of a structured program of linguistic and cultural elements, showing teachers and learners the ground to be covered and summarizing the route taken in previous lessons. Many textbooks show the cultural topics in the outlines of their contents.

Although some teachers – and many students – expect to cover everything in a textbook, most EFL training courses emphasize that the textbook is a *resource:* a set of materials and activities from which the most appropriate or useful items will be chosen. Other parts may be briefly dealt with or ignored, and supplementary material will often be brought in by the teacher, because the textbook is unlikely to cover everything. However, for many teachers the textbook remains the major source of cultural content, because in their situation supplementary materials on target cultures are simply not available.

A textbook is also a *trainer:* for inexperienced or untrained teachers, the explanations and guidance, the step-by-step instructions of a teacher's guidebook, can be very useful. Textbooks are seen as embodying current research and theory. Teachers can learn from them, not least about culture.

A textbook is thus seen as an *authority:* it is reliable, valid, and written by experts. The cultural content is therefore taken at face value and often unjustifiably considered as correct, or even as the only interpretation. Views that books are accepted as facts, as true and indisputable documents in some cultures, are themselves culture-bound. Less experienced teachers, and perhaps some whose native language is not English, may understandably reify textbooks in this way and fail to look at them critically. Often a textbook carries the authorization of important publishers or ministries of education, together with the further authority that many EFL teachers have no choice as to which text to use: a school administrator, or the ministry itself, may take such decisions on behalf of all teachers within their purview.

Even more experienced teachers can, however, become overdependent on textbooks (Shannon, 1987; Richards, 1993). The textbook may then become a *de-skiller;* teachers may not use a more creative, interpretative or critical approach to using materials, as they were trained to do. The textbook does it for them. Their role becomes marginalized to that of merely "going over" the cultural content, rather than engaging with it in a cognitive, interactive process of teaching.

Finally, the textbook can be seen as *ideology*, in the sense that it reflects a worldview or cultural system, a social construction that may be imposed on teachers and students and that indirectly constructs their view of a culture. This aspect often passes unrecognized. On analysis, there may be an identifiably interest-based perspective, revealed by such questions as "In whose interests is this text written and why?" English textbooks can function as a form of cultural politics by inclusion (or exclusion) of aspects of social, economic, political, or cultural reality (De Castell, Luke, & Luke, 1989; Apple & Christian-Smith, 1991). The country of origin, commercial interests, and the views or interests of decision makers who choose a book can be important factors leading to changes in cultural content. This is shown in the efforts of newly independent countries to produce their own textbooks. It is also seen in countries in Eastern Europe that have chosen to use different ("democratic") textbooks in a post-Soviet society. The role of textbooks as cultural commodities has been demonstrated by Kwong's (1985) study of language textbooks in China, showing how they reflect a changing political and moral culture, and by Stray's (1994) analysis of the influential processes of cultural transmission of Latin grammars in nineteenth-century England.

This ideological level can be considered in another important aspect: the beliefs, attitudes, and values of the users concerning what textbooks are for and how they should be used. This level has been substantially researched regarding textbooks for the development of native-language reading (Garner & Alexander, 1994), but not for EFL. It makes a difference whether the book is seen in transmission terms ("the book will give us knowledge") or in a more dialogic, interactive, or interpretative manner ("we will discuss the content, debate and argue with it to develop our own knowledge and interpretation"). The book may become a cultural icon or symbol, but what that symbol represents varies from culture to culture. We would think of this level as part of a culture of learning (see the section titled "Textbooks Based on Target Culture").

Richards (1993, p. 49) clearly articulates the more reflective, resource-based view of the use of textbooks: "I see textbooks as sourcebooks rather than coursebooks. I see their role as facilitating teaching, rather than restricting it. However in order to be able to serve as sources for creative teaching, teachers need to develop skills in evaluating and adapting published materials."

To learn to evaluate materials is now a normal part of EFL or ESL teacher training. The usual way to do this is by getting the teachers to analyze a course book against the points in an evaluative checklist.

Textbook evaluation checklists

Some published checklists do not mention culture (e.g., Dwyer, 1984; Brown, 1995, pp. 146–150, 159–166, 176–177). In others, evaluation of cultural content is only present by implication in such questions as, "In what ways do the materials involve your learners' values, attitudes and feelings?" (Breen & Candlin, 1987, pp. 13–28).

Some checklists simply (but importantly) draw attention to possible stereotypes of races and cultures in textbooks (e.g., Harmer, 1991, pp. 281–284; McDough & Shaw, 1993, pp. 63–79). Others alert teachers to possible varieties of target cultures, but actually only mention Britain or the United States (Savignon, 1983, pp. 169–175). The portrayal of cultural variation is important; otherwise learners will be led to see only a unified, monolithic culture. Both inter- and intra-cultural variation need to be represented.

Slightly more thorough is Cunningsworth's list (1984), which asks whether a cultural setting is acceptable to learners, and whether culture is only a setting for the linguistic material. Skierso (1991, pp. 432–453) queries the extent to which cultural content is integrated in the texts, dialogues, and exercises. Cunningsworth (1984) also asks whether the cultural contexts help learners in perceiving and categorizing social situations they may find themselves in; that is, he draws attention to cultural skills as well as to cultural knowledge. This point is elaborated by Skierso (1991, pp. 432–453) and Snow (1996, pp. 231–250), who distinguish cultural recognition from cultural production. Students may need to recognize the meaning of target group behavior but they may not wish to follow it. Some may have mixed feelings about "Western" cultures and such cultures therefore need to be presented in an objective and sensitive manner. Cunningsworth (1995) encourages teachers to ask whether the social and cultural contexts are, in fact, interpretable by students. He further argues (ibid., p. 90) that language textbooks are bound to express some social and cultural values. These are often not explicit and are unstated. Any detailed evaluation should therefore aim to detect and examine such unstated values. This would go beyond looking out for stereotypes.

It is clear that current checklists differ widely in the emphasis and detail given to the role of culture in EFL textbooks. Few mention historical dimensions, or comparative frames of reference in which several target cultures might be discussed, or the development of intercultural communicative skills (Damen, 1987 is one exception). Few ask whether the cultural content is presented with evaluative comment or clear author (or other) viewpoints (Damen does so). Few ask whether uncomfortable social realities – such as unemployment, poverty, racism – are omitted from textbooks. Sheldon (1988, pp. 237–246) includes this point. One can conclude that items presented in checklists reflect their authors' interest and awareness in culture. It is noticeable that questions about culture, if present, are nearly always placed at the end of a checklist, almost as an afterthought.

Among the more thorough lists of criteria for textbook evaluation is Byram's (1993a) list, which focuses on cultural content. Byram examines the extent and manner in which a textbook includes a focus on each of the areas shown in Figure 2. He includes a comparative element (e.g., British students might compare their stereotypes of Germans with German stereotypes of the British as a step to recognizing the nature of stereotypes and transcending them, or at least putting them into perspective).

Byram (1989, p. 72–74) cites Huhn's useful criteria (1978) for evaluating the treatment of the cultural content in language textbooks, shown in Figure 3.

Risager (1991) has used similar criteria to examine elementary EFL textbooks used in Scandinavia. She indicates that her analysis shows tendencies that seem generalizable to the whole of Western Europe. She shows that in the social and geographic definition of textbook characters, the people featured are predominantly middle-class, young people, isolated individuals (rather than family members) who are often tourists or visitors to urban centers. They engage in rather trivial linguistic interaction in mainly leisure activities or consumer situations. They reveal few feelings or opinions and never engage in social, moral, or philosophical problems. Most cultural information is bland. There is little historical

Criteria for textbook evaluation

Focus on *cultural content:*

- **social identity and social groups**
  (social class, regional identity, ethnic minorities)
- **social interaction**
  (differing levels of formality; as outsider and insider)
- **belief and behavior**
  (moral, religious beliefs; daily routines)
- **social and political institutions**
  (state institutions, health care, law and order, social security,
  local government)
- **socialization and the life cycle**
  (families, schools, employment, rites of passage)
- **national history**
  (historical and contemporary events seen as markers of
  national identity)
- **national geography**
  (geographic factors seen as being significant by members)
- **stereotypes and national identity**
  (what is "typical," symbols of national stereotypes)

Figure 2   Criteria for textbook evaluation (after Byram, 1993a).

Evaluating treatment of cultural content in textbooks

- giving factually accurate and up-to-date information
- avoiding (or relativizing) stereotypes by raising awareness
- presenting a realistic picture
- being free from (or questioning) ideological tendencies
- presenting phenomena in context rather than as isolated facts
- explicitly relating historical material to contemporary society
- making it clear how personalities are products of their age

Figure 3   Evaluating the treatment of cultural content of textbooks (after Huhn, 1978; cited in Byram, 1989).

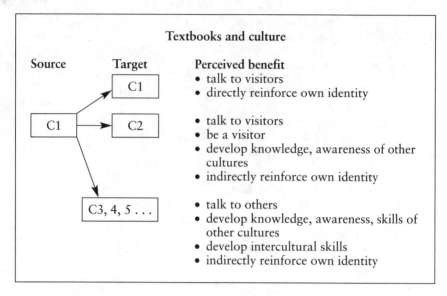

Figure 4   Textbooks and culture.

background or cultural comparison – target countries are considered in isolation. There is an avoidance of indication of the authors' attitude and no invitation to critical analysis.

In order to see whether such a depressing picture applies more generally around the world, we have examined a range of ELT textbooks.

Textbooks based on source cultures

Our examination of textbooks reveals gaps in the evaluation checklists considered so far. They are predicated on the notion that the cultures mirrored in EFL textbooks will be target cultures, that questions of cultural identity are unproblematic, and that for the most part culture will be construed in terms of declarative knowledge (knowing that) rather than as procedural knowledge (knowing how) or the development of intercultural skills. Yet, there are English-language textbooks for which none of these are the case. This presents English teachers with several paradoxes.

Figure 4 shows three patterns in English textbooks reflecting cultures. C1 refers to learners' own culture, the *source culture*. C2 refers to a *target culture* where the target language is used as a first language (there may be many, of course, as with English). C3, 4, 5 refer to cultures that are neither a source culture nor a target culture; these are a variety of cultures in English- or non-English-speaking countries around the world, using

English as an international language. These might be termed *international target cultures*.

There are EFL textbooks, produced at a national level for particular countries, that mirror the source culture, rather than target cultures, so that the source and target cultures are identical. A textbook for Venezuela, *El libro de inglés* (Nuñez, 1988), for example, has a text describing the country's chief geographic features – yet this can hardly be new content information for the Venezuelan ninth grade students with whom the book is used. The book gives details of a major national hero, Simón Bolívar, but again the content is very familiar to these students. When students practice asking for and giving directions, the setting is in Caracas, or other major Venezuelan cities. Places outside Venezuela are mentioned, but prime attention is given to the source culture, that of the learners, rather than to target cultures.

Similarly, the cultural content of an EFL textbook for Turkey, *Spotlight on English* (Dede & Emre, 1988), is primarily Turkish rather than a target culture. It is about Turkish food, Turkish history, and Turkish weather, discussed in English. When the textbook characters travel, they travel exclusively inside Turkey, although some characters are English-speaking visitors to Turkey. The implication is that students learn English to talk to visitors who come to their country, but they are not expected to travel to target countries or to learn about target cultures. If they do talk to visitors, they can only do so from within their Turkish cultural frameworks because they have not encountered cultural alternatives and are therefore likely to carry their home culture with them in their use of English. Thus, paradoxically, unless an English-speaking visitor is already familiar with Turkish culture, the visitor may not understand; visitor and host will speak English but communicate on different cultural wavelengths, unaware of the other's cultural view – a classic setup for miscommunication.

A third example is *English for Saudi Arabia* (Al-Quraishi, Watson, Hafseth, & Hickman, 1988), in which virtually every setting is located in the source culture. When the textbook characters greet one another, talk about professions, make Arabian coffee, or talk about going on pilgrimage to Mecca, they are predominantly Saudi Arabians performing culturally familiar activities in their own country with their own citizens (in English). All the maps in the book are maps of the home country. When there is a text about currency, it discusses only the Saudi riyal. In such textbooks, learners see members of their own culture, in their own context, who are not different from themselves, except that they all speak English.

There are reasons why it is the source culture that features so strongly in such textbooks. There is a need for learners to talk about their culture with visitors. A deeper reason is that such materials are usually designed to help students become aware of their own cultural identity. Thus, in many

African countries it was important for ELT textbooks to reflect local cultures in postcolonial times. Both these aims are unlikely to be realized, however, unless teachers and students have a degree of reflection on the nature of culture, and have some idea of cultural contrasts (as well as cultural aspects likely to be held in common).

Regarding identity, there is an argument that until learners' first cultural identity is established, it may be harmful to learn about other cultures. In this view, it is acceptable for younger students to learn EFL but not for them to learn about English-speaking cultures. This argument depends on the separability of language and culture, yet, as stated earlier, many scholars in the field (e.g., Byram, 1989) maintain that such separation is impossible (and undesirable) if communicative competence is the goal.

There are also counterexamples that demonstrate how widespread inclusion of foreign culture elements in textbooks does not necessarily threaten ethnic identity. Lebanon is one example. Lebanese people, like other groups, have their own personal and social identities, and perhaps different loyalties to different groups within the country. They suffered 16 years of war (1975–1991) but there is a strong feeling among the Lebanese that their cultural identity is Lebanese. At every level of schooling, students learn two languages: Arabic (the official language and native language of nearly all students) and French (75% of students) or English (25%). Many learn to use a third or fourth language. Most school textbooks (not only the foreign language ones) are in French or English, largely imported from Europe or the United States. The cultural content of these textbooks is that of the country of their origin, not Lebanese. As a result, more than half of the Lebanese are bilingual; they are familiar with other cultures and are generally regarded as very cosmopolitan, yet very few think of themselves as French, or American, or British; their ethnic identity as Lebanese is basically not in question, nor felt to be under threat – certainly not from source culture textbooks.

A more theoretical argument can be developed, which relates cultural identity to intercultural competence. This argument reveals a paradox with the use of EFL materials that predominantly mirror source cultures.

Identity can be seen (Ting-Toomey, 1993, p. 74) as the "mosaic sense" of ways in which people identify themselves along various dimensions: nationality, ethnic group, native language, occupation, age, gender, and so on. How a person thinks of his or her identity varies in intensity and in the salience of any of these dimensions, according to different contexts. Although people have some stable sense of a generalized self, major aspects of identity are dynamic and are "framed, negotiated, modified, confirmed, and challenged through communication and contact with others" (Collier & Thomas, 1988, p. 112). In this view, identity is negotiated in communication in different contexts. Hence, in intercultural contexts, cultural identity is also negotiated. As a further step, *intercultural communication competence* can be defined as an "effective identity negotiation process in novel communication episodes" (ibid., p. 73) or as "the demonstrated ability to negotiate mutual meanings, rules, and positive outcomes . . . the most important of which is confirmation of the preferred identity" (Collier & Thomas, 1988, p. 108). The paradox with the use of EFL materials containing largely source cultures is that, although the reason often given for their use is that this will help students to develop their own cultural identity, it effectively deprives the learners of realizing that identity. Since the materials mirror mainly their own culture, students have little opportunity to engage in intercultural negotiation with a text portraying another culture, and so they are unable to engage in a dialogue with the text to identify and confirm their own cultural identity, or to ascertain its similarities and differences with that of another cultural group.

A dialogue from a Malagasy EFL textbook, *English Third Steps* (n.a., 1978, pp. 11–12) shows how the paradox of using source cultures can, on occasion, operate:

Koffi: Is circumcision practised in Madagascar?
Baly: Yes. It's practised all over the country. If you're not circumcised you'll never be considered a true man.
Koffi: It's exactly the same in our tribe. When does it take place in your country?
Baly: Well, usually from June to September. It's generally a family celebration. But in some regions it's a communal festivity which is performed every eleven years. . . . Our boys are usually circumcised at the age of three, four or five. (*Koffi laughs*) Why are you laughing?
Koffi: Well, in our tribe, the "candidate" for circumcision visits his relatives and friends. He declares he's made up his mind to become a "man." He invites them to attend the operation which will be carried out at the village place. You know, we are circumcised at the age of twenty-five. . . .
Baly: Good heavens! What if the boy cries?
Koffi: If he cries? If he cries, I'm telling you, man, no girl will marry him.

Students are told that Baly is Malagasy and Koffi is from Africa. The text is accompanied by a photograph illustrating the operation that is being discussed. If this dialogue is intended as a model of how to talk about local customs in the source culture, then it is not difficult to imagine that it could be a cause of some embarrassment if shared with others from the wider English-speaking world: visitors to the country might receive unexpected explanations or be asked awkward questions.

There is a resolution to this kind of paradox: The teacher can mediate the textbook in classroom interaction, indicating which aspects of the source culture would be interesting or problematic for target language speakers. Such compensatory action would, however, demand a measure of intercultural knowledge, skills, and awareness from the teacher.

Textbooks based on target culture

There are a large number of EFL textbooks that focus on target cultures. Many conform closely to Risager's (1991) analysis, outlined earlier, and some deserve Brumfit's description of being "Masses of rubbish that is skilfully marketed" (1980, p. 30). Commercial values clearly influence the design and content of textbooks, but there are changes. Social and environmental issues are now selling points. Thus, not only do recent EFL textbooks include materials designed to promote awareness of race, gender, and environmental issues, but these points are highlighted in the publishers' promotional materials.

An effective example of this contemporary approach to social cultural realism in elementary-level textbooks is *Success – Communicating in English* (Walker, 1994), which is set in the United States but marketed worldwide. The multicultural nature of American society is portrayed by including members of minority groups, shown positively in responsible positions or professional roles. By providing information in simple graphic formats, issues concerning health, crime, the environment, and the role of women are raised. In a typical explicit move to counter stereotypes, some texts feature husbands as being responsible for child care and housework, while their wives are breadwinners.

Another page (Book 2, p. 109), under the heading "What are you concerned about?" gives details of contemporary social, moral, or economic issues (e.g., child abuse). The text delineates aspects of such problems but – an important point – does not provide solutions. Students are asked to share their own opinions and concerns.

Parts of this textbook exemplify Luke's (1989) distinction between "closed" and "open" texts. A *closed* text shows an unproblematic world that confirms or reinforces learners' views and beliefs. The text seems to be complete already, so there is no need for student response or interpretation. An *open* text, in contrast, invites a range of possible interpretations, elaborations, and learner responses. It is (deliberately) incomplete to encourage the students to interact with the text in ways that go beyond simple manipulation of text language. An open text encourages cognitive or emotional involvement and draws on what students bring to the text. The page in Walker (1994) referred to in the preceding paragraph can be seen as an open text.

A second example of a more realistic, open textbook is *English G* (Hennig, 1991). This is intended for advanced-level German EFL students. The target culture focus is the United States. The book has units tackling most aspects of culture mentioned in Byram's list (1993a), quoted earlier. One theme is "Blacks in America." This theme is set in a detailed historical framework covering times of slavery to the more recent elections of black men and women to the U.S. Senate and state governorships. Students are invited to construe alternative interpretations of progress made by black Americans through examining data comparing black and white income groups and percentages of college graduates, managers and professionals, or elected officials. Further alternative perspectives are offered in the interviews with black families of differing social backgrounds, the collective interviews being juxtaposed with factual information. On the whole, these texts are open, offering more complex, in-depth versions of the target culture.

A third example, which again has marked open qualities, is *Learning English, Topline* (Bülow, Forman, & Vettel, 1992), an advanced reader and workbook for German EFL students. The cultural focus is balanced between seven units on the United States, six on the United Kingdom, one on India, and one on Ireland. This textbook has an enormous variety of cultural coverage, focusing on modern history and social, political, technological, religious, and artistic topics. It includes extracts from more than one hundred authors, representing a wide range of voices. Students are encouraged to analyze authors' points of view. The book is amply illustrated with factual material, contemporary illustrations, and explanatory graphics. It is, of course, much easier to introduce this richness of material to advanced learners.

It is easy to assume that textbooks should reflect a target culture. However, a survey of Greek students by Prodromou (1992) reveals that some students have mixed views on the cultural focus of their English lessons. Among 300 students, 60% wanted to focus on British culture (C2), 26% on American culture (C2), 36% on "the culture of other countries" (either C2 or C3, C4, C5), and 27% on Greek culture (C1).

Textbooks aimed at international target cultures

A third category of cultural content in EFL textbooks involves those books that include a wide variety of cultures set in English-speaking countries or in other countries where English is not a first or second language, but is used as an international language. The rationale for such *international target cultures* is that English is frequently used in international situations by speakers who do not speak it as a first language. An example of such a situation is when Belgian teachers have taught English in China to Chinese factory technicians who need English to speak to Italian and German engineers; English is not the first language of any of these groups.

A preintermediate EFL textbook that aims at international target cultures is *One World, Secondary English* (Priesack & Tomscha, 1993), which is accompanied by cassettes featuring not only a range of native-speaker accents but also some from nonnative speakers from around the world. Book 3 has units focusing on British history, Australian geography,

Spanish tourism, the Chinese New Year, a Canadian story, Greek mythology, and other topics. However, these are fragmented topics, in Risager's terms (1991). Each is restricted to a single unit. There is no cultural thread to link the topics together.

This difficulty is avoided in *Panorama* (Potter, 1990), an elementary to intermediate series, by the use of themes. One theme of an American family living in Rio de Janeiro allows some focus on Brazilian culture compared with American culture, spread over three books. A second theme of visits allows a linked focus on Istanbul, Marrakech, Seoul, and Buenos Aires, with further comparisons with Bangkok and Tokyo. Elsewhere, the themes of job applications for a job in Milan, and of an international conference in Nairobi, extend such international targets over a number of units. This seems to avoid fragmentation.

While such textbooks offer interesting cultural mirrors, the learning of culture and the development of intercultural skills depend in large part on how the textbooks are used in the classroom, that is, on the quality of interaction between students, texts, and teachers. Beyond textbooks, what is required is a methodology of cultural learning. Allwright's point (1981, p. 9) was not made about cultural aspects of textbooks, but it surely applies to these aspects: "The whole business of the management of language learning is far too complex to be satisfactorily catered for by a pre-packaged set of decisions embodied in teaching materials." What is needed are appropriate methods for teaching and learning culture in the EFL classroom that will facilitate a reflective use of the best available materials.

Culture learning as dialogue

As we have argued, intercultural competence takes place in situations of negotiating meaning and identity in the context of other cultures. Culture learning through textbooks might also be seen as a process of dialogue in which students negotiate meaning and identity vicariously with the author of the textbook and its cultural content. However, this is mediated in the classroom with a teacher who manages the way in which the students see the culture mirrored in the textbook. The teacher may also thereby mediate ways in which students see themselves. Teachers are thus "ambassadors of culture" (Nayar, 1986; quoted in Nelson, 1995 p. 30).

There is, then, a three-party dialogue with the culture content when the textbook is used in classroom interaction, as shown in Figure 5. In this dialogue, neither the teacher nor the students are blank slates regarding the target culture. They may have some previous knowledge of it (e.g., the teacher may be a native-speaking participant).

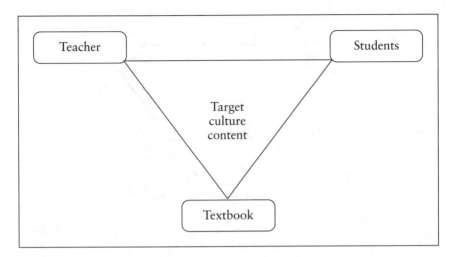

Figure 5   A three-party dialogue with culture content.

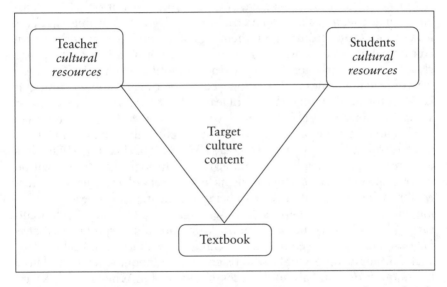

Figure 6   Teacher and students bring cultural resources to the textbook.

If they do not have much knowledge of the target culture, we can still recognize that they bring cultural resources to the dialogue with the textbook, shown in Figure 6. These resources are their understanding of their own source culture, which can be exploited in an ethnographic or reflective approach.

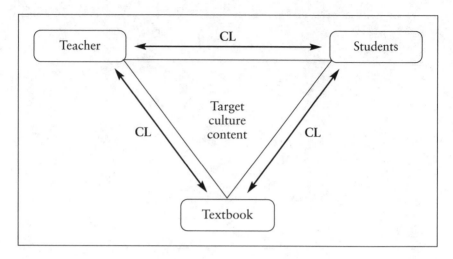

Figure 7   Cultures of learning mediating the learning of target culture content (CL = culture of learning).

Further, in an EFL classroom, culture learning is not only a *content-based dialogue,* it is also a *medium-based dialogue* of learning. Students learn about target cultures, but their way of learning is part of their own culture, acquired in most cases long before entering a foreign language classroom. Similarly, teachers may teach about target cultures, but their way of teaching is not solely influenced by their professional training. It is also influenced by their culture of learning. The *culture of learning* that students and teachers bring to the classroom is a taken-for-granted frame-work of expectations, attitudes, values, and beliefs about what constitutes good learning (Jin & Cortazzi, 1993, 1995; Cortazzi & Jin, 1996). It is acquired in early socialization patterns and through the internalization of roles and expectations that students learn at school. It influences teach-ers through the imprint of years of being a student, prior to teacher train-ing, and years of apprenticeship observing others teaching. Such a cul-ture of learning becomes a framework of cultural interpretation that is unconsciously employed in later teaching. It becomes an invisible yard-stick for judgments about how to teach or learn, about whether and how to ask questions, and about what textbooks are for. When textbooks are written, they are also predicated on a culture of learning (see Figure 7).

A culture of learning not only mediates the learning of target culture content – it may also deny such learning by creating barriers of differ-ences of interpretation.

The problem is that the students' and their teacher's culture of learn-ing may not be consonant with each other, and either could be out of syn-chronization with the target culture. Source cultures then dominate the interaction so that the culture content becomes filtered or distorted by the participants' approach to interaction with the text.

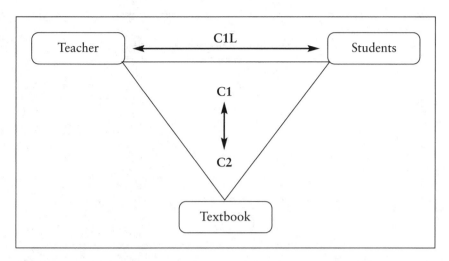

Figure 8   Teacher and students share the same culture of learning. C1L = source culture of learning; C1 = source culture; C2 = target culture.

One paradox that emerges is the possibility that teacher and students may share the same culture of learning but use an EFL textbook based on a quite different culture of learning. Although the teacher-student inter- action shows a congruence of cultures of learning, this cultural medium does not, perhaps, match the cultural content of the textbook; nor does it match the medium expected to be used by its authors. It is possible, even probable, that the source culture will, in fact, dominate the dialogic exploitation of the text, as shown in Figure 8. This is a paradox because the teacher is in an ideal position to understand the students' approach to the text, by being familiar with their culture of learning. However, pre- cisely because the teacher shares this culture of learning it is difficult for him or her to transcend it in order to match the target culture with a tar- get culture of learning. Another paradox may arise from a different sit- uation, shown in Figure 9, where the teacher may be a native speaker of English, using his or her own culture of learning to teach EFL. This is ap- parently a better opportunity for students – they can learn the target cul- ture with a native speaker using a target culture methodology. However, there is still a mismatch which can create barriers: students may expect a different culture of learning from the teacher, and, not seeing evidence of it, they may conclude that the teacher is a poor teacher because he or she is not teaching in expected ways. This situation can be improved if the teacher understands the students' culture of learning.

However, the paradox is that the more the teacher moves toward the students' expectations, the greater the distance he or she is from the tar- get culture. Also, some students – and some teachers – may well feel that to change their culture of learning is to change their culture, which raises the problems of identity discussed earlier. There is a further problem

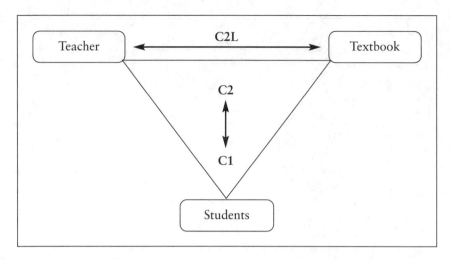

Figure 9   Teacher and textbook share the same culture of learning. C2L = target culture of learning; C2 = target culture; C1 = source culture.

because it is likely that teachers (in Figure 8) and students (in Figures 8 and 9) have successfully employed their cultures of learning in other subjects in the curriculum.

A third situation, shown in Figure 10, has already been discussed in earlier sections. In this situation, students and the textbook share the same culture, which is the source culture; but the teacher may come from another culture, with another culture of learning. This pattern may cause a failure of teaching and learning, unless the teacher is familiar with the students' culture of learning.

The possibilities mentioned above are simplifications. As we have shown, there is not a single target culture; rather, there are target cultures (C2), source culture (C1), and international target cultures (C3, C4, C5 . . .). Furthermore, there are many EFL or ESL situations where students do not come from a single cultural background. They may represent many cultures and many cultures of learning. In these ways, the dialogue of cultures of learning is a multiparty one, and it takes place on several levels. The cultural mirror in the EFL materials and methods is many-faceted.

Western teachers and Chinese students

Some of these points can be illustrated by looking at the situation of Western teachers (i.e., from the United Kingdom, the United States and Canada, Australia, New Zealand, and Western Europe) interacting with Chinese university students in China (Jin & Cortazzi, 1993, 1995; Cor-

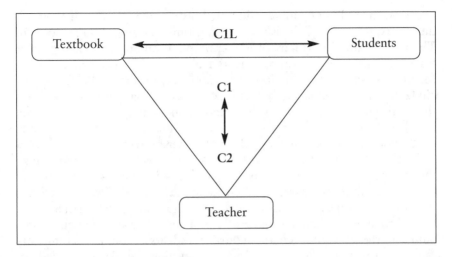

Figure 10 Students and textbook share the source culture of learning.

tazzi & Jin, 1996). The following account presents only tendencies, which will not apply to all individuals.

The Western teachers, in general, approach the classroom use of textbooks as a resource (see Figure 1) that they exploit selectively, attempting to involve students in active discussion. They expect students' participation which will include a critical evaluation of texts, revealing students' independent thinking.

Many Chinese students, however, approach textbooks as teachers and authorities (see Figure 1). They expect the teacher to expound the book – they will learn through attentive listening, because the teacher is also an authority and provider of knowledge. They apparently accept this knowledge from the textbook uncritically, but in their minds they have their own thinking. They hesitate to express this thinking because their culture of learning includes the notion that one cannot really create or contribute something new until one has mastered the field or relevant techniques – that is, after long apprenticeship. Also, they reflect carefully before participating, in order to be sure their point is valid and useful. Further, they incorporate their care for social relationships into their learning environment, which includes their respect for teacher and fellow students, their concern for "face" issues, for not "showing off," for group harmony, and so on.

These contrasting cultures of learning lead to variant interpretations of the classroom interaction that accompanies the use of textbooks. For example, asking questions about the cultural content of the textbook seems, for the teacher, very useful. The teacher will ask questions and encourage students to do so, in the belief that this reflects student activity and learning. Many Chinese students, however, believe that if they ask questions, there is a high risk of wasting time or being thought foolish. The teacher should, as part of lesson preparation and teaching, predict learners' questions, so some students feel no need to ask, but will wait for the anticipated explanation. If no explanation comes, then they conclude that this aspect is not important or that they may find answers from the textbook and materials if they read them again and try to solve the problem themselves. Other students reflect carefully before they ask – they have good questions, but they ask the teacher individually after class in order not to disturb the class. Others ask after class in order to minimize the loss of face if the question seems foolish – their classmates will not hear them ask if they ask alone. This frustrates some Western teachers, who find their time after class taken up with questions, that, in their view, should have been asked during class, especially if they are good questions. Similarly, the Western teachers encourage students to volunteer comments in class – this will show interest and the speaker will be considered active. In the students' perspective, however, this is showing off. It also prevents the teacher from talking and thus it is negatively evaluated, because it is the teacher, not other students, who should be transmitting knowledge.

These mismatches in cultures of learning can affect participants' interpretations of one another: perceptions of others' behavior are attributed to the cultural categorization of the others' group and conclusions are drawn about their general status and ability – sometimes quite mistakenly.

Western teachers agree that Chinese students are hardworking, well motivated, and friendly. However, the students seem unwilling to speak; they are passive and rather resistant to pair or group work. They seem oriented to exams and memorization, but not to the processes of learning.

The Chinese students like to have Western teachers. They are good models for pronunciation and have the authority of being native speakers and sources of cultural knowledge. However, these teachers are seen as less knowledgeable and helpful for learning grammar and vocabulary than Chinese teachers, perhaps because the Western teachers emphasize communication rather than linguistic knowledge and mental activity. Some Western teachers are thought to be poor at teaching, because they stress pair and group discussion instead of teaching the students themselves.

Some current reforms in the EFL national curriculum in China are movements in the direction of a Western-oriented style of learning (Han, Lu, & Doug, 1995); how far these are successful remains to be seen. The situation of Western teachers and Chinese students has, of course, other complexities, other variations, and contemporary developments (see Cortazzi & Jin, 1996). However, we hope that the above analysis, which is based on research in China, demonstrates that paying heed to cultural materials and methods is insufficient. Attention also needs to be given to teachers' and students' ways of learning, and, by extension, each side needs to pay attention to the other side's culture of learning. Yet, it is important to emphasize that in language classrooms there are not inevitably cultural problems. All around the world, there are teachers and students who successfully engage in cultural learning.

Teaching culture

There seem to be several broad solutions to the kinds of problems we have identified. First, a broader definition of the cultural content of texts is called for, and a corresponding requirement is that textbook evaluation lists have greater sophistication about cultural elements, as discussed earlier. Second, we believe that teachers and students should take a more reflective or ethnographic stance toward cultural content and methodology, in order to raise their awareness of intercultural issues. Third, it would be a useful development if more textbooks included explicit intercultural elements and if teachers were more conscious of intercultural competence, in the way that many are now conscious of communicative competence. We will elaborate on the second and third points below.

For EFL teachers to develop a reflective stance toward classroom experience is now regarded as a major path to professional development (Wallace, 1991; Richards & Lockhart, 1994). It has also been argued that teachers must become colearners, along with their students, in a cooperative approach to classroom interaction (Wenham, 1991). This idea is also a part of Confucian philosophy of education: "Jiao xue xiang zhang" (Teaching and learning influence and improve each other). (Confucius). These developments suit the need for language teachers and students to construct an interpretative approach to learning culture in which, as is likely, the teacher may be learning. This would mean that the development of cultural awareness (Tomalin & Stempleski, 1993) is a priority.

Developing cultural awareness means being aware of members of another cultural group: their behavior, their expectations, their perspectives and values. It also means attempting to understand their reasons for their actions and beliefs. Ultimately, this needs to be translated into skill in communicating across cultures and about cultures. This can be encouraged by developing an ethnographic stance toward cultural learning. This is following the approach demonstrated for the ethnography of communication (Saville-Troike, 1989) and for ethnography in language classroom research (van Lier, 1988), but extended explicitly to help students (and teachers) to understand the process of understanding culture, both their own and target cultures (Zarate, 1991, 1995). For example, Zarate suggests presenting learners with photographs of different tennis clubs. Students are given the task of ranking the clubs (e.g., formal-informal; public-private) through detailed attention to interpreting what they see. The teacher then helps them to understand (and extend) the cultural

frameworks they use on the task. With encouragement, students can realize *how* to learn about cultures, and such learning skills may include
learning how to learn from one another, particularly in multicultural
groups (Nelson, 1995, p. 33).

More explicit teaching is being developed in several countries. In an
elementary-level textbook, *English for China* (Alexander, Grant, & Liu,
1992), there is a text comparing British, Chinese, American, and Australian take-out food. Another, on the topic "Good Manners," includes
the following passage (Book 4, p. 89):

Ideas of what are good manners are not always the same in different countries.
For example, in Britain or America it is not polite to ask people how much
money they get in their jobs. People don't like talking about the cost of things
around the home, though in America they don't mind so much. But both in
Britain and America it is not polite to ask people how old they are.

There are other interesting differences between China and foreign countries.
In China, if someone says something good about you, it is polite to answer,
'No, not at all!' In Britain or America, a person answers 'Thank you', with a
big smile. This may be bad manners in China, but good manners in Britain or
America.

This is a constructive attempt to be explicit about intercultural behavior
and communication, especially in view of the limited language available
at this level. The text might be made more open by asking students how
target culture members might interpret the Chinese examples mentioned
(and vice versa). This would help students into an interpretative framework rather than simply teaching cultural rules.

Further examples are textbooks whose entire content is focused on
cross-cultural communication (Genzel & Cummings, 1986; Levine, Baxter, & McNulty, 1987; Hartmann, 1989; Levine & Adelman, 1993). These
include culture assimilators that present situations in which students must
make choices. They are then given feedback on the cultural consequences
of their choices. The setting in these books is predominantly American,
which may constrain their international use. However, there are difficulties in designing international target culture materials, as shown in photo
dictionaries. An example is Rosenthal and Freeman (1994), which has
an excellent range of photographs for vocabulary learning, intended for
Chinese learners of English as well as for English learners of Chinese.
However, this book is not a two-way cultural mirror: All the photographs
illustrate American and Canadian or British culture; there are none portraying anything Chinese.

Conclusions

EFL textbooks reflect not only the target cultures, but also source cultures and international cultures. EFL methods also reflect cultures, some-

times in ways that are overlooked, as cultures of learning. Cultural mismatches can occur, but knowledge and awareness of cultural approaches may alleviate problems. Ethnographic stances and explicit teaching may develop both students' and teachers' cultural knowledge.

The participants in classroom interaction are also major cultural resources; on them ultimately depends the full realization of the cultural content of textbooks. In this way, the method determines the use of the medium; medium and method are culturally interdependent. They reflect each other in a hall-of-mirrors effect.

A cultural focus on intercultural competence has communicative ends, but there are further important advantages: It may not only encourage the development of identity, but also encourage the awareness of others' identities and an element of stabilization in a world of rapid change. As Meyer (1991, p. 137) says, "Intercultural competence includes the capacity of stabilising one's self-identity in the process of cross-cultural mediation, and of helping other people to stabilise their self-identity."

Whatever the appearance to the contrary, few EFL materials are culturally neutral. Textbook evaluation checklists have their cultural slants, too. Even definitions of intercultural competence vary cross-culturally, as does its enactment (Martin, 1993, p. 20). Inevitably, then, our account will also have its cultural twists and turns, but we hope that we have woven together a few useful threads.

References

(N.a.). (1978). *English third steps*. Ministry of Education, Malagasy Republic.

Alderson, J. C., & Beretta, A. (Eds.). (1992). *Evaluating second language education*. Cambridge: Cambridge University Press.

Alexander, L., Grant, N. J. H., & Liu, D. (1992). *Junior English for China*. Beijing: People' s Education Press and Longman.

Allwright, R. (1981). What do we want teaching materials for? *English Language Teaching Journal, 36*(1), 5–18.

Al-Quarishi, K. D., Watson, M., Hafseth, J., & Hickman, D. (1988). *English for Asudi Arabia*. Riyadh: Ministry of Education.

Apple, M. W., & Christian-Smith, L. K. (1991). *The politics of the textbook*. New York: Routledge.

Arnaudet, M., & Barrett, M. E. (1984). *Approaches to academic reading and writing*. Englewood Cliffs, NJ: Prentice Hall.

Aston, G. (1995). Say "thank you": Some pragmatic restraints in conversational closings. *Applied Linguistics 16*(1), 57–86.

Atkinson, D. (1991). Discourse analysis and written discourse conventions. *Annual Review of Applied Linguistics, 11*, 57–76.

Auerbach, E., & McGrail, L. (1991). Rosa's challenge: Connecting classroom and community contexts. In S. Benesch (Ed.), *ESL in America: Myths and possibilities* (pp. 96–111). Portsmouth, NH: Boynton/Cook Heinemann.

Bachman, L. (1990). *Fundamental considerations in language testing*. Oxford: Oxford University Press.

Bakhtin, M. M. (1981). *The dialogic imagination*. M. Holquist (Ed.), C. Emerson & M. Holquist (Trans.). Austin: University of Texas Press.

Bakhtin, M. M. (1986). *Speech genres and other essays*. M. Holquist & C. Emerson (Eds.), and V. McGee (Trans.). Austin: University of Texas Press.

Bakhtin, M. M. (1990). *Art and answerability*. M. Holquist & V. Liapunov (Eds.). Austin: University of Texas Press.

Balk, M. (1995). *Language, ideology and power: English textbooks of two Koreas*. Seoul, Korea: Thaehaksa.

Bardovi-Harlig, K. (1992). Pragmatics as part of teacher education. *TESOL Journal, 1*(1), 28–32.

Bardovi-Harlig, K., & Hartford, B. (1993). Learning the rules of academic talk: A longitudinal study of pragmatic change. *Studies in Second Language Acquisition, 19*(3), 279–304.

Bardovi-Harlig, K., Hartford, B., Mahan-Taylor, R., Moorage, M., & Reynolds, D. (1991). Developing pragmatic awareness: Closing the conversation. *ELT Journal, 45*(1), 4–15.

Barro, A., Byram, M., Grimm, H., Morgan, C., & Roberts, C. (1993). Cultural studies for advanced language learners. In D. Graddol, L. Thompson, & M. Byram (Eds.), *Language and culture* (pp. 55–70). Clevedon, UK: BAAL and Multilingual Matters.

Barthes, R. (1977). *Image-music-text*. New York: Hill and Wang.

Bateson, G. (1972). *Steps to an ecology of mind*. New York: Balantine.

Beebe, L., Takahashi, T., & Uliss-Weltz, R. (1990). Pragmatic transfer in ESL refusals. In R. Scarcella, E. Andersen, & S. Krashen (Eds.), *Developing communicative competence in a second language* (pp. 75–94). New York: Newbury House.

Benesch, S. (1993). ESL, ideology, and the politics of pragmatism. *TESOL Quarterly, 27*(4), 705–717.

Bentahila, A., & Davies, E. (1989). Culture and language use: A problem for foreign language teachers. *IRAL, 27*, 99–112.

Bergman, M., & Kasper, G. (1993). Perception and performance in native and nonnative apology. In G. Kasper & S. Blum-Kulka (Eds.), *Interlanguage pragmatics* (pp. 82–107). New York: Oxford University Press.

Berk, M., & Diaz, R. (1992). *Private speech*. Hillsdale, NJ: Lawrence Erlbaum.

Berman, R., & Slobin, D. (1994). *Relating events in narratives. A crosslinguistic developmental study*. Hillsdale, NJ: Lawrence Erlbaum.

Bhatia, V. (1993). *Analysing genre: Language use in professional settings*. London: Longman.

Biber, D. (1988). *Variation across speech and writing*. Cambridge: Cambridge University Press.

Bickner, R., & Peyasantiwong, P. (1988). Cultural variation in reflective writing. In A. Purves (Ed.), *Writing across languages and cultures: Issues in contrastive rhetoric* (pp. 160–175). Newbury Park, CA: Sage.

Biq, Y.-O. (1990). Question words as hedges in Chinese. In L. F. Bouton & Y. Kachru (Eds.), *Pragmatics and Language Learning, 1*, 141–158.

Birdsong, D. (1992). Ultimate attainment in second language acquisition. *Language, 68*, 706–755.

Bloom, A. (1981). *The linguistic shaping of thought*. Hillsdale, NJ: Lawrence Erlbaum.

Blum-Kulka, S. (1989). Playing it safe: The role of conventionality in indirectness. In S. Blum-Kulka, J. House, & G. Kasper (Eds.), *Cross-cultural pragmatics: Requests and apologies* (pp. 37–70). Norwood, NJ: Ablex.

Blum-Kulka, S., House, J., & Kasper, G. (Eds.). (1989). *Cross-cultural pragmatics: Requests and apologies*. Norwood, NJ: Ablex.

Blum-Kulka, S., & Olshtain, E. (1984). Requests and apologies: A cross-cultural study of speech act realization patterns (CCSARP). *Applied Linguistics, 5*(3), 196–213.

Boas, F. (1911). Language and thought: Handbook of American Indian languages. *Bulletin of the Bureau of American Ethnology Number 30*, Part I. Reprinted in J. M. Valdes (Ed.) (1986), *Culture bound: Bridging the cultural gap in language teaching*. Cambridge: Cambridge University Press.

Borkin, A., & Reinhart, S. (1978). Excuse me and I'm sorry. *TESOL Quarterly, 12*(1), 57–69.

Bodde, D. (1991). *Chinese thought, society and science: The intellectual and social background of science and technology in pre-modern China*. Honolulu: University of Hawaii Press.

Boster, J. (1991). The information economy model applied to biological similarity judgment. In L. Resnick, J. Levine, & S. Teasley (Eds.), *Perspectives on socially shared cognition* (pp. 203–225). Washington DC: American Psychological Association.

Bourdieu, P. (1991). *Language and symbolic power.* Cambridge: Harvard University Press.

Bouton, L. F. (1988). A cross-cultural study of the ability to interpret implicatures in English. *World Englishes, 7*(2), 183–197.

Bouton, L. F. (1989). So they got the message, but how did they get it? *IDEAL, 4,* 119–149.

Bouton, L. F. (1990). The effective use of implicature in English: Why and how it should be taught in the ESL classroom. In L. Bouton & Y. Kachru (Eds.), *Pragmatics and Language Learning, 1,* 43–52.

Bouton, L. F. (1992a). Culture, pragmatics, and implicature. In H. Nyyssonen & L. Kuure (Eds.), *Acquisition of language – Acquisition of culture* (pp. 35–61). Jyvaskyla, Finland: AFinLA.

Bouton, L. F. (1992b). The interpretation of implicatures in English by NNS: Does it come automatically – without being explicitly taught? In L. Bouton & Y. Kachru (Eds.), *Pragmatics and Language, 3,* 183–197.

Bouton, L. F. (1994). Conversational implicature in a second language: Learned slowly when not deliberately taught. *Journal of Pragmatics, 24,* 157–167.

Breen, M. P., & Candlin, C. N. (1987). Which materials? A consumer's and designer's guide. In L. E. Sheldon (Ed.), *ELT textbooks and materials: Problems in evaluation and development.* London: Modern English Publications.

Britton, J., Burgess, T. Martin, N. McLeod, A. & Rosen, H. (1975). *The development of writing abilities.* London: Macmillan.

Brown, A., & Campione, J. (1994). Guided discovery in a community of learners. In K. McGilly (Ed.), *Classroom lessons: Integrating cognitive theory and classroom practice* (pp. 229–270). Cambridge: MIT Press.

Brown, J. D. (1995). *The elements of language curriculum: A systematic approach to program development.* Boston: Heinle and Heinle.

Brumfit, C. J. (1980). Seven last slogans. *Modern English Teachers, 7*(1), 30–31.

Bülow, F. M., Bulow, F. W., & Vettel, F. (1992). *Learning English, Topline.* Stuttgart: Klett.

Butterworth, G. (1993). Context and cognition in models of cognitive growth. In P. Light & G. Butterworth (Eds.), *Context and cognition: Ways of learning and knowing* (pp. 1–13). Hillsdale, NJ: Lawrence Erlbaum.

Buttjes, D. (1991). Mediating languages and cultures: The social and intercultural dimension restored. In D. Buttjes & M. Byram (Eds.), *Mediating languages and cultures: Towards an intercultural theory of foreign language education.* (pp. 3–16). Clevedon, UK: Multilingual Matters.

Buttjes, D., & Byram, M. (Eds.). (1991). *Mediating languages and cultures: Towards an intercultural theory of foreign language education.* Clevedon, UK: Multilingual Matters.

Byram, M. (1989). *Cultural studies in foreign language education.* Clevedon, UK: Multilingual Matters.

Byram, M. (1991). Teaching culture and language: Towards an integrated model. In D. Buttjes & M. Byram (Eds.), *Mediating languages and cultures: Towards an intercultural theory of foreign language education* (pp. 17–32). Clevedon, UK: Multilingual Matters.

Byram, M. (1993a). Language and culture learning: The need for integration. In M. Byram (Ed.), *Germany, its representation in textbooks for teaching German in Great Britain* (pp. 3–16). Frankfurt am Main: Diesterweg.

Byram, M. (1993b). Criteria for textbook evaluation. In M. Byram (Ed.), *Germany, its representation in textbooks for teaching German in Great Britain* (pp. 87–101). Frankfurt am Main: Diesterweg.

Byram, M., & Morgan, C. (1994). *Teaching-and-learning language-and-culture*. Clevedon, UK: Multilingual Matters.

Cameron, D., Frazer, E., Harvey, P., Rampton, M. B. H., and Richardson, K. (1992). *Researching language: Issues of power and method*. London, Routledge.

Canagarajah, A. S. (1993). Comments on Ann Raimes's "Out of the woods: Emerging traditions in the teaching of writing": Up the garden path: Second language writing approaches, local knowledge, and pluralism. *TESOL Quarterly, 27*(2), 301–310.

Canale, M. (1983). From communicative competence to communicative language pedagogy. In J. C. Richards & R. Schmidt (Eds.), *Language and communication* (pp. 2–28). London: Longman.

Canale, M., & Swain, M. (1980). Theoretical bases of communicative approaches to second language teaching and testing. *Applied Linguistics, 1*(1), 1–47.

Carbaugh, D. (1989). *Talking American: Cultural discourses on Donahue*. Norwood, NJ: Ablex.

Carbaugh, D. (1990). Communication rules in Donahue discourse. In D. Carbaugh (Ed.), *Cultural communication and intercultural contact*. Hillsdale, NJ: Lawrence Erlbaum.

Carlson, S. (1988). Cultural differences in writing and reasoning skills. In A. Purves (Ed.), *Writing across languages and cultures: Issues in contrastive rhetoric* (pp. 109–137). Newbury Park, CA: Sage.

Carson, J., & Leki, I. (Eds.). (1993). *Reading in the composition classroom*. Boston: Heinle and Heinle.

Celce-Murcia, M., Donnyei, Z., & Thurrell, S. (1995). Communicative competence: A pedagogically motivated model with content specifications. *Issues in Applied Linguistics, 6*(2), 5–35.

Chafe, W. (1985). Linguistic differences produced by differences between speaking and writing. In D. R. Olson, N. Torrance, & A. Hildyard (Eds.), *Literature, language, and learning: The nature and consequences of reading and writing* (pp. 105–123). Cambridge: Cambridge University Press.

Chen, J. (1990). *Confucius as a teacher: Philosophy of Confucius with special reference to its educational implications*. Beijing: Foreign Languages Press.

Cheng, I. (1976). *Clara Ho Tung: A Hong Kong lady, her family and her times*. Hong Kong: Chinese University Press.

Choi, Y.-H. (1988). Text structure in Korean students' argumentative writing in English. *World Englishes, 7*(2), 129–142.

Clyne, M. (1983). Linguistics and written discourse in particular languages. Contrastive studies: English and German. *Annual Review of Applied Linguistics, 3*, 38–49.

Clyne, M. (1987). Discourse structure and discourse expectations: Implications for Anglo-German academic communication. In L. Smith (Ed.), *Discourse across cultures: Strategies in World Englishes* (pp. 73–83). New York: Prentice Hall.

Coates, J. (1983). *The semantics of the modal auxiliaries*. Beckenham, UK: Croom Helm.

Cohen, A., & Olshtain, E. (1981). Developing a measure of sociolinguistic competence: The case of apology. *Language Learning, 31*(1), 113–134.

Cohen, A., Olshtain, E., & Rosenstein, D. (1986). Advanced EFL apologies: What remains to be learned. *International Journal of the Sociology of Language, 62*(1), 51–74.

Cole, M., & Engestrom, R. (1993). A cultural-historical approach to distributed cognition. In G. Salomon (Ed.), *Distributed cognitions: Psychological and educational considerations* (pp. 1–46). Cambridge: Cambridge University Press.

Collier, M. J., & Thomas, M. (1988). Cultural identity: An interpretive perspective. In Y. Y. Kim & W. Gudykunst (Eds.), *Theories in multicultural communication* (pp. 99–119). Newbury Park, CA: Sage.

Collins, P. (1991). The modals of obligation and necessity in Australian English. In K. Aijmer & B. Altenberg (Eds.), *English corpus linguistics* (pp. 145–165). New York: Longman.

Condon, J. (1986). "So near the United States." In J. M. Valdes (Ed.), *Culture bound: Bridging the cultural gap in language teaching* (pp. 85–93). Cambridge: Cambridge University Press.

Connor, U. (1987). Argumentative patterns in student essays: Cross-cultural differences. In U. Connor & R. Kaplan (Eds.), *Writing across languages: Analysis of L2 text* (pp. 57–71). Reading, MA: Addison-Wesley.

Connor, U. (1996). *Contrastive rhetoric*. Cambridge: Cambridge University Press.

Connor, U., & Kaplan, R. (Eds.). (1987). *Writing across languages: Analysis of L2 text*. Reading, MA: Addison-Wesley.

Connor, U., & Lauer, J. (1985). Understanding persuasive essay writing: linguistic/rhetoric approach. *Text, 5*(4), 309–326.

Connor, U., & Lauer, J. (1988). Cross-cultural variation in persuasive student writing. In A. Purves (Ed.), *Writing across languages and cultures: Issues in contrastive rhetoric* (pp. 109–137). Newbury Park, CA: Sage.

Coppieters, R. (1987). Competence differences between native and non-native speakers. *Language, 63,* 544–573.

Cortazzi, M., & Jin, L. (1996). Cultures of learning: Language classrooms in China. In H. Coleman (Ed.), *Society and the language classroom* (pp. 169–206). Cambridge: Cambridge University Press.

Cunningsworth, A. (1984). *Evaluating and selecting EFL teaching materials*. London: Heinemann.

Cunningsworth, A. (1995). *Choosing your coursebook*. London: Heinlemann.

Cushman, D., & Kincaid, D. L. (1987). Introduction and initial insights. In D. L. Kincaid (Ed.), *Communication theory: Eastern and Western perspectives* (pp. 1–10). San Diego, CA: Academic Press.

Damen, L. (1987). *Culture learning: The fifth dimension in the language classroom*. Reading, MA: Addison-Wesley.

Danesi, M. (1986). The role of metaphor in second language pedagogy. *Rassegna italiana di linguistica applicata, 18*(3), 1–10.

Danesi, M. (1993). Metaphorical competence in second language acquisition and second language teaching: The neglected dimension. In J. E. Alatis (Ed.), *Language, communication, and social meaning* (Georgetown University roundtable on languages and linguistics, 1992) (pp. 489–500). Washington, DC: Georgetown University Press.

de Bot, K., Ginsberg, R. B., & Kramsch, C. (1991). *Foreign language research in cross-cultural perspective.* Amsterdam: John Benjamins.

De Castell, S., Luke, A., & Luke, C. (1989). (Eds.). *Language, authority and criticism: Readings on the school textbook.* London: Falmer Press.

Dede, M., & Emre, M. (1988). *Spotlight on English.* Ankara: Hitit Product.

Devine, J. (1982). A question of universality: Conversational principles and implications. In M. A. Clarke & J. Handscombe (Ed.), *On TESOL 1982* (pp. 191–209). Washington, DC: TESOL.

Dinges, N. (1983). Intercultural competence. In D. Landis & R. W. Brislin (Eds.), *Handbook of intercultural training,* vol. 1 (pp. 176–202). New York: Pergamon.

Dissanayake, W. (1985). Towards a decolonized English: South Asian creativity in fiction. *World Englishes, 4*(2), 233–242.

Dissanayake, W. (1990). Self and modernism in Sri Lankan poetry in English. *World Englishes, 9*(2), 225–236.

Donato, R. (1994). Collective scaffolding in second language learning. In J. P. Lantolf & G. Appel (Eds.), *Vygotskian approaches to second language research* (pp. 33–56). Norwood, NJ: Ablex.

Donato, R., & Brooks, F. (1994). Looking across collaborative tasks: Capturing L2 discourse development. Paper presented at the 1994 AAAL Conference, Baltimore, Maryland.

Dorr-Bremme, D. (1990). Contextualization cues in the classroom: Discourse regulation and social control functions. *Language in Society, 19*(3), 379–402.

Drotner, K. (1992). Modernity and media panics. In M. Skovmand & K. Christian Schrøder (Eds.), *Media cultures: Reappraising transnational media* (pp. 42–62). London: Routledge.

Dwyer, M. A. (1984). A preliminary checklist for materials development. *English Teaching Forum* (April), 8–10.

Eggington, W. (1987). Written academic discourse in Korean: Implications for effective communication. In U. Connor & R. Kaplan (Eds.), *Writing across languages: Analysis of L2 text* (pp. 53–168). Reading, MA: Addison-Wesley.

Eisenstein, M., & Bodman, J. (1993). Expressing gratitude in American English. In G. Kasper & S. Blum-Kulka (Eds.), *Interlanguage pragmatics* (pp. 64–81). New York: Oxford University Press.

Elbow, P. (1973). *Writing without teachers.* London: Macmillan.

Engestrom, R. (1995). Voice as communication. *Mind, Culture, and Activity: An International Journal, 2,* 192–216.

Ervin, S. (1968). An analysis of the interaction of language, topic, and listener. In J. Fishman (Ed.), *Readings in the sociology of language* (pp. 161–187). The Hague: Mouton.

Ervin-Tripp, S. (1976). Is Sybil there? The structure of some American English directives. *Language in Society, 5,* 25–66.

Ervin-Tripp, S., Strage, A., Lampert, M., & Bell, N. (1987). Understanding requests. *Linguistics, 25,* 107–143.

Flowerdew, J., & Miller, L. (1995). On the notion of culture in L2 lectures. *TESOL Quarterly, 29*(2), 345–373.

Fodor, J. (1972). Some reflections on L. S. Vygotsky's *Thought and language.* *Cognition, 68,* 83–95.

Foucault, M. (1980). *Power/knowledge: Selected interviews and other writings, 1972–1977.* New York: Pantheon Books.

Fowler, R. (1988). Critical linguistics. In K. Malmkjaev (Ed.), *The linguistic encyclopedia.* New York: Routledge.

Fox, H. (1994). *Listening to the world: Cultural issues in academic writing.* Urbana, IL: National Council of Teachers of English.

Frawley, W., & Lantolf, J. P. (1985). Second language discourse: A Vygotskian perspective. *Applied Linguistics, 6,* 19–44.

Gardner, H. (1984). The development of competence in culturally defined domains: A preliminary framework. In R. Schweder & R. LeVine, (Eds.), *Culture theory* (pp. 257–275). Cambridge: Cambridge University Press.

Garner, R., & Alexander, L. (Eds.). (1994). *Beliefs about text and instruction with text.* Hillsdale, NJ: Lawrence Erlbaum.

Gee, J. P. (1990). *Social linguistics and literacies.* London: Falmer Press.

Geertz, C. (1973). *The interpretation of cultures.* New York: Basic Books.

Geertz, C. (1983). *Local knowledge.* New York: Basic Books.

Genzel, R. B., & Cummings, M. G. (1986). *Culturally speaking: A conversation and culture text for learners of English.* Singapore: HarperCollins.

Gibbons, J. (1987). *Code-mixing and code choice: A Hong Kong case study.* Clevedon, UK: Multilingual Matters.

Gibbs, R. (1984). Literal meaning and psychological theory. *Cognitive Science, 8,* 275–304.

Goffman, E. (1963). *Behavior in public places: Notes on the social organization of gatherings.* New York: Free Press.

Goffman, E. (1971). *Relations in public.* New York: Harper and Row.

Goffman, E. (1981). *Forms of talk.* Philadelphia: University of Pennsylvania Press.

Goody, E. (1995). Introduction: Some implications of a social origin of intelligence. In E. Goody (Ed.), *Social intelligence and interaction* (pp. 1–33). Cambridge: Cambridge University Press.

Grabois, H. (1997). Love and power: Word associations, lexical organization and second language acquisition. Unpublished doctoral dissertation, Cornell University, Ithaca, New York.

Green, G. M. (1989). *Pragmatics and natural language understanding.* Hillsdale, NJ: Lawrence Erlbaum.

Greene, M. (1993). Beyond insularity: Releasing the voices. *College ESL, 3*(1), 1–14.

Grice, H. P. (1975). Logic and conversational implicature. In P. Cole (Ed.), *Syntax and semantics* (pp. 411–458). New York: Academic Press.

Grice, H. P. (1978). Further notes on logic and conversation. In P. Cole (Ed.), *Syntax and semantics: Pragmatics* (pp. 113–127). New York: Academic Press.

Grice, H. P. (1981). Presupposition and conversational implicature. In P. Cole (Ed.), *Radical pragmatics* (pp. 183–198). New York: Academic Press.

Gudykunst, W. (1989). Cultural variability in ethnolinguistic identity. In S. Ting-Toomey & F. Korzenny (Eds.), *Language, communication, and culture* (pp. 222–243). Newbury Park, CA: Sage.

Gumperz, J. (1972). Introduction. In J. Gumperz & D. Hymes (Eds.), *Directions in sociolinguistics* (pp. 1–25). New York: Holt, Rinehart and Winston.

Gumperz, J. (1982). *Discourse strategies.* Cambridge: Cambridge University Press.

Gumperz, J. (1992). Contextualization and understanding. In A. Duranti & C. Goodwin (Eds.), *Rethinking context: Language as an interactive phenomenon* (pp. 229–252). Cambridge: Cambridge University Press.

Gumperz, J., & Hymes, D., (Eds.). (1972). *Directions in sociolinguistics: The ethonography of communication.* New York: Holt, Rinehart and Winston.

Hall, D., & Ames, R. T. (1987). *Thinking through Confucius.* Albany: State University of New York Press.

Hall, E. (1969). *The hidden dimension.* Garden City, NY: Doubleday.

Hall, E. (1976). *Beyond culture.* Garden City, NY: Doubleday.

Hall, E., & Hall, M. (1987). *Hidden differences: Doing business with the Japanese.* Garden City, NY: Doubleday.

Hall, J. K. (1993a). Oye, oye lo que ustedes no saben: Creativity, social power and politics in the oral practice of chismeando. *Journal of Linguistic Anthropology, 3*(1), 75–98.

Hall, J. K. (1993b). The role of oral practices in the accomplishment of our everyday lives: The sociocultural dimension of interaction with implications for the learning of another language. *Applied Linguistics, 14*(2), 145–166.

Hall, J. K. (1995). (Re)creating our worlds with words: A sociohistorical perspective of face-to-face interaction. *Applied Linguistics, 16*(2), 34–46.

Halliday, M. A. K. (1973). *Explorations in the function of language.* London: Edward Arnold.

Halliday, M. A. K. (1978). *Language as social semiotic.* London: Edward Arnold; Baltimore: University Park Press.

Halliday, M. A. K. (1985). *An introduction to functional grammar.* London: Edward Arnold.

Halliday, M. A. K. (1993). The act of meaning. In J. Alatis (Ed.), *Language, communication and social meaning* (pp. 7–21). Georgetown University Roundtable on Languages and Linguistics, 1992. Washington, DC: Georgetown University Press.

Halliday, M. A. K., & Hasan, R. (1976). *Cohesion in English.* London: Longman.

Hammer, M. R. (1989). Intercultural communication competence. In M. K. Asaute & W. B. Gudykunst (Eds.), *Handbook of interactional and intercultural communication* (pp. 247–260). Newbury Park, CA: Sage.

Han, Q. S., Lu, C., & Dong, Y. F. (1995). Quan mian guan che jiao xue da gang, nu li ti gao jiao xue zhi liang [Carrying out the national curriculum and making an effort to improve teaching quality] *Wai yu jie* [The world of foreign languages], No.1 (44–49).

Hansen, C. (1983). *Language and logic in ancient China.* Ann Arbor: University of Michigan Press.

Hansen, C. (1985). Punishment and dignity in China. In D. Munro (Ed.), *Individualism and holism: Studies in Confucian and Taoist values.* Ann Arbor, MI: Center for Chinese Studies.

Harmer, J. (1991). *The practice of English language teaching.* London: Longman.

Harris, R. (1981). *The language myth.* London: Duckworth.

Harrison, B. (Ed.), (1990). *Culture and the language classroom.* London: Modern English Publications/British Council.

Hartmann, P. (1989). *Clues to culture, a cross-cultural reading/writing book.* New York: Random House.

Hennig, U. J. (1991). *English G,* Band A6, 10th class. Frankfurt am Main: Cornetson.

Hermeren, L. (1978). *On modality in English.* Lund Studies in English, 53. Lund, Sweden: Gleerup.

Hinds, J. (1976). *Aspects of Japanese discourse.* Tokyo: Kaitakusha.

Hinds, J. (1980). Japanese expository prose. *Papers in Linguistics: International Journal of Human Communication, 13,* 117–158.

Hinds, J. (1983a). Linguistics and written discourse in particular languages. Contrastive studies: English and Japanese. *Annual Review of Applied Linguistics, 3,* 78–84.

Hinds, J. (1983b). Contrastive rhetoric: Japanese and English. *Text, 3*(2), 183–195.

Hinds, J. (1984). Retention of information using a Japanese style of presentation. *Studies in Language, 8*(1), 45–69.

Hinds, J. (1987). Reader versus writer responsibility: A new typology. In U. Connor & R. Kaplan (Eds.), *Writing across languages: Analysis of L2 text* (pp. 141–152). Reading, MA: Addison-Wesley.

Hinkel, E. (1994). Native and nonnative speakers' pragmatic interpretations of English texts. *TESOL Quarterly, 28*(2), 353–376.

Hinkel, E. (1995). The use modals verbs as a reflection of cultural values. *TESOL Quarterly, 29*(3), 325–344.

Hirokawa, R. (1987). Communication within the Japanese business organization. In D. L. Kincaid (Ed.), *Communication theory: Eastern and Western perspectives* (pp. 137–160). San Diego, CA: Academic Press.

Holmes, J. (1984). Hedging your bets and sitting on the fence: Some evidence for hedges as support structures. *Te Reo, 27*(1), 47–62.

Holmes, J., & Brown, D. (1987). Teachers and students learning about compliments. *TESOL Quarterly, 21*(4), 523–546.

Holquist, M. (1990). *Dialogism: Bakhtin and his world.* New York: Routledge.

Houtkoop-Steenstra, H. (1991). Opening sequences in Dutch telephone conversations. In D. Boden & D. Zimmerman (Eds.), *Talk and social structure: Studies in ethnomethodology and conversation analysis.* Cambridge: Polity Press.

Huang, M. C. (1996). Achieving cross-cultural equivalence in a study of American and Taiwanese requests. Unpublished doctoral dissertation, University of Illinois, (Urbana-Champaign).

Huebler, A. (1983). *Understatements and hedges in English.* Amsterdam: John Benjamins.

Huhn, P. (1978). Landeskune um Lehrbuch: Aspekte der Analyse, Kritik und Korrektiven Behandlung. In W. Kuhlwein & G. Radden (Eds.), *Sprache and Kultur.* Tubingen: Gunter Narr.

Hvitfeldt, C. (1992). Oral orientation in ESL academic writing. *College ESL, 2*(1), 29–39.

Hwang, S. J. J. (1987). *Discourse features of Korean narration.* Arlington, TX: Summer Institute of Linguistics and University of Texas.

Hymes, D. (1967). Models of the interaction of language and social setting. *Journal of Social Issues, 23*(2), 8–28.

Hymes, D. (1970). The ethnography of speaking. In J. Fishman (Ed.), *Readings in the sociology of language* (pp. 99–138). New York: Mouton.

Hymes, D. (1971). Sociolinguistics and the ethnography of speaking. In E. Ardener (Ed.), *Social anthropology and language* (pp. 47–93). London: Tavistock.

Hymes, D. (1972a). Models of the interaction of language and social life. In J. J. Gumperz & D. H. Hymes (Eds.), *Directions in sociolinguistics: The ethnography of communication* (pp. 35–71). New York: Holt, Rinehart and Winston.

Hymes, D. (1972b). *Reinventing anthropology*. New York: Pantheon Books.

Hymes, D. (1974). *Foundations in sociolinguistics: An ethnographic approach*. Philadelphia: University of Pennsylvania Press.

Hymes, D. (1996). *Ethnography, linguistics, narrative inequality*. Bristol, PA: Taylor and Francis.

Hymes, D. (Ed.), (1964). *Language in culture and society: A reader in linguistics and anthropology*. New York: Harper and Row.

Irujo, S. (1986). Don't put your leg in your mouth: Transfer in the acquisition of idioms in a second language. *TESOL Quarterly, 20*, 287–304.

Irujo, S. (1993). Steering clear: Avoidance in the production of idioms. *International Review of Applied Linguistics, 31*, 205–219.

Ivanic, R. (1994). I is for interpersonal: Discoursal construction of writer identities and the teaching of writing. *Linguistics and Education, 6*(1), 3–16.

Jacobs, R. (1995). *English syntax: A grammar for English language professionals*. Oxford: Oxford University Press.

Jenkins, R. (1992). *Pierre Bourdieu*. London: Routledge.

Jenks, C. (1993). *Culture*. London: Routledge.

Jin, L., & Cortazzi, M. (1993). Cultural orientation and academic language use. In D. Graddol, L. Thompson, & M. Byram (Eds.), *Language and culture* (pp. 84–97). Clevedon, UK: BAAL and Multilingual Matters.

Jin, L., & Cortazzi, M. (1994). This way is very different from Chinese ways: EAP needs and academic culture. In T. Dudley-Evans & M. Hewings (Eds.), *Evaluation and course design in EAP* (pp. 205–216). London: Macmillan.

Jin, L., & Cortazzi, M. (1995). A cultural synergy model for academic language use. In P. Bruthiaux, T. Boswood, & B. Du-Babcock (Eds.), *Explorations in English for professional communication* (pp. 41–56). Hong Kong: City University of Hong Kong.

Johns, A. (1997). *Text, role, and context*. Cambridge: Cambridge University Press.

Johnson, D. (1994). Who is "we"?: Constructing communities in U.S.-Mexico border discourse. *Discourse and Society, 5*(2), 207–231.

Johnson, D. (1995). Constructing social groups in discourse. Paper presented at the Ninth Annual International Conference on Pragmatics and Language Learning, Urbana-Champaign, Illinois, March.

Johnson, J., & Newport, E. (1989). Critical period effects in second language learning: The influence of maturational state on the acquisition of English as a second language. *Cognitive Psychology, 21*, 60–99.

Johnson, D., & Roen, D. (1989). Introduction. In D. Johnson & D. Roen (Eds.), *Richness in writing* (pp. 1–14). New York: Longman.

Johnson, R. K. (Ed.), (1989). *The second language curriculum*. Cambridge: Cambridge University Press.

John-Steiner, V. (1985). The road to competence in an alien land: A Vygotskian perspective on bilingualism. In J. V. Wertsch (Ed.), *Culture, communication, and cognition: Vygotskian perspectives* (pp. 348–371). Cambridge: Cambridge University Press.

Johnstone-Koch, B. (1983). Presentation as proof: The language of Arabic rhetoric. *Anthropological Linguistics, 25*(1), 47–59.

Jordan, E. (1992). Culture in the Japanese language classroom: A pedagogical paradox. In C. Kramsch & S. McConnell-Ginet (Eds.), *Text and context: Cross-disciplinary perspectives on language study* (pp. 156–168). Lexington, MA: D. C. Heath.

Jowett, B. (1990). The dialogues of Plato. In J. Mortimer (Ed.), *Great books of the Western world,* vol. 6. Chicago: Encyclopaedia Britannica.

Kachru, B. (1981). Socially realistic linguistics: The Firthian tradition. *International Journal of the Sociology of Language, 31,* 65–89.

Kachru, B. (1982). Meaning in deviation: Toward understanding non-native English texts. In B. Kachru (Ed.), *The other tongue: English across cultures* (pp. 325–350 [2d ed., 1992]). Urbana: University of Illinois Press.

Kachru, B. (1985). Standards, codification and sociolinguistic realism: The English language in the outer circle. In R. Quirk & H. Widdowson (Eds.), *English in the world: Teaching and learning the language and literatures* (pp. 11–30). Cambridge: Cambridge University Press.

Kachru, B. (1986). *The alchemy of English.* Oxford: Pergamon Press.

Kachru, B. (1987). The bilingual's creativity: Discoursal and stylistic strategies in contact literatures. In L. Smith (Ed.), *Discourse across cultures: Strategies in World Englishes* (pp. 125–140). New York: Prentice Hall.

Kachru, B. (Ed.), (1982). *The other tongue: English across cultures.* Oxford: Pergamon.

Kachru, B. (Ed.), (1992). *The other tongue: English across cultures,* 2d ed. Urbana: University of Illinois Press.

Kachru, Y. (1983). Linguistics and written discourse in particular languages: Contrastive studies: English and Hindi. *Annual Review of Applied Linguistics, 3,* 50–77.

Kachru, Y. (1987). Cross-cultural texts, discourse strategies and discourse interpretation. In L. Smith (Ed.), *Discourse across cultures: Strategies in World Englishes* (pp. 87–100). New York: Prentice Hall.

Kachru, Y. (1988). Writers in Hindi and English. In A. Purves (Ed.), *Writing across languages and cultures: Issues in contrastive rhetoric* (pp. 109–137). Newbury Park, CA: Sage.

Kachru, Y. (1992). Culture, style and discourse: Expanding poetics of English. In B. Kachru (Ed.), *The other tongue: English across cultures,* 2d ed., (pp. 340–352). Urbana: University of Illinois Press.

Kachru, Y. (1995a). Cultural meaning and rhetorical styles: Toward a framework for contrastive rhetoric. In B. Seidlhofer & G. Cook (Eds.), *Principles and practice in applied linguistics: Studies in honor of Henry G. Widdowson* (pp. 171–184). London: Oxford University Press.

Kachru, Y. (1995b). Culture, meaning and rhetorical style: Issues in writing research. Paper presented at the annual meeting of the Teachers of English to Speakers of Other Languages (TESOL), Long Beach, California.

Kachru, Y. (1996). Language and cultural meaning: Expository writing in South Asian English. In R. Baumgardner (Ed.), *South Asian English: Structure, use and users* (pp. 127–140). In the series *English in the Global Context.* Urbana: University of Illinois Press.

Kachru, Y. Culture and argumentative writing in world Englishes. In L. Smith (Ed.), (to appear). Honolulu: University of Hawaii Press.

Kachru, Y. (In press). Culture and communication in India. To appear in S. N. Sridhar & N. Mattoo (Eds.), *Ananya.*

Kaplan, R. (1966). Cultural thought patterns in inter-cultural education. *Language Learning, 16*, 1–20. Reprinted in K. Croft (Ed.) (1980), *Readings on English as a second language for teachers and teacher trainees* (pp. 399–418). Cambridge, MA: Winthrop.

Kaplan, R. (1972). *The anatomy of rhetoric: Prolegomena to a functional theory of rhetoric.* Philadelphia: Center for Curriculum Development.

Kaplan, R. (1987). Cultural thought patterns revisited. In U. Connor & R. Kaplan (Eds.), *Writing across languages: Analysis of L2 text* (pp. 9–20). Reading, MA: Addison-Wesley.

Kaplan, R. (1988). Contrastive rhetoric and second language learning: Notes toward a theory of contrastive rhetoric. In A. Purves (Ed.), *Writing across languages and cultures: Issues in contrastive rhetoric* (pp. 275–304). Newbury Park, CA: Sage.

Kasper, G. (1997). Can pragmatic competence be taught? (Net Work #6) (HTML document). Honolulu: University of Hawaii, Second Language Teaching and Curriculum Center. http://www.lll.hawaii.edu/nflrc/NetWorks/NW6/ [access: May 2, 1997].

Kasper, G., & Blum-Kulka, S. (Eds.). (1993). *Interlanguage pragmatics.* New York: Oxford University Press.

Kasper, G., & Dahl, M. (1991). Research methods in interlanguage pragmatics. *Studies in Second Language Acquisition, 13*(1), 215–247.

Kasper, G., & Schmidt, R. (1996). Developmental issues in interlanguage pragmatics. *Studies in Second Language Acquisition, 18*(1), 149–169.

Katchen, J. (1982). A structural comparison of American English and Farsi expository writing. *Papers in Linguistics, 15*, 165–180.

Kearney, M. (1984). *World view.* Novato, CA: Chandler and Sharp.

Keenan, E. O. (1976). The universality of conversational postulates. *Language and Society, 5*, 67–79.

Keil, F. C. (1989). *Concepts, kinds, and cognitive development.* Cambridge: MIT Press.

Keyes, D. (1966). *Flowers for Algernon.* New York: Harcourt, Brace and World.

Kim, Y. Y. (1991). Intercultural communication competence. In S. Ting-Toomey & F. Korzenny (Eds.), *Cross-cultural interpersonal communication* (pp. 259–275). Newbury Park, CA: Sage.

Kincaid, D. L. (1987). Communication East and West: Points of departure. In D. L. Kincaid (Ed.), *Communication theory: Eastern and Western perspectives* (pp. 1–17). San Diego, CA: Academic Press.

Kolers, P. A. (1963). Interlingual word associations. *Journal of Verbal Learning and Verbal Behavior, 2*, 291–300.

Kordes, H. (1991). Intercultural learning at school: Limits and possibilities. In D. Buttjes & M. Byram (Eds.), *Mediating languages and cultures: Towards an intercultural theory of foreign language education* (pp. 287–305). Clevedon, UK: Multilingual Matters.

Kowal, M., & Swain, M. (1994). Using collaborative language production tasks to promote students language awareness. *Language Awareness, 3*(2), 73–93.

Kramsch, C. (1991). Culture in language learning: A view from the States. In K. de Bot, R. B. Ginsberg, & C. Kramsch (Eds.), *Foreign language research in cross-cultural perspective* (pp. 217–240). Amsterdam: John Benjamins.

Kramsch, C. (1993a). *Context and culture in language teaching.* Oxford: Oxford University Press.

Kramsch, C. (1993b). Language study as border study: Experiencing difference. *European Journal of Education, 28*(3), 349–358.

Kress, G. (1994). Critical sociolinguistics. In R. E. Asher (Ed.), *The encyclopedia of language and linguistics*. Vols. 1–10. Oxford: Pergamon.

Kroll, B. (Ed.), (1990). *Second language writing: Research insights for the classroom*. Cambridge: Cambridge University Press.

Kwong, J. (1985). Changing political culture and changing curriculum: An analysis of language textbooks in the People's Republic of China. *Comparative Education, 21*(2), 197–208.

Labov, W. (1972). *Sociolinguistic patterns*. Philadelphia: University of Pennsylvania Press.

Labov, W. (1988). The judicial testing of linguistic theory. In D. Tannen (Ed.), *Linguistics in context: Connecting observation and understanding*. Norwood, NJ: Ablex.

Lakoff, G., & Johnson, M. (1980). *Metaphors we live by*. Chicago: University of Chicago Press.

Latulippe, L. (1992). *Writing as personal product*. Englewood Cliffs, NJ: Prentice Hall.

Lau, D.C. (1983). *Confucius: The analects (Lun y)*. Hong Kong: Chinese University Press.

Lave, J., & Wenger, E. (1991). *Situated learning: Legitimate peripheral participation*. Cambridge: Cambridge University Press.

Lee, L. C. (1992). Issues of identity. In L. C. Lee (Ed.), *Asian Americans: Collages of identities* (pp. 1–8). Ithaca, NY: Asian American Studies Program, Cornell University.

Lee, S.-H. (1987). The teachings of Yi Yulgok: Communication from a neo-Confucian perspective. In D. L. Kincaid (Ed.), *Communication theory: Eastern and Western perspectives* (pp. 101–114). San Diego, CA: Academic Press.

Leech, G. (1983). *The principles of pragmatics*. London: Longman.

Lee-Wong, S. (1994). Imperatives in requests: Direct or impolite: Observations from Chinese. *Pragmatics, 4*(4), 491–515.

Leki, I. (1991). Twenty-five years of contrastive rhetoric: Text analysis and writing pedagogies. *TESOL Quarterly, 25*(1), 123–143.

Leki, I. (1995). *Academic writing: Techniques and tasks*. 2d ed. New York: St. Martin's Press.

Levine, D. R., & Adelman, M. B. (1993). *Beyond language, cross-cultural communication*. 2d ed. Englewood Cliffs, NJ: Regents/Prentice Hall.

Levine, D. R., Baxter, J., & McNulty, P. (1987). *The culture puzzle, cross-cultural communication for English as a second language*. Englewood Cliffs, NJ: Prentice Hall.

Levinson, S. P. (1983). *Pragmatics*. Cambridge: Cambridge University Press.

Light, P., & Butterworth, G. (Eds.) (1993). *Context and cognition: Ways of learning and knowing*. Hillsdale, NJ: Lawrence Erlbaum.

Lovejoy, L. (1981). On the not-so-obvious: Pragmatics in ELT. *English Language Teaching Journal, 35*(1), 22–26.

Lowenberg, P. (1986). Non-native varieties of English: Nativization, norms and implications. *Studies in Second Language Acquisition, 8*(1), 1–18.

Lu, M.-Z. (1994). Professing multiculturalism: The politics of style in the contact zone. *College Composition and Communication, 45*(4), 442–458.

Lucy, J. A. (1996). The scope of linguistic relativity: An analysis and review of empirical research. In J. J. Gumperz & S. C. Levinson (Eds.), *Rethinking linguistic relativity* (pp. 37–69). Cambridge: Cambridge University Press.

Luke, A. (1989). Open and closed texts: The ideological/semantic analysis of textbook narratives. *Journal of Pragmatics, 13,* 53–80.

Luke, K.-K., & Richards, J. C. (1982). English in Hong Kong: Functions and status. *English World-wide, 3*(1), 47–64.

Lum, W. T. (1992). Matrices, paradoxes, and personal passions. In L. C. Lee (Ed.), *Asian Americans: Collages of identities* (pp. 31–40). Ithaca, NY: Asian American Studies Program, Cornell University.

Luria, A. R. (1973). *The working brain: An introduction to neuropsychology.* New York: Basic Books.

Lynch, B. K. (1996). *Language program evaluation.* Cambridge: Cambridge University Press.

Lyons, J. (1981). *Language and linguistics.* Cambridge: Cambridge University Press.

Lyster, R. (1994). The effect of functional-analytic teaching on aspects of French immersion students' sociolinguistic competence. *Applied Linguistics, 15*(3), 263–287.

Mandelbaum, J., & Pomerantz, A. (1991). What drives social action? In K. Tracy (Ed.), *Understanding face-to-face interaction* (pp. 151–166). Hillsdale, NJ: Lawrence Erlbaum.

Manes, J., & Wolfson, N. (1981). The compliment formula. In F. Coulmas (Ed.), *Rasmus Rask studies in pragmatic linguistics: Conversational routine explorations in standardized communication situations and prepatterned speech* (pp. 115–132). The Hague: Mouton.

Mao, L. M. (1991). I conclude not: Toward a pragmatic account of metadiscourse. *Rhetoric Review, 11*(2), 265–289.

Mar-Molinero, C. (1992). Cultural representations in foreign language teaching: A critique of four BBC courses. *Language, Culture and Curriculum, 5*(1), 1–10.

Martin, J. (1992). *Towards a theory of text for contrastive rhetoric: An introduction to issues of text for students and practitioners of contrastive rhetoric.* New York: Peter Lang.

Martin, J. N. (1993). Intercultural communication competence: A review. In R. L. Wiseman & J. Koester, *Intercultural communication competence* (pp. 16–29). Newbury Park, CA: Sage.

Martin, J. N. (Ed.). (1989). Intercultural communication competence. *International Journal of Intercultural Relations, 13,* 76–98.

Master, P. (1991). Active verbs with inanimate subjects in scientific prose. *English for Specific Purposes, 10*(1), 15–33.

Matalene, C. (1985). Contrastive rhetoric: An American writing teacher in China. *College English, 47,* 789–807.

Matthews, S., & Yip, V. (1994). *Cantonese: A comprehensive grammar.* London: Routledge.

Maynard, S. (1993). *Discourse modality: Subjectivity, emotion and voice in the Japanese language.* Amsterdam: John Benjamins.

McCarthy, M. (1994). It, this, and that. In M. Coulthard (Ed.), *Advances in written text analysis* (pp. 266–275). New York: Routledge.

McCunn, R. (1988). *Chinese American portraits: Personal histories (1828–1988).* San Francisco: Chronicle Books.

McDough, J., and Shaw, C. (1993). *Materials and methods in ELT: A teacher's guide.* Oxford: Blackwell.

Medgyes, P. (1992). Native or non-native: Who's worth more? *ELT Journal,* 46(4), 340–349.

Memering, D., & O'Hare, F. (1983). *The writer's work.* Englewood Cliffs, NJ: Prentice Hall.

Mendelsohn, D., Laufer, R., & Seskus, J. (1984). *Functioning in English.* Toronto: Hodder and Stoughton, with Dominie Press.

Meyer, M. (1991). Developing transcultural competence: Case studies of advanced language learners. In D. Buttjes & M. Byram (Eds.), *Mediating languages and cultures: Towards an intercultural theory of foreign language education* (pp. 136–158). Clevedon, UK: Multilingual Matters.

Miller, P., & Hoogstra, L. (1992). Language as tool in the socialization and apprehension of cultural meanings. In T. Schwartz, G. White, & C. Lutz (Eds.), *New directions in psychological anthropology* (pp. 83–101). Cambridge: Cambridge University Press.

Moerman, M. (1988). *Talking culture: Ethnography and conversation analysis.* Philadelphia: University of Pennsylvania Press.

Mohan, B., & Yeung Lo, W. A. (1985). Academic writing and Chinese students: Transfer and developmental factors. *TESOL Quarterly, 19*(3), 515–534.

Moll, L. (Ed.) (1990). *Vygotsky and education: Instructional implications and applications of sociohistorical psychology.* New York: Cambridge University Press.

Morain, G. (1986). Kinesics and cross-cultural understanding. In J. M. Valdes (Ed.), *Culture bound: Bridging the cultural gap in language teaching* (pp. 64–76). Cambridge: Cambridge University Press.

Morson, G., & Emerson, C. (1990). *Mikhail Bakhtin: Creation of a prosaics.* Stanford, CA: Stanford University Press.

Mura, D. (1992). Preparations (turning Japanese: A Sansei memoir). In L. C. Lee (Ed.), *Asian Americans: Collages of identities* (pp. 9–24). Ithaca, NY: Asian American Studies Program, Cornell University.

Myers, G. (1989). The pragmatics of politeness in scientific articles. *Applied Linguistics, 10*(1), 1–35.

Nayar, P. B. (1986). Acculturation or enculturation: Foreign students in the Untied States. In P. Byrd (Ed.), Teaching across cultures in the university ESL program. Washington, D.C.: National Association of Foreign Student Affairs, pp. 1–13.

Nelson, C. (1991). New Englishes, new discourses, new speech acts. *World Englishes, 10*(3), 317–323.

Nelson, G. (1995). Considering culture: Guidelines for ESL/EFL textbook writers. In P. Byrd (Ed.), *Material writers guide* (pp. 23–42). New York: Heinle & Heinle.

Newman, F., & Holzman, L. (1993). *Lev Vygotsky: Revolutionary scientist.* London: Routledge.

Nuñez, D. (1988). *El libro de inglés.* Caracas: Maracay.

Ohta, A. S. (1991). Evidentiality and politeness in Japanese. *Issues in Applied Linguistics, 2*(2), 183–210.

Oliver, R. (1971). *Communication and culture in ancient India and China.* Syracuse, NY: Syracuse University Press.

Olshtain, E. (1983). Sociocultural competence and language transfer: The case of Apology. In S. Gass & L. Selinker (Eds.), *Language transfer in language learning* (pp. 232–249). Rowley, MA: Newbury House.

Olshtain, E., & Cohen, A. (1991). Teaching speech act behavior to nonnative speakers. In M. Celce-Murcia (Ed.), *Teaching English as a second or foreign language* (pp. 154–165). New York: Newbury House.

Olshtain, E., & Weinbach, L. (1993). Interlanguage features of the speech act of complaining. In G. Kasper & S. Blum-Kulka (Eds.), *Interlanguage pragmatics* (pp. 108–121). New York: Oxford University Press.

Ostler, S. (1987). English in parallels: A comparison of English and Arabic prose. In U. Connor & R. Kaplan (Eds.), *Writing across languages: Analysis of L2 text* (pp. 169–184). Reading, MA: Addison-Wesley.

Owen, C. (1993). Corpus-based grammar and the Heineken effect: Lexico-grammatical description for language learners. *Applied Linguistics, 14*(2), 167–187.

Palincsar, A. S., & Brown, A. L. (1984). Reciprocal teaching of comprehension-fostering and comprehension-monitoring activities. *Cognition and Instruction, 2,* 117–175.

Pandharipande, R. (1983). Linguistics and written discourse in particular languages: Contrastive studies: English and Marathi. *Annual Review of Applied Linguistics, 3,* 118–136.

Park, Y. M. (1988). Academic and ethnic background as factors affecting writing performance. In A. Purves (Ed.), *Writing across languages and cultures: Issues in contrastive rhetoric* (pp. 261–273). Newbury Park, CA: Sage.

Patthey-Chavez, G. G., and C. Gergen. (1992). Culture as an instructional resource in the multiethnic composition classroom. *Journal of Basic Writing, 11/1,* 75–91.

Paulston, C. (1975). Linguistic and communicative competence in the ESOL classroom. *TESOL Quarterly, 8/3,* 347–362.

Pavlenko, A. (1997). *Bilingualism and cognition.* Unpublished doctoral dissertation, Cornell University, Ithaca, New York.

Pavlenko, A., & Lantolf, J. P. (1997). Voices from the margins: Second language learning as a (re)construction of self. Paper presented at the Annual Meeting of the American Association for Applied Linguistics, Orlando, Florida, March.

Pennington, M. (1994). *Forces shaping a dual-code society: An interpretive review of the literature on language use and language attitudes in Hong Kong.* Research Report No. 35, Department of English, City Polytechnic of Hong Kong.

Perelman, C. (1992). Rhetoric. In *Encyclopaedia Britannica,* vol. 26, p. 759. Chicago: Encyclopaedia Britannica.

Perkins, D., & Salomon, G. (1989). Are cognitive skills context-bound? *Educational Researcher, 18*(1), 16–25.

Pierce, B. N. (1995). Social identity, investment, and language learning. *TESOL Quarterly, 29*(1), 9–31.

Pierson, H. D. (1987). Language attitudes and language proficiency: A review of selected research. In R. Lord & H. N. L. Cheng (Eds.), *Language education in Hong Kong* (pp. 2–30). Hong Kong: Chinese University Press.

Pierson, H. D. (1993). Societal accommodation to English and Putonghua in Cantonese-speaking Hong Kong. Paper presented at the Thirty-fourth International Conference on Asian and North African Studies, Hong Kong, August.

Pollio, H., Barlow, J., Fine, H., & Pollio, M. (1977). *The poetics of growth: Figurative language in psychology, psychotherapy, and education.* Hillsdale, NJ: Lawrence Erlbaum.

Poole, D. (1991). Discourse analysis in ethnographic research. *Annual Review of Applied Linguistics, 11,* 42–56. Cambridge: Cambridge University Press.

Potter, M. (1990). *Panorama.* London: Macmillan.

Pratt, M. L. (1991). Arts of the contact zone. *Profession, 91,* 33–40.

Prentice, D. J. (1987). Malay (Indonesian and Malaysian). In B. Comrie (Ed.), *The world's major languages* (pp. 913–935). Oxford: Oxford University Press.

Priesack, T., & Tomscha, T. (1993). *One world, secondary English.* New York: Prentice Hall.

Prodromou, L. (1992). What culture? Which culture? Cross-cultural factors in language learning. *ELT Journal, 46*(1), 39–49.

Purves, A. (Ed.), (1988). *Writing across languages and cultures: Issues in contrastive rhetoric.* Newbury Park, CA: Sage.

Quinn, N., & Holland, D. (1987). Culture and cognition. In D. Holland & N. Quinn (Eds.), *Cultural models in language and thought* (pp. 3–40). Cambridge: Cambridge University Press.

Quirk, R., Greenbaum, S., Leech, G., & Svartvik, J. (1985). *A comprehensive grammar of the English language.* New York: Longman.

Raimes, A. (1991). Out of the woods: Emerging traditions in the teaching of writing. *TESOL Quarterly, 25*(3), 407–430.

Raimes, A. (1992). *Exploring through writing.* 2d ed. New York: St. Martin's Press.

Ratner, C. (1991). *Vygotsky's sociocultural psychology and its contemporary application.* New York: Plenum Press.

Rea-Dickens, P., & Germaine, K. (1992). *Evaluation.* Oxford: Oxford University Press.

Reeder, K., & Wakefield, J. (1987). The development of young children's speech act comprehension: How much language is necessary? *Applied Psycholinguistics, 8,* 1–18.

Reid, J. (1983). *Teaching ESL Writing.* Englewood Cliffs, NJ: Prentice Hall.

Reid, J. (1989). English as a second language composition in higher education: The expectations of the academic audience. In D. Johnson & D. Roen (Eds.), *Richness in writing* (pp. 193–206). New York: Longman.

Reynolds, D. (1993). Illocutionary acts across languages: Editorializing in Egyptian English. *World Englishes, 12*(1), 35–46.

Richards, J. C. (1980). Conversation. *TESOL Quarterly, 14,* 413–432.

Richards, J. C. (1993). Beyond the textbook: The role of commercial materials in language teaching. *Perspectives, 5*(1), 43–53.

Richards, J. C., & Lockhart, C. (1994). *Reflective teaching in second language classrooms.* Cambridge: Cambridge University Press.

RiSager, K. (1991). Cultural references in European textbooks: An evaluation of recent tendencies. In D. Buttjes & M. Byram (Eds.), *Mediating languages and cultures: Towards an intercultural theory of foreign language education* (pp. 180–192). Clevedon, UK: Multilingual Matters.

Robinson, G. (1988). *Cross-cultural understanding.* New York: Prentice Hall.

Robinson, G. (1991). Second culture acquisition. In J. E. Alatis (Ed.), *Linguistics and language pedagogy: State of the art* (pp. 114–122). Washington, DC: Georgetown University Press.

Robinson-Stuart, G., & Nocon, H. (1996). Second culture acquisition: Ethnography in the foreign language classroom. *Modern Language Journal, 80*, 431–449.

Rodby, J. (1992). *Appropriating literacy: Writing and reading in English as a second language.* Portsmouth, NH: Boynton/Cook.

Rogoff, B. (1990). *Apprenticeship in thinking: Cognitive development in social context.* New York: Oxford University Press.

Rogoff, B., & Lave, J. (Eds.). (1984). *Everyday cognition: Its development in social contexts.* Cambridge: Harvard University Press.

Rosaldo, M. (1984). Toward an anthropology of self and feeling. In R. Shweder & R. LeVine (Eds.). *Culture theory* (pp. 137–157). Cambridge: Cambridge University Press.

Rose, K. (1994a). On the validity of discourse completion tests in non-Western contexts. *Applied Linguistics, 15*(1), 1–14.

Rose, K. (1994b). Pragmatic consciousness-raising in an EFL context. In L. F. Bouton & Y. Kachru (Eds.), *Pragmatics and language learning 5, 2–63.* University of Illinois, Urbana-Champaign.

Rose, K. (1995). Nonnative-speaking teachers and the teaching of pragmatics. Paper presented at the Third International Conference on Teacher Education in Second Language Teaching, City University of Hong Kong, March.

Rose, K. (1997). Pragmatics in the classroom: Theoretical concerns and practical possibilities. In L. F. Bouton (Ed.), *Pragmatics and Language Learning, 8, 267–295.* University of Illinois at Urbana-Champaign.

Rosenshine, B., & Meister, C. (1994). Reciprocal teaching: A review of the research. *Review of Educational Research, 64*(4), 479–530.

Rosenthal, M. S., & Freeman, D. B. (1994). *Longman English-Chinese photo dictionary.* London: Longman.

Rubin, D. (Ed.). (1995). *Composing social identity in written language.* Hillsdale, NJ: Lawrence Erlbaum.

Said, E. (1978). *Orientalism.* New York: Pantheon Books.

Sanders, R. E. (1987). *Cognitive foundations of calculated speech.* Albany: SUNY Press.

Sanders, R. E. (1995). Neo-rhetorical theory: The enactment of role-identities as interactive and rhetorical. In S. Sigman (Ed.), *The consequentiality of communication* (pp. 155–183). Hillsdale, NJ: Lawrence Erlbaum.

Sapir, E. ([1921] 1961). *Culture, language, and personality.* Berkeley: University of California Press.

Savignon, S. (1983). *Communicative competence: Theory and classroom practice, texts and contexts in second language learning.* Reading, MA: Addison-Wesley.

Saville-Troike, M. (1989). *The ethnography of communication.* Oxford: Blackwell.

Scarcella, R. (1984). How writers orient their readers to expository essays: A comparative study of native and non-native English writers. *TESOL Quarterly, 18*(4), 671–688.

Scarcella, R. (1990). Communication difficulties in second language production, development, and production. In R. Scarcella, E., Anderson, & S. Krashen (Eds.), *Developing communicative competence in a second language* (pp. 337–352). New York: Newbury House.

Scarcella, R. (1994). *Power through the written word.* Boston: Heinle and Heinle.

Scarcella, R., & Lee, C. (1989). Different paths to writing proficiency in a second language? A preliminary investigation of ESL writers of short-term and long-term residence in the United States. In M. Eisenstein (Ed.), *The dynamic interlanguage* (pp. 137–153). New York: Plenum Press.

Schegloff, E. (1972). Sequencing in conversational openings. In J. Gumperz & D. Hymes (Eds.), *Directions in sociolinguistics*. New York: Holt, Rinehart and Winston.

Schiffrin, D. (1987). *Discourse markers*. Cambridge: Cambridge University Press.

Schmidt, R. (1993). Conscious learning and interlanguage pragmatics. In G. Kasper & S. Blum-Kulka (Eds.), *Interlanguage pragmatics* (pp. 21–42). New York: Oxford University Press.

Schmidt, R. (1994). Deconstructing consciousness in search of useful definitions for applied linguistics. *AILA Review, 11*, 11–26.

Scollon, R. (1991). Eight legs and one elbow: Stance and structure in Chinese English compositions. *Proceedings of the Second North American Conference on Adult and Adolescent Literacy*. Hong Kong.

Scollon, R. (1993). Maxims of stance. *Research Report No. 26*. Hong Kong: City Polytechnic of Hong Kong.

Scollon, R. (1994). As a matter of fact: The changing ideology of authorship and responsibility in discourse. *World Englishes, 13*(1), 33–46.

Scollon, R. (1995). From sentences to discourses, ethnography to ethnographic: Conflicting trends in TESOL research. *TESOL Quarterly, 29*(2), 381–384.

Scollon, R. (1998). *Mediated discourse as social interaction: A study of news discourse*. London: Longman.

Scollon, R., & Scollon, S. (1981). *Narrative, literacy and face in interethnic communication*. Norwood, NJ: Ablex.

Scollon, R., & Scollon, W. S. (1991). Topic confusion in English-Asian discourse. *World Englishes, 10*(2), 113–125.

Scollon, R., & Scollon, S. Wong. (1995). *Intercultural communication*. Oxford: Blackwell.

Scollon, S. (1993). Metaphors of self and communication English and Chinese. *Working Papers of the Department of English City Polytechnic of Hong Kong, 5*, 41–62.

Shannon, P. (1987). Commercial reading materials, a technological ideology, and the de-skilling of teachers. *The Elementary School Journal, 87*(3), 307–329.

Sharwood-Smith, M. (1981). Consciousness-raising and the second language learner. *Applied Linguistics, 7*(3), 239–256.

Shatz, M., & L. McCloskey. (1984). Answering appropriately: A developmental perspective on conversational knowledge. In S. Kuczaj (Ed.), *Discourse development: Progress in cognitive development research* (pp. 19–36). New York: Springer-Verlag.

Sheldon, L. E. (1988). Evaluating ELT textbooks and materials. *ELT Journal, 42*(4), 237–246.

Shen, F. (1989). The classroom and the wider culture: Identity as a key to learning English composition. *College Composition and Communication, 40*(4), 459–466.

Shore, B. (1996). *Culture in mind. Cognition, culture, and the problem of meaning*. New York: Oxford University Press.

Shweder, R. (1984). A colloquy of culture theorists. In R. Shweder & R. LeVine (Eds.), *Culture theory* (pp. 1–26). Cambridge: Cambridge University Press.

Shweder, R., and LeVine, R. (Eds.), (1984). *Culture theory*. Cambridge: Cambridge University Press.

Skierso, A. (1991). Textbook selection and evaluation. In M. Celce-Murcia (Ed.), *Teaching English as a second or foreign language* (pp. 432–453). Boston: Heinle and Heinle.

Skovmand, M. (1992). Barbarous TV international: Syndicated *Wheel of Fortune*. In M. Skovmand & K. Christian Schrøder (Eds.), *Media cultures: Reappraising transnational media* (pp. 84–103). London: Routledge.

Smith, L. (1987). Introduction: Discourse strategies and cross-cultural communication. In L. Smith (Ed.), *Discourse across cultures: Strategies in World Englishes* (pp. 1–7). New York: Prentice Hall.

Smith, L. (Ed.), (1987). *Discourse across cultures: Strategies in World Englishes*. New York: Prentice Hall.

Smoke, T. (1992). *A writer's workbook*. New York: St. Martin's Press.

Snow, C. (1989). Understanding social interaction and language acquisition: Sentences are not enough. In M. Bornstein & J. Bruner (Eds.), *Interaction in human development* (pp. 83–103). Hillsdale, NJ: Lawrence Erlbaum.

Snow, D. (1996). *More than a native speaker: An introduction for volunteers teachign abroad*. Alexandria, VA: TESOL.

Snow, C., Cancino, H., de Temple, J., & Schley, S. (1991). Giving formal definitions: A linguistic or metalinguistic skill? In E. Bialystok (Ed.), *Language processing in bilingual children* (pp. 90–112). Cambridge: Cambridge University Press.

Snow, C., Perlman, R. Y., Gleason, J. B., & Hooshyar, N. (1990). Developmental perspectives on politeness: Sources of children's knowledge. *Journal of Pragmatics, 14*(2), 289–305.

Snow, C., Shonkoff, F., Lee, K., & Levin, H. (1986). Learning to play doctor: Effects of sex, age, and experience in the hospital. *Discourse Processes, 9*, 461–473.

Sokolov, A. N. (1972). *Inner speech and thought*. New York: Plenum Press.

Spack, R. (1985). Literature, reading, writing and the ESL student. *TESOL Quarterly, 19*(4), 703–725.

Spencer-Oatey, H. (1993). Conceptions of social relations and pragmatic research. *Journal of Pragmatics, 20*, 27–47.

Stewart, E. (1972). *American cultural patterns: A cross-cultural perspective*. Yarmouth, ME: Intercultural Press.

Stigler, J., Shweder, R., & Herdt, G. (Eds.). (1990). *Cultural psychology*. Cambridge: Cambridge University Press.

Stone, A., & Forman, E. (1988). Cognitive development in language-learning disabled adolescents: A study of problem-solving performance in an isolation-of-variables task. *Learning Disabilities Research, 3*(2), 107–114.

Stray, C. (1994). Paradigms regained: Towards a historical sociology of the textbook. *Journal of Curriculum Studies, 26*(1), 1–29.

Strevens, P. (1987). Cultural barriers to language learning. In L. Smith (Ed.), *Discourse across cultures: Strategies in World Englishes* (pp. 169–179). New York: Prentice Hall.

Swales, J. (1990). *Genre analysis*. Cambridge: Cambridge University Press.

Swales, J., & Feak, C. (1994). *Academic writing for graduate students*. Ann Arbor: University of Michigan Press.

Szalay, L. B. (1984). An in-depth analysis of cultural/ideological belief systems. *Mankind Quarterly, 25,* 71–100.

Szalay, L. B., and Brent, J. (1967). The analysis of cultural meanings through free verbal associations. *Journal of Social Psychology, 72,* 161–187.

Szalay, L. B., Lynse, D. A., & Bryson, J. A. (1972). Designing and testing cogent communications. *Journal of Cross-Cultural Psychology, 3,* 247–258.

Szalay, L. B., & Windle, C. (1968). Relative influence of linguistic versus cultural factors on free verbal associations. *Psychological Reports, 22,* 43–51.

Tadros, A. (1994). Predictive categories in expository text. In M. Coulthard (Ed.), *Advances in written text analysis* (pp. 69–82). New York: Routledge.

Takahashi, T., & Beebe, L. (1993). Cross-linguistic influence in the speech act of correction. In G. Kasper & S. Blum-Kulka (Eds.), *Interlanguage pragmatics* (pp. 138–157). New York: Oxford University Press.

Takaki, R. (1989). *Strangers from a different shore: A history of Asian Americans.* New York: Penguin Books.

Tannen, D. (1986). *This is not what I meant: How controversial style makes or breaks relations with others.* New York: William Morris.

Taylor, G., & Chen, T. (1991). Linguistic, cultural, and subcultural issues in contrastive discourse analysis: Anglo-American and Chinese scientific texts. *Applied Linguistics, 12*(2), 319–336.

Teo, A. (1995). Analysis of newspaper editorials: A study of argumentative structure. Unpublished doctoral dissertation, University of Illinois: Urbana-Champaign.

Tharp, R., & Gallimore, R. (1988). *Rousing minds to life: Teaching, learning and schooling in social context.* Cambridge: Cambridge University Press.

Thomas, J. (1983). Cross-cultural pragmatic failure. *Applied Linguistics, 4*(1), 91–112.

Thomas, J. (1984). Cross-cultural discourse as "unequal encounter": Toward a pragmatic analysis. *Applied Linguistics, 5*(2), 226–235.

Thompson, J. (1990). *Ideology and modern culture.* Stanford, CA: Stanford University Press.

Thumboo, E. (1985). Twin perspectives and multi-ecosystems: Tradition for a commonwealth writer. *World Englishes, 4*(2): 213–221.

Thumboo, E. (1990). Conversion of the tribes: Societal antecedents and the growth of Singapore poetry. *World Englishes, 9*(2), 155–173.

Ting-Toomey, S. (1993). Communicative resourcefulness, an identity negotiation perspective. In R. L. Wiseman & J. Koester (Eds.), *Intercultural communication competence* (pp. 72–111). Newbury Park, CA: Sage.

Tirkkonen-Condit, S. (1985). Argumentative text structure and translation. Unpublished doctoral dissertation, University of Jyvaskyla, Finland.

Tomalin, B., & Stempleski, S. (1993). *Cultural awareness.* Oxford: Oxford University Press.

Tsao, F.-F. (1983). Linguistics and written discourse in particular languages: Contrastive studies: English and Mandarin. *Annual Review of Applied Linguistics, 3,* 99–117.

Tsujimura, A. (1987). Some characteristics of the Japanese way of communication. In D. L. Kincaid (Ed.), *Communication theory: Eastern and Western perspectives* (pp. 115–126). San Diego, CA: Academic Press.

Tucker, A. (1995). *Decoding ESL: International students in the American college classroom.* Portsmouth, NH: Boynton/Cook.

Tulviste, P. (1991). *The cultural-historical development of thinking.* New York: Nova Science.

Turner, J. A. (1982). *Kwang Tung or five years in South China.* Hong Kong: Oxford University Press.

Turner, V. (1974). *Dramas, fields and metaphors.* Ithaca, NY: Cornell University Press.

Ushakova, T. N. (1994). Inner speech and second language acquisition: An experimental-theoretical approach. In J. P. Lantolf & G. Appel (Eds.), *Vygotskian approaches to second language research* (pp. 135–156). Norwood, NJ: Ablex.

Vahapassi, A. (1988). The problem of selection of writing tasks in cross-cultural study. In A. Purves (Ed.), *Writing across languages and cultures: Issues in contrastive rhetoric* (pp. 51–78). Newbury Park, CA: Sage.

Valdes, G. (1992). Bilingual minorities and language issues in writing. *Written Communication, 9*(1), 85–136.

Valdes, J. M. (Ed.), (1986). *Culture bound: Bridging the cultural gap in language teaching.* Cambridge: Cambridge University Press.

Valentine, T. (1988). Developing discourse types in non-native English: Strategies of gender in Hindi and Indian English. *World Englishes, 7*(2), 143–158.

Valentine, T. (1991). Getting the message across: Discourse markers in Indian English. *World Englishes, 10*(3), 325–334.

Valentine, T. (1995). What's the point? Storytelling by women of India. In Y. Kachru (Ed.), *Language, gender and power.* Special issue of *Studies in the Linguistic Sciences 25*(2).

van Lier, L. (1988). *The classroom and the language learner: Ethnography and second-language classroom research.* London: Longman.

Vandrick, S. (1995). Privileged ESL university students. *TESOL Quarterly, 29*(2), 375–380.

Vyas, B., Tiwari, B., & Srivastav, R. (1972). *hindī vyākaran aur racnā* (Hindi grammar and composition). New Delhi, India: National Council of Educational Training and Research.

Vygotsky, L. S. (1978). *Mind in society.* Cambridge: Harvard University Press.

Vygotsky, L. S. (1981). The genesis of higher mental functions. In J. V. Wertsch (Ed.), *The concept of activity in Soviet psychology* (pp. 144–189). Armonk, NY: Sharpe.

Vygotsky, L. S. (1986). *Thought and language.* Cambridge: MIT Press.

Walker, M. (1994). *Success – communicating in English,* Books 1&2. New York: Addison-Wesley.

Wall, A. (1987). *Say it naturally.* New York: CBS College Publishing.

Wallace, M. J. (1991). *Training foreign language teachers: A reflective approach.* Cambridge: Cambridge University Press.

Weitzman, E. (1993). Interlanguage requestive hints. In G. Kasper & S. Blum-Kulka (Eds.), *Interlanguage pragmatics* (pp. 123–137). New York: Oxford University Press.

Weizman, E. (1989). Requestive hints. In S. Blum-Kulka, J. House, & G. Kasper (Eds.), *Cross-cultural pragmatics: Requests and apologies* (pp. 71–95). Norwood, NJ: Ablex.

Wenham, M. (1991). Education as interaction. *Journal of Philosophy of Education, 25*(2), 235–246.

Wertsch, J. V. (1985). *Vygotsky and the social formation of mind.* Cambridge: Harvard University Press.

Wertsch, J. V. (1987). Collective memory: Issues from a sociohistorical perspective. *Quarterly Newsletter of the Laboratory of Comparative Human Cognition, 9*(1), 19–22.

Wertsch, J. V. (1991). *Voices of the mind.* Cambridge: Harvard University Press.

White, L., & Genesee, F. (1996). How native is near-native? The issue of ultimate attainment in adult second language acquisition. *Second Language Research, 12,* 233–265.

White, R. V. (1988). *The ELT curriculum, design, innovation and management.* Oxford: Blackwell.

Whorf, B. (1956). *Language, thought, and reality: Selected writing of Benjamin Lee Whorf.* Cambridge: MIT Press.

Williams, J. (1985). *Style.* Glenview, IL: Scott, Foresman.

Winkler, A., & McCuen, J. R. (1984). *Rhetoric made plain.* New York: Harcourt Brace Jovanovich.

Winner, E. (1982). *Invented worlds: The psychology of the arts.* Cambridge: Harvard University Press.

Wiseman, R. L., & Koester, J. (1993). *Intercultural communication competence.* Newbury Park, CA: Sage.

Wolfson, N. (1983). An empirically based analysis of compliments. In N. Wolfson & E. Judd (Eds.), *Sociolinguistics and language acquisition* (pp. 82–85). Rowley, MA: Newbury House.

Wolfson, N. (1989). *Perspectives: Sociolinguistics and TESOL.* Rowley, MA: Newbury House.

Wolfson, N., & Judd, E. (1983). *Sociolinguistics and language acquisition.* Rowley, MA: Newbury House.

Wong, H. (1990). The use of rhetorical questions in written argumentative discourse. In L. Bouton & Y. Kachru (Eds.), *Pragmatics and Language Learning, 1,* 187–208.

Wong, S. L. (1987). The language learning situation of Asian immigrant students in the U.S.: A socio- and psycholinguistic perspective. *NABE Journal, 11*(3), 203–234.

Wong, S. L. (1992). Centers: A meditation on Asian American identity and aesthetics. In L. C. Lee (Ed.), *Asian Americans: Collages of identities* (pp. 87–100). Ithaca, NY: Asian American Studies Program, Cornell University.

Wu, H.-F., De Temple, J., Herman, J., & Snow, C. (1994). "L' animal qui fait oink! oink!": Bilingual children's oral and written picture descriptions in English and French under varying conditions. *Discourse Processes, 18,* 141–164.

Yorio, C. (1989). Idiomaticity as an indicator of second language proficiency. In K. Hyltenstam and L. K. Obler (Eds). *Bilingualism across the lifespan: Aspects of acquisition, maturity, and loss* (pp. 55–72). Cambridge: Cambridge University Press.

Yoshida, K. (1990). Knowing vs. behaving vs. feeling: Studies on Japanese bilinguals. In L. A. Arena (Ed.), *Language proficiency* (pp. 19–40). New York: Plenum Press.

Yum, J.-O. (1987). Korean philosophy and communication. In. D. L. Kincaid

(Ed.), *Communication theory: Eastern and Western perspectives* (pp. 71–86). San Diego, CA: Academic Press.

Zarate, G. (1991). The observation diary: An ethnographic approach to teacher education. In D. Buttjes & M. Byram (Eds.), *Mediating languages and cultures: Towards an intercultural theory of foreign language education* (pp. 248–260). Clevedon, UK: Multilingual Matters.

Zarate, G. (1995). Cultural awareness and the classification of documents for the description of foreign culture. *Language Learning Journal, 11,* 24–25.

Zhang, Y. (1995). Strategies in Chinese requesting. In G. Kasper (Ed.), *Pragmatics of Chinese as a native and target language* (Technical Report No. 5 (pp. 23–67). Honolulu, Hawaii, Second Language Teaching and Curriculum Center.

Zinchenko, V. P. (1996). Developing activity theory: The zone of proximal development and beyond. In B. Nardi (Ed.), *Context and consciousness: Activity theory and human–computer interaction* (pp. 286–321). Cambridge: MIT Press.

Index